SO CLOSE

Infertile and addicted to hope

TERTIA ALBERTYN

Oshun

Oshun

Published by Oshun Books
an imprint of Struik Publishers
(a division of New Holland Publishing (South Africa) (Pty) Ltd)
PO Box 1144, Cape Town, 8000
New Holland Publishing is a member of Johnnic Communications Ltd.

First published in 2006

1 2 3 5 7 9 10 8 6 4 2

PUBLISHING MANAGER: Michelle Matthews
EDITOR: Linda Cilliers
COVER DESIGN: Bridgitte Chemaly
TEXT DESIGN AND TYPESETTING: Bridgitte Chemaly
PRODUCTION MANAGER: Valerie Kömmer
AUTHOR PHOTO: Sean Wilson

Set in 11.5 pt on 15 pt Sabon

Reproduction by Hirt & Carter (Cape) (Pty) Ltd
Printed and bound by Paarl Print,
Oosterland Street, Paarl, South Africa

ISBN-10: 1 77020 003 7
ISBN-13: 9781770200036

And the day came when the risk to remain tight in a bud
was more painful than the risk it took to blossom.

– ANAÏS NIN

FOR ALL MY CHILDREN, LIVING AND GONE

In memory of Ben, 04/01/2004–14/01/2004

Acknowledgements

There are so many people whom I would like to thank, who have influenced my life and consequently this book. Literally hundreds of people. It has been that long a journey.

To all the people at Oshun who made this book happen. Michelle, Linda, Ceridwen, thank you. And thank you to my darling friends Tess Lyons and Meriel Bartlett, for helping me with the first edits of this book. And all the handholding and support!

To all the medical people who helped me along the way. Dr Victor Hulme, Dr Lut Geerts, Dr Paul Strong, Sheila Faure, Louis Vlok, Kimenthra Raja, Vicky Hindmarch, Sister Ann. But mostly, a heartfelt thank you to my dear Dr Sulaiman Heylen. Dr H, words can never be enough to thank you for all you have done for me. You were more than just my fertility doctor; you were my shrink, my GP, my friend and my saviour. Thank you dear doctor, from the bottom of my heart.

Then, to all my friends in the computer. You have no idea how much you have helped me along the way. There were many times I wished I could reach through my screen and hold your hands on the other side of the world.

To my real-life friends: Thank you. Thank you for not giving up on me. I know it must have been very hard at times to be my friend.

To my sisters, my brother and my father and my extended family: Thank you. Thank you for loving me when I was so hard to love.

To my kids, Adam and Kate: You'd better love your mommy forever after reading this book! I will be docking your pocket money to repay your debt. Mommy loves you, my precious little miracles.

To my darling husband: I adore you, you are one of the best investment decisions I have ever made. Thanks for being so strong, thank you for never giving up on the dream. I love you, so very much.

Then, to my mother: Oh Mother, how can I ever thank you enough for everything you have done for me? I love you my darling mother, I am honoured to be your daughter.

Lastly, to all my infertile sisters out there: My heart aches for you, what a painful, lonely path you walk. I'll never forget from where I came. I will carry all of you in my heart always. May all your dreams and wishes come true; may your aching, empty arms be filled.

Foreword

And they lived 'Happily ever after'. The End?

The end is only the beginning. What happened to Snow White and Prince Charming two, five or ten years down the line? After the marriage there is usually the desire, and indeed the expectation, to have a family. Most of the time desire, expectation and outcome fall into place. I want a child, I expect to fall pregnant, I enjoy trying, I have organised the nursery, chosen the name, told my family and friends. And *voila*!

For many, however (13–24% of couples worldwide to be exact), it is not so simple.

Unless you have had the experience of infertility, directly or indirectly, it is impossible to understand the journey from desire to outcome; The Infertility Route. Tertia Albertyn has documented her experience. It is an unbridled, authentic step-by-step journey, characterised by everything that anyone who has travelled this route knows – not believes, but *knows* – deeply and viscerally.

The joyous highs, the devastating lows, the overwhelming anxiety, the cautious anticipation, the financial burden, the effect on the relationship, the imagined symptoms, the waiting and waiting and waiting and so much more. Have you ever bought a home pregnancy test and cried by yourself in the early hours of the morning? Have you ever wished that all panties in the world were black? Have you fantasised about just how you will tell your mother that you are pregnant? Have you ever closed your eyes and thought of England and wished that this 'love making' be over with as quickly as possible? Have you ever wondered why everyone around you seems to be contributing to the population of the country except you? Have you ever … ? The paths of each individual and couple may be different, but the identification with Tertia and her experience is unquestionable.

It is rare (and an honour) to witness and participate in a journey written from the point of view of participant and observer. It is only with the highest level of self-awareness and insight that it is possible to BE your story, open your heart and mind and invite others in.

This is a groundbreaking documentary for anyone who travels The Infertility Route and anyone who wishes to understand. Most of all, it is for everyone who feels they can't do it again. Not again. Whatever the 'it' is … usually another IVF or some invasive treatment that has taken its toll financially, emotionally, socially and sometimes spiritually.

It is Tertia's story – but it's also everybody's story – about possibility even probability, courage, tenacity, determination and the undoubted value and healing power of support.

Please do not be discouraged by Tertia's experience of nine IVFs, and most especially the devastating loss and depth of pain regarding the death of her and Marko's beloved first born, Ben. Rather be inspired by the outcome – the birth of her twins Adam and Kate. There are many on the rollercoaster who are successful first or second time around.

The gift of the book is that you CAN and you WILL have a baby – for sure! You might have to move your goalposts, you might have to shift your mindset in the process, but one way or another with some of the courage, determination, support and the optimistic world view that is demonstrated by Tertia and her husband Marko, it will happen.

And that, above all, is her gift to you.

Dorianne Weil 'Dr. D'
Clinical Psychologist

PROLOGUE

I am so close, so close I can almost taste it. Surely I will get there this time. Surely, please God, let it happen this time.

Here I stand, on the brink of what I hope will be my last in vitro (IVF) cycle. If this – my ninth attempt – doesn't work, I don't know whether I can do another one ever again. This is quite possibly the most terrifying thing I have ever done. It is taking every single ounce of whatever bit of strength I have left.

I know there are people who think I'm crazy – barking mad for doing this again, after what I've been through. I can sense people having to forcibly restrain themselves from begging me to stop – people who are dying to express thoughts I really don't want to hear:

'Please just stop! We can't take it any more. We can't see you go through this agony again. Please. Just. Give. Up.'

I think they think if I continue down this road, I may lose my mind.

They don't know I lost it long ago.

So many people ask me how I have the strength to carry on with these fertility treatments. They say I am brave, how much they admire me. Brave? I don't know. Stubborn? Maybe. Determined? Probably. What they don't know is that as terrifying as it is to do yet another fertility treatment, the alternative is way, way scarier. The alternative is *not* trying and therefore facing the possibility of a childless future. And that, for me, is terrifying – a future not worth considering. So, I don't think I am being brave at all. I am just too terrified *not* to try again.

It's been a long, shit, hard, heartbreaking ride. Never in my wildest imagination, my worst nightmares, did I ever imagine I would be standing here, four years down the line, about to embark on my ninth IVF – my twelfth infertility treatment in total. Never. And yet I feel as if I am so close to achieving my dream of a living, healthy child. With each IVF attempt it seems we get closer to the dream. And that is why I have to carry on, why I have to put my long-suffering husband and myself through yet another procedure. Because I can sense how close we are to our dream – so very close.

But I'm getting ahead of myself. Let me take you back to the beginning, to where it all started. Or didn't start.

MY NAME IS TERTIA AND I'M AN INFERTILE

Before I introduce you to my reproductive bits and recount their miserable failings, I suppose I had better tell you a bit more about myself. I'm more than just my baby-making bits. Which is just as well, because otherwise I'd be forced to describe myself as 'Faulty, factory reject: For recreational use only'.

I am 36 years old and I live in Cape Town, South Africa. I've been married for five years to a great guy called Marko, whose good points far outweigh his pain-in-the-arse points. And whose good qualities are enough to make me want to create some mini-me's with him.

I'm not a particularly patient person. I'm not good at waiting for things. I'm an instant-gratification kind of a girl – I want it, and I want it now! I've never been good at denying myself. Which got me into all sorts of trouble during my misspent yet terribly entertaining youth. And which makes my infertility a particularly unfunny kind of cosmic joke.

Domestic things are not my forte: I'm an appalling cook. In fact, I hate cooking. Cooking, to me, is a supreme waste of energy when you can get absolutely fantastic ready-made stuff from Wool-worths. No mess, no fuss. Woollies, the microwave and I have maintained a happy *ménage à trois* for many years. I'm also not particularly fond of housework. Nor am I any good at it.

However, for all our faults, Marko and I are a match made in your average person's version of heaven. Imperfectly perfect for each other. For all my lack of domestic skills, the man loves me, and love, they say, is blind.

I like who I am. I could probably be described as unusual look-ing. I don't care what people think about me and I don't bow to society's expectations or norms about how I *should* behave, or how I *should* look. I love that about me. I think I secretly enjoy shocking people a little.

I drink too much, I swear too much. I have a terribly addictive personality. I've given up smoking at least five times, hopefully for good this time! I have no self-control and I eat all the wrong foods. I am quite possibly the world's worst dieter. I just hate denying myself.

I get bored quickly. I am impatient. I'm easily distracted. I'm a terrible procrastinator. I am funny, clever, kind. I am honest and decent, deeply loved and very loving. I am loyal and driven, serious and silly.

I am also infertile. Which is the hardest part about being me.

WHEN MARKO MET TERTIA

Before discovering my infertility, the hardest part about being the 20-something Tertia was balancing work and play – work kept interrupting play! I was a social girl. With a great life, a fabulous social circle and a series of fairly entertaining, mostly transient boyfriends. Marriage, future husbands or even just long-term boyfriends were the last things on my mind. And then I met Marko.

I'd love to tell you some romantic story about how I met Marko at a poetry reading, how our eyes met across a crowded room, and how we felt an instant connection and knew in that moment that we were meant to be together, forever. The real version of events is a little less romantic, but a lot more real.

Marko and I met in a bar.

At the time, I absolutely loved being single. I had a great group of girlfriends and we moved in a pack, partying every weekend until the sun came up. Having a permanent boyfriend was not part of the deal. Three months was the normal lifespan of my relationships and as that landmark approached and Marko was still very much in the picture, my girlfriends began chorusing, 'When? When will you dump him?'

'As soon as he starts annoying me,' I assured them.

Three months had passed and what was this? He hadn't started to irritate me. He hadn't turned all weak and pathetic. I still liked him. A lot. The passion-tinted spectacles, usually tossed aside after 90 days, came off but instead of revealing a sub-intelligent, immature, annoying, self-absorbed psycho, time was proving Marko to be the same strong-but-kind, serious-yet-funny person I'd met in the beginning. A thoroughly decent guy. This was the real deal.

My friends gradually began to realise that this platinum member of the singles club was taking a one-way trip to the Land of Serious Relationships.

In June 1999, we moved into a small house together. We started buying things together – a *big* step for me, as this was a major *commitment*. And the more I learned about him, the more I liked him. That was when I started to think that this could be a long-term thing. Perhaps all the domestic, suburban stuff made the thought of 'settling down' and having children more appealing. I was 30 and all partied out; I was ready for a new chapter in my life.

Marko is the first guy whom I have never been able to wrap around my little finger; he gives as much shit as he gets, he stands up to me, he didn't turn into a wimp within six months of our dating, and he has never irritated or disappointed me. I liked him just as much after three months, six months, a year, as in the first month of our relationship. It was obvious; I had to marry him. Of course it didn't hurt that he was damn sexy!

Realising it was getting serious and that an engagement was on the horizon, I gave him strict instructions on the ideal marriage proposal. I told him that no one had ever asked me the big question before – nor was anyone likely to do so again. So when he did pop the question, it had to be done properly – the old-fashioned way. That included his asking my father for my hand in marriage, choosing a ring and going down on his knees. All that he did. Of course I said yes.

I knew that I would want to start trying for a baby straight away, so I decided to give up my 20-a-day cigarette habit. I even set a date – 27 November 1999, the day after my 31st birthday and the weekend after finishing my MBA.

Six months later, on 22 April 2000, we had the perfect wedding – for us. It was small and intimate, a morning affair. No dancing. Marko doesn't dance.

What convinced me that Marko was The One was the fact that my parents liked him. I adore my parents. They mean the world to me and their approval was very important. My girlfriends liked him, too. And he didn't annoy me. Of course, now that I'm married to him, he annoys me immensely. Just kidding. Well, mostly kidding.

Marko is my soul mate, my partner, my best friend. He is my perfect match. With him, I hit the jackpot.

IN THE BEGINNING, THERE WAS …
UM … NOT A LOT OF ACTION AT ALL

For most people, having a child involves sex. They don't question the assumption that sex will do the trick. Until it doesn't. Looking back, I think I always kind of knew that it would not happen as easily for me as it did for others. Of course, I had no idea just how much of a struggle it would be. Why did I think I might struggle? Well, there were a few little clues along the way.

The most glaringly obvious was the lack of regularity in my natural menstrual cycle. Foolishly, I thought my birth control pills were controlling my cycle. In hindsight, the only thing the pills controlled was how many pairs of shoes I had in my closet. What a complete waste of money that was! When I think of all the pairs of Nine West shoes I could have owned, I feel like weeping.

While going through my wild, sowing-my-(seedless)-oats stage in my twenties, the non-existence of a normal menstrual cycle was wonderful instead of woeful. No periods. Yay! Except, of course, for the occasional time or two I thought I'd accidentally got knocked up. I spent many a night praying, nay, begging, that I wasn't pregnant. God must be very confused. Years of praying, 'Oh please God, let me not be pregnant', followed by years of, 'Oh please God, let me be pregnant.'

The other sign that should have alerted me to my faulty reproductive bits was that in spite of some vociferous and enthusiastic sans-contraception honeymoon shagging during my ovulatory period (a rare occurrence indeed – the ovulation, that is, not the sex. Although the sex was later to become increasingly rare – more on that later), no baby resulted. Marko and I had a divine honeymoon. We went to the beach, drank cocktails, shagged … a thoroughly pleasant time. And although baby making was the last thing on my mind, I couldn't help but idly wonder whether conception might not be the result of the copious shagging.

It was probably around then that my baby-wanting switch was flicked. The one that says, 'I am ready for this. On every level. I want this. Now.' It was more than whimsy, or thinking that having a child sometime soon might be a good idea. It was a conscious decision, which awoke in me an innate and primal desire that would never, ever be satisfied with anything less than a child. Once that switch was flicked, there was no turning it off.

Two weeks after our honeymoon, I had a period. All normal, to be expected. Good. The next month, I wait for my period to arrive … and wait … it never arrives. In my supreme innocence, I even did a home pregnancy test. Negative, of course. I was a little disappointed, but not hugely surprised. The next month, still no period. Three months later, I still do not have a period.

Even with my rudimentary knowledge of the reproductive system, I know that in the absence of a bun in the oven, no periods usually means no ovulation, and no ovulation means sweet bugger all chance of having a baby. Being the anal, A-type, instant-gratification, I-want-it-and-I-want-it-now type of girl that I am, I decide to get help. Forthwith!

I ask around and my sister-in-law tells me about a doctor near Panorama Medi-clinic. The doctor, let's call her Dr M, is apparently good and evidently quite popular, as the first available appointment was weeks away. Well, popular is good, I suppose. Dr M is nice enough – efficient, pleasant, all the usual stuff. She seems unconcerned at my erratic periods and suggests that tall, thin women sometimes struggle to conceive. Her response makes me feel slightly less worried. I am tall and thin(nish). This apparently happens sometimes. Fine.

She takes my medical history, checks me out and assures me

that on the surface I seem to have all the bits needed to make a baby. She suggests we start at the beginning, with Trying For A Baby 101, where the woman takes her temperature every morning to establish her fertile period. In the infertility world this process is known as temping.

She hands me a sheet of graph paper, on which I am to plot my temperature every morning. I dash off to the chemist and buy a basal body temperature (BBT) thermometer. Every morning at the same time (and it has to be at the same time, every time), just after opening my eyes but before doing anything else, I pop the thermometer in my mouth and lie there clenching my full bladder, writing down my registered temperature. Hardly romantic stuff.

The next step is to watch out for the anticipated spike in temperature, which indicates ovulation. Dutifully, Marko and I are then to shag like rabbits and hope that somehow his sperm will meet with my egg and, boom! A baby will be made.

This all sounds very easy, and it should be. I wake up every morning and take my temperature. I plot it and join the dots, looking out for the spike. Instead of a beautiful graph with an elegant spike in the middle, my graph looks decidedly flat and unspiky. But I persevere. I carry on taking my temperature and plotting the results on the graph every morning. And I watch and wait for the spike.

And wait.

Nothing. Nada. Niks. Fôkôl. Not an effing spike to be seen. Nothing. Flat line. I am either dead and don't know it, or these ovaries of mine are even more useless than I feared.

About a million of my friends and acquaintances have babies in the meantime – without the help of a thermometer and a stupid piece of graph paper. First Belinda, then Leanne, then Melanie, then Janine … over a period of a year, four of my five closest friends have babies. Back to Dr M I go. I'm starting to feel a little antsy. And embarrassed. I can't seem to get this right. Why is it so difficult?

Dr M suggests that my system may be out of synch and perhaps needs a kick-start. She prescribes a five-day course of progesterone to simulate the second half of a normal cycle and thus force my body into having a period. The pills do what they're supposed to do and a few days later I get a period for the first time in months. Yippee! I can start a fresh cycle of plotting, charting and hoping.

The temping thing gets boring very quickly. It's so slow. No action. I don't like that at all. Absolutely nothing is happening. Not a spike to be seen. But I don't give up. I do another month of the thermometer thing, take more progesterone, have a period, then spend another month plotting the graph and taking more progesterone.

I react very badly to the progesterone. It makes me feel terrible, depressed, spotty and fat. I hate it. The more depressed I get, the more I withdraw into myself. I don't want to go out anymore. I feel fat and ugly. As my body gets bigger, my world gets smaller. I change from someone who is the life and soul of the party to someone who just wants to stay at home. Ugly. Old. Miserable.

After some months of this and no baby to show for it, I realise things are not going well. I write a long, impassioned letter to Dr M, telling her how I feel. I pour my heart out. I don't hear a word from her. That silence helps me make the decision that it's time to move on. I need to see someone specialising in this infertility stuff. Someone who cares beyond the R500 consultation fee I represent. Dr M may be good at what she does, but her bedside manner sucks.

I call my friend Gill, who also struggled to have a child. She isn't available, but her husband answers the phone and tells me about their doctor and how fabulous he is. Perfect. If Gill's husband likes the man, so should Marko. It's important for one's husband to like the man who spends so much time peering at one's fanny. I am relieved that I'm taking the next step. I don't think an ordinary gynaecologist is going to work for me. I fear my issues are bigger than that.

The new doctor works at a place called the Cape Fertility Clinic in Claremont, Cape Town, which is a bit far, but it is fine, manageable. It's not like I'll be going there a million times. I like the sound of the clinic. I like that they are experts in fertility treatment. I have never been one to be satisfied with second-string expertise, with dealing with the B-team. I call the clinic and make what is the first of many appointments with a man who will come to play a huge role in my life for the next few years.

Dr Heylen. What a wonderful man. What a wonderful doctor.

I must say I feel much better now. It feels like we're finally doing something purposeful. This buggering around with charts and temperatures and doctors who don't take me seriously is not for me. And thank God I'm off the pesky progesterone!

It is September 2000. I've been trying for only six months. On the one hand it's a very short time; on the other, it's forever. I'm ready to embark on the next stage of my journey – a stage, I'm sure, (based on what I've read and heard) which will include some capital outlay, a course of hormonal medication and quite possibly some fairly high-tech fertility treatments. That's OK. I'll do what it takes. As nervous as I am, I'm also excited.

I am so ready. Bring it on.

TESTING, TESTING 1-2-3

It is October 2000, and time for my first appointment at the fertility clinic. I'm going on my own. That's fine; I prefer it that way. Of course, it would be nice to have my husband with me, but Marko just stresses me out when it comes to things like this. He gets all worked up if things don't work exactly according to schedule; he's the sort to get agitated in traffic. Better to go without him – initially, at least.

I'm quite nervous; it seems like such a big step. At the back of my mind, I fret that they will find something horribly wrong with me. The high-tech fertility world is so foreign. Another part of me is excited; I just love the science of it all. As I walk into the waiting room, I suddenly want Marko with me. Only couples there. Oh well, tough shit. Probably better this way.

Dr Heylen looks youngish, early forties I'd guess, and so handsome! He has a fairly thick Belgian accent and speaks softly. It takes me a while to make out what he is saying. He comes across as kind, caring and knowledgeable. I like him already. A lot. We discuss my history, my menstrual cycle, all sorts of things. He is quietly confident. He says that, on the face of it, it seems like a fairly simple issue to address.

He explains the normal process of an infertility work-up. He says in 30 percent of cases the 'problem' lies with the woman, in another 30 with the man and in yet another 30 with both partners. Ten percent of infertile couples are labelled as 'unexplained'. This is the worst diagnosis, because the doctors basically mean, 'we have no idea what the hell is wrong with you.' It's a crap diagnosis. If you don't know what is wrong with you, how on earth can you try to fix it?

Dr H suggests that we do a complete infertility work-up on both Marko and me. In other words, test what can be tested, look at what can be looked at and then decide on a course of action based on the results. For me, this means blood tests, operations and a fair bit of pain and suffering. All that will be required of Marko is a quick 'fiddle' in the loo. OK, that sounds a bit harsh, but seriously, that's what it is! He has to give a 'sample'. I have to have instruments fiddling around my insides.

But there is some justice in the world! The jar into which the sample has to be collected is really small. So the poor bugger has to jerk off and then make sure the stuff goes into the jar and not on his hand, on the floor or next to the jar. Or else he has to do it all over again. And apparently doing it twice in a row, under enormous time constraints, is almost impossible. Or so I'm told.

I leave the appointment feeling optimistic. Dr Heylen strikes me as being more than competent, the clinic seems wonderful – they have a fantastic success rate. Plus, I now have so many options other than just taking my temperature and helplessly waiting for something to happen. There's ovulation induction – a simple ovulation stimulation process, where I take a few pills to stimulate ovulation; artificial insemination – where they stimulate ovulation and put the sperm directly back into the uterus; and the big daddy of them all – in vitro fertilisation, or IVF as it is commonly known. IVF is where they take your eggs out, mix them with the sperm in the laboratory and put the resulting embryo back into your womb, creating what is colloquially known as a test tube baby.

I like having options; it makes me feel less out of control, less like I'm staring down the barrel of a gun. Though I hope I don't have to explore too many of these options; it's hellishly expensive, this infertility lark. Around R15 000 an IVF attempt. Shit, that's a lot of money.

But I'm getting ahead of myself again. First we have to do the testing to determine why we're not getting pregnant.

I bring the collection jar home with the instruction sheet – no shit! Seriously! An instruction sheet. I mean, really, how difficult can it be?

1. Remove cap from jar
2. Unzip pants
3. Disinter penis
4. Jerk off
5. Aim penis towards jar
6. Release sample into jar
7. Ensure no spillage
8. Wipe jar clean and close cap
9. Hand jar to wife to rush off to laboratory

To be fair, the instruction sheet was more about not using soaps and lotions and making sure the sample is handed in at the lab within 90 minutes or so. Sperm has a limited shelf life outside the body, so you need to get it to the lab as soon as possible.

Poor Marko. I just know he's going to hate this. I leave the collection jar with the sheet on the bathroom counter – a little surprise for him when he brushes his teeth tonight. I giggle nervously. Shit, is he going to hate this!

The sample can be given in any time from now until November. It's all up to Marko. Of course, if it were me, I'd get it over and done with as soon as possible. But it's not me. The jar and instruction sheet stand menacingly on the bathroom counter collecting dust for about two months. Marko thinks if he ignores it, it will go away.

THE SCIENCE

Laparoscopy

A laparoscopy is described as a direct visualisation of the peritoneal cavity, ovaries, outside of the tubes and uterus by using a laparoscope. The laparoscope is an instrument somewhat like a miniature telescope with a fibre optic system, which brings light into the abdomen. It is about as big around as a fountain pen and twice as long.

An instrument to move the uterus during surgery will be placed in the vagina. Carbon dioxide (CO_2) is put into the abdomen through a special needle that is inserted just below the navel. This gas helps to separate the organs inside the abdominal cavity, making it easier for the physician to see the reproductive organs during the laparoscopy. The gas is removed at the end of the procedure.

Sounds fabulous, hey? Not.

Source: http://www.ivf.com

A laparoscopy is scheduled for the end of November to check out my insides, to see whether all is OK down below. I wish it were sooner. Hurry up and wait. I've been doing a lot of waiting lately. By now, I've all but given up any hope of falling pregnant on my own. It seems like an impossibility. Infertility treatment seems to be my only hope, and while we sit around waiting for appointments and operations, it feels like time is ticking by.

In the meantime, we have to start with Marko's contribution to the testing process. Marko is not charmed. I find it all a bit hilarious. I take to calling him 'my little wanker'. I think it's hysterical. He does not find my amusement funny at all. I stop calling him a wanker. I thought all men loved it! And here is a perfectly legitimate reason to do it. But apparently wanking is different when you're doing it for science instead of fun.

Some fertility clinics in other parts of the world have fancy … um … collection rooms – basically cubicles where the man can do his thing with appropriate aids or props like saucy magazines. Unfortunately, my clinic has nothing like that, so it's either the public loo down the passage (where occupational hazards include a bad case of tennis elbow or being caught wanking in the loo by the cleaner), or jerk off in the privacy of your own home, rushing the sample to the lab afterwards. Clearly my man is not going to choose the public loo, so the whole thing has to be done at home.

The problem, of course, is that because sperm doesn't live long outside the body, the whole procedure has to be planned with military precision. Which basically means we ... um ... make that I ... have to rush the sample off to the laboratory straight afterwards. It's about an hour's drive in the traffic. I have only 90 minutes to get the sperm there. If I hit traffic I'm fucked.

The morning of The Great Wank eventually arrives. We can no longer put it off. It's pointless for me to go through any procedure unless we find out whether we have sperm issues or not.

Marko makes me wait *outside* the house, on the front lawn, with the front door, passage door and bathroom door closed while he gets busy. I'm not allowed to laugh, make jokes or mention the word wank. So I wait outside, dressed and ready for the race to the lab, hazard lights flashing, police escort, aforementioned Special Cargo safely tucked into the waistband of my pants (keeping it at body temperature is essential). Operation Wank underway.

He calls me inside and looks at the jar with worry on his face. 'Doesn't look like very much, does it?' I assure him it's fine. I'm just so damn relieved he managed to do it and get the stuff in the small jar. I grab the jar and race off. The whole way to the lab I have visions of cops pulling me over for speeding, me explaining why I'm in a hurry, producing the jar as proof. 'Look officer, I have to get this to the lab within the next 30 minutes. It's my husband's semen. No really! Promise, it really is semen, wanna taste?'

Luckily, nothing exciting happens and I get the sample there on time. We have to wait a week for the results. They test three aspects of the sperm. Motility (that the little buggers can swim), the number or count (how many of them there are) and the morphology (that they are 'normally' shaped – i.e. capable of penetrating and fertilising an egg). Marko's results come back as excellent for count or number and good for motility, but his morphology score is lower than it should be, meaning there are too many abnormally shaped sperm.

Marko is not at all impressed with the results. Even though one knows logically that fertility has nothing to do with sexuality, or with being a man or a woman, it is hard not to take this stuff personally. It does make you feel uncomfortable; it can make you very depressed. Marko is clearly taking this all quite personally and decides that someone is lying. Or has made a mistake. The lab, the doctor, someone. It's silly, because there's nothing wrong with him. The morphology result was eight percent and it's supposed to be ten percent or something. Hardly cause for concern.

Dr H tells us Marko is fine, and that he could father a child without any fertility assistance. It would appear the problem does indeed lie with me. Which is fine. I'd far rather it be me than him.

So that's Marko's testing out of the way. My turn next.

SHOULD PLAY THE LOTTERY
WITH THESE KIND OF ODDS

It's the day of the operation. Marko drops me off at Newlands Surgical Clinic. My friend Sue, who moved to America, tells me that when someone there goes to hospital the entire family goes along and waits around in the passages and waiting rooms, just like you see in the movies. Certainly not in South Africa: at least not my family.

Marko slows down just enough for me to jump out at the traffic light. This suits me just fine; he's an enormous pain in the arse when it comes to hospitals, airports and any potentially bureaucratic and/or stressful situation. But he is especially painful at hospitals. He gets annoyed with the staff, with the rules, with the lack of any sense of urgency. I think it makes him feel out of control, something he does not like. The whole experience just stresses him out. Which is not particularly good news for us, because over the next five years or so we spend a lot of time in hospitals. Actually, let me rephrase that – *I* spend a lot of time in hospitals. Sometimes (only when required) with him, but most times on my own or with my mother.

It's a day procedure – in and out the same day. Dr H will sedate me and then have a look at my uterus, my tubes, my ovaries. Once I come around he will tell me what he found and then I will go home and recover. Simple.

All goes according to plan. Dr H comes to tell me what he found down below. The good news is that my tubes are clear. He did, however, find some stage II endometriosis (there are four stages, stage four being the worst), a relatively common condition among women. He managed to remove most of the endometriosis via the laparoscopy. All other bits appear to be in working order. All good.

I text Marko to come and pick me up. He arrives 30 minutes later and helps me pack my things. All that is now required is for me to pee. Then we can go home. Perfect.

Except.

Except that in apparently *one percent* of laparoscopy procedures, the patient is unable to pass urine and will therefore require an overnight stay with a catheter until she is able to pee on her own. Naturally, I fall smack bang in the middle of that completely obscure one percent.

Believe me when I say I try to pee. I sit and read. I wait. I strain. I let the tap run. I tell Marko to take a walk or go to the shop or do something. The thought of him huffing and puffing outside is enough to give even the most seasoned performer a bad case of stage fright.

Try as I might, nothing comes out. It's as if they accidentally sedated my bladder. There is nothing I can do. They can't let me go home without having urinated, and to be honest, if I don't get a catheter in right now, I might just explode from all the water I've drunk to force my bladder into action.

So there I am – no toothbrush, no PJs, nothing. I tell Marko to go home and come back in the morning. I'm not going anywhere that night.

I lie in my hospital bed and turn my head to look out into the dark night. I wonder where this journey will end. Part of me is optimistic; it should be an easy fix, no? There's nothing terribly wrong with either of us, is there? Nothing to it, right? Except there's this niggling worry, this lingering fear that it may not be as straightforward as I think. That this may in fact be the start of something far bigger, far harder, than anything I could ever have imagined. I shake my head as if to remove the dark thoughts. I lie back and force myself to sleep.

Artificial Insemination 101

THE SCIENCE

Before I lose you completely, let me explain what artificial insemination is all about.

During an artificial insemination (AI) or, as it is most commonly referred to, IUI (intra-uterine insemination) cycle, the doctor gives you hormone therapy (pills or injections) to stimulate your ovaries into producing an egg or two (usually about three or four). The normal woman produces one egg each month; the hormone therapy or ovulation stimulation gives your ovaries a big push to produce at least one, usually more. During the stimulation phase you are scanned every few days to see that your ovaries are doing their thing, and also to make sure that the hormone therapy doesn't hyperstimulate the ovaries, a potentially dangerous situation that can lead to hospitalisation – even death.

Once the doctor has determined through the use of regular ultrasounds and blood tests that the eggs are sufficient in size and number, he will administer a shot to trigger ovulation 36 hours later, at which time the scheduled artificial insemination will take place. The precise timing of the trigger shot is vital, especially when you move on to more high-tech infertility procedures.

On the morning of the insemination, your partner will do what is needed to produce sperm, get it in the collection jar and get it to the lab on time. It is then washed and spun and the misshaped sperm taken out, leaving behind the good swimmers. Or you can user donor sperm. Same process.

The nicely washed and spun good swimmers are then loaded into a catheter thingy, which the doctor threads into your uterus to gently inject the sperm into your uterus. The thinking is that the good swimmers will swim along enthusiastically towards one (or two) of the recently released eggs and make a baby.

It's very similar to how baby making through shagging works, but sans penis and with a little help from the doctor. Some people go the DIY route, i.e. using a 'donation' from a friend and a turkey baster.

That, in a nutshell, is how artificial insemination works.

Of course, it works nothing like that for me.

READY, STEADY, GO!

It is January 2001 and I am beyond excited. We are finally doing something about this baby-making mission of ours. Mine. Ours. Whatever. It is time for my first AI cycle.

Yes, even though there is nothing officially wrong with or missing from either of us, and even though with enough time and patience we might get pregnant on our own, I didn't want to wait, I didn't want to leave it to chance. We are moving ahead with the artificial insemination. I'm so excited to eventually get to the 'go' stage. Feels like I've been waiting forever. Surely it will work. It just has to work.

Infertility is a whole different universe. All the acronyms, all the procedures. Stuff I become very familiar with, stuff I wish I didn't have first-hand experience of.

When you're trying for a baby, everything revolves around your monthly cycle and what cycle day you are on. The whole process is driven around cycle days. So, as instructed, on Cycle Day One (CD1), the first day of my period, I see Dr H. He runs through the how and when of what will happen. The protocol I am going to be following is the entry-level fertility cycle, Trying for a Baby with Help 101. Hopefully, it will be relatively cheap, relatively easy, relatively painless. And very successful. Hopefully.

The most basic ovulation stimulation drug is one called Clomid, of which there are various brand names and generics. It sounds perfect for me, because from what we can see, my only problem seems to be failure to ovulate. Everything else seems fine. My tubes, my uterus, Marko's sperm. It's all very encouraging. Especially the part that says, 'If the lack of ovulation is the only cause of infertility, most women on Clomid treatment will achieve a pregnancy within four to six months of treatment.' I can handle four to six months of treatment.

How Clomid works

There are various causes of infertility, one of them being anovulation (lack of ovulation), common among women with infrequent or absent periods. Such women don't secrete enough Luteinising Hormone (LH) and Follicular Stimulating Hormone (FSH) at the right time during the cycle, resulting in an immature egg that is not released. In such cases, the most commonly prescribed drug is Clomiphene Citrate also known by its brand names Clomid or Serophene. If the lack of ovulation is the only cause of infertility, most women on Clomid treatment will achieve a pregnancy within four to six months of treatment.

Structurally similar to oestrogen, Clomid works as a selective oestrogen modulator, by attaching itself to the oestrogen receptor sites in the brain, disallowing them to bind with naturally circulating oestrogen. In response, the hypothalamus releases more Gonadotropin Releasing Hormone (GnRH), stimulating the pituitary to drain more LH and FSH, which then causes the ovary to produce more eggs and follicles, resulting in ovulation. Generally, a woman taking Clomid doubles or triples the amount of oestrogen production in that cycle compared with pre-treatment cycles.

From http://www.babyhopes.com/articles/clomid.html

THE SCIENCE

So, my protocol for this first cycle will be as follows:

I'll take 100mg Clomid a day from Cycle Day Three (CD3) to Cycle Day Eight (CD8). On CD10, I'll go in for a scan to see how many follicles I've grown. These follicles will hopefully release eggs at the time of ovulation and turn into a baby somewhere along the line.

I leave the appointment on a high. It feels so good to be doing *something*, to have a plan of action, to have the fertility drugs in my sweaty paws. It feels like I've been waiting for ages just to get to start the process. It's actually been nine months. How's that for irony?

I start popping my little baby-making pills. You know how, whenever you read a book or see a movie about a woman going through an infertility cycle she is always a high-maintenance, weepy, hormonal mess? She is on Clomid! Progesterone might be the hormone from hell, but oh my God, Clomid turns me into a psychotic bitch within 24 hours of ingesting the first tablet – a raging lunatic, an illogical, impatient, unstable bitch on wheels. It's funny; Clomid is the marijuana of fertility drugs, considering what's coming down the track. By the time I do my last IVF, I'll be shooting up the speedball crack-cocaine equivalent of Clomid, but of all the drugs I take, simple old, benign-looking Clomid affects me the most.

Marko and I go out for lunch at the Tygervalley mall. I'm irritated, bloated, frustrated and hungry. I'm never at my best when I'm hungry. Combine that with a dose of Clomid and I completely lose the plot. We order our food. We make idle conversation while we wait. Even his breathing irritates me. I'm tempted to tell him to 'stop breathing so loudly, for fucksake.'

Eventually, after what feels like ages, our food arrives. They have brought me the wrong fucking order. The waitress, who is either terminally stupid or stoned, realises the mistake and says she's sorry, she will bring the correct food right away. I'm so hungry that I tell her I'll eat whatever she has brought. But she assures me it won't take long. I graciously tell Marko to start eating while I wait.

And wait. And wait.

I'm fucking starving. I can feel my temper rising. Marko finishes his meal and my food has still not arrived.

I am about to explode. I look around the restaurant for our waitress and I see her *eating her staff meal*! Marko has finished his food, my food is nowhere to be seen and our waitress is *eating her fucking staff meal*! I completely lose it. I jump up and march across to the manager and give him the biggest earful of his life. I am in tears. I stomp back to the table as my food arrives. I start eating. Slowly the rage recedes and I start feeling increasingly sheepish.

I look across the table at Marko and say, 'I think I might have overreacted there. I'm not hungry anymore, let's go.'

'You'll finish your food first and then we'll go,' he says through gritted teeth.

I'm telling you, that Clomid stuff is evil.

IUI #1. AND #2. AND #3.

I eventually finish the last of the pills and manage to find my elusive sanity again.

It is CD10 – the first ultrasound scan. I'm so nervous. Yet I'm excited to see how many eggs I have brewing inside. I skip off work early and look at the other women in the waiting room of the fertility clinic. No one talks. In fact, almost all avoid eye contact. How strange. I'm dying to talk; I want to know their diagnoses, how far along they are with the process, what they're in for. Stuff. But no one talks. Many are there with their husbands or partners. I'm on my own again. Where do these men find the time and patience to accompany their wives to all the appointments?

I sit across the desk from Dr H. We exchange pleasantries. *Just scan me already!* I'm dying to know how many eggs there are. I've done my homework. I know we want about three or four, no more – else they may cancel my cycle, or they may convert me to an IVF. With more than four eggs, you run too high a risk of multiples. And although the thought of twins or even triplets sounds romantic, a multiple pregnancy is dangerous, both for the mother and the babies. Women's bodies weren't designed to carry more than one baby at a time. I'm hoping for three – no, make that *four* – eggs. What the hell! May as well go for broke.

Eventually it is time for the scan. I go into the exam room to get ready. Broeks off, hop onto the exam table. This is always the moment of discomfort: how do I tell him I'm ready? What is the proper etiquette when telling your fanny doctor you're ready and waiting

– broeks off and legs spread? 'Honey, I am ready, come right in!' I usually settle for clearing my throat and mumbling, 'ready'.

Dr H comes in, switches on the ultrasound machine, puts a condom over the probe and inserts the fanny wand. I *hate* this part. It is humiliating and uncomfortable and invasive. God, how I hate it. On the other hand, I know that only through an ultrasound will I know what's going on inside me. I have a love-hate relationship with that thing. I wish there were another way of looking at my insides. From the top would be nice. Yeah, right.

Dr H scans and looks at the display monitor. I can't make out what is what; it all looks like so many shadows and blotches. I can tell by his reaction that the news is not good. He turns to me and says, 'This is not what I expected to see.'

I have no follicles. Nothing. Not a fucking iota. I should have at least one or two by now. It looks like the Clomid hasn't worked.

I am crushed. How can the Clomid not have worked? It's supposed to work. What about that whole, 'if the lack of ovulation is the only cause of infertility, most women on Clomid treatment will achieve a pregnancy within four to six months of treatment' thing? How the fuck am I going to get pregnant if I can't even make one fucking egg? Good God, is my body that fucked up that fertility drugs won't – can't – work?

I can't help myself. I start crying. I try my best not to. I hate that I'm crying in front of the doctor. I hate being a high-need, high-maintenance patient. It's just that I'm so disappointed, so devastated. I was so sure that this would do the trick, that all I needed was something to make me ovulate. That if I could just make an egg, I would have a baby. That's how it's supposed to work.

Oh fuck, what now?

Dr Heylen, in his typically calm manner, tells me it's not over. That in some cases Clomid does not work and the patient has to move on to stronger drugs, in other words, injectable hormone therapy. Apparently the marijuana of the infertility world doesn't quite cut it for me. I'll have to start moving on to the harder stuff. I'll have to start shooting up.

Oh fuck. Injections. Ouch! Not only is it bloody sore, it is also much, much more expensive. A course of Clomid costs a hundred bucks or so. One hormone injection costs R200. That's a flipping lot of money.

I ask Dr H how many injections I'd need. He can't say for sure – he says some people need six per cycle, others 30. Oh God, *30* injections! Those poor, poor women. It must cost them a flipping fortune. I hope I don't get anywhere near needing 30 injections per cycle. I'll be broke! Dr H suggests I start off with six and come back in a few days for another scan, to see whether the injections have done what the pills failed to do.

I leave the doctor's office, clutching my bag of syringes, needles and fertility drugs. I am shell-shocked. Empty, poorer, barren. So very barren. And scared. Suddenly the stakes have been upped by several notches. Doing a cycle of a few pills costing a few hundred is fine. Doing a cycle where I have to be injected, with drugs that cost thousands – that's a whole other ballgame.

I get in my car and the dam wall breaks. I start sobbing – ugly, heart-wrenching sobs. I'm just so crushingly disappointed. I was so hopeful. And I am scared. I am scared that nothing will work. That this is the start of a downward spiral.

On my way home, Marko phones to ask how the scan went. I sob harder. He can't understand a word I'm saying. He tells me to pull over. I choke back the sobs, because I can hear he's getting upset with me. For me. I'm crying so hard, he's worried that I will have an accident. My tears are scaring him. I force myself to stop crying, I force the tears down. I'll deal with them later.

I start the injections. I have six vials of Pergonal, at R200 a vial. I'm sure heroin is cheaper. And makes you feel better. If heroin would get me pregnant, I'd be shooting up in the blink of an eye, no problem.

You get two kinds of injectable fertility drugs – one lot is administered subcutaneously, just under the skin, which means you can inject yourself. The other kind needs to be administered intramuscularly, which means in your butt. Which is kind of difficult to do yourself. Pergonal is the intramuscular kind. So I need to find someone to give me the jabs.

The local 24-hour ER at the hospital down the road does it for free. That is where I go every day at the same time for my injections. I wish Marko would do it for me, but he refuses. He says he doesn't want to hurt me. So off I go at the same time every day, waiting around, asking whichever nurse is free to inject me and then I go on my way again. It's a huge pain in the arse, really.

The injections seem to be working. Barely. After a course of ten, I manage to produce two pathetic eggs. It's time for the insemination.

The next injection due is the trigger shot, the one that induces ovulation. It has to be timed to the minute, exactly 36 hours before the scheduled insemination. My insemination is scheduled for three o'clock on Tuesday afternoon. Which means I have to have the trigger shot at three o'clock Monday morning.

I set the alarm clock for half past two in the morning. I get up, pull on my tracksuit and drive the ten kilometres to the ER. It is busy and the waiting room is packed with weekend revellers who are finding themselves on the wrong side of lucky. I feel like a fraud – like I'm wasting everyone's time. But I need my shot and I need it at exactly three. I wind my way through people slouched around the waiting room. I softly whisper to the receptionist that I need someone to administer an injection.

'What injection?' She booms back.

'It's for my fertility treatment,' I whisper.

'IS THERE ANYONE WHO CAN GIVE THIS LADY HER FERTILISATION INJECTION?!' she hollers to the staff behind her.

Previously passed-out occupants of the waiting room perk up and look around to see who is about to get her 'fertilisation' jab. I decide there and then it's the last time I'm doing this. Marko can bloody well bite the bloody bullet and do the injections.

Tuesday arrives and it's time for the insemination. Once again Marko has to do his thing, and once again I *race* to the clinic with his 'donation' tucked into the waistband of my pants. I hand over the sample. I notice another collection jar on the counter. I squint to read the name. I want to make sure they have the correct name on my jar. God, can you imagine them mixing up the sperm!

I recognise the name on the other jar. It's an unusual name. It belongs to a lecturer I had on my MBA course. I turn around and sure enough, there he is with his wife. We nod to acknowledge each other. I giggle to myself, 'I know what you've been doing …' I feel like winking at him. I don't.

They prepare the sperm for the insemination and an hour later I'm on the exam table about to have the swimmers placed directly into my uterus. This is a quick, simple process. It seems almost anti-climactic after the whole build-up. I expect thunder and light-ening; at least soft music and candlelight. But it's a quickie. In and out and done with. Then the man leaves the room.

It seems so strange that this could be the moment of possible conception – my husband is not even there. Some couples hold hands during or after the insemination, to make the moment less about science and more about … um … I don't know. Love? Me? I'm just glad Marko isn't there, huffing and puffing and impatiently glancing at his watch. After lying there for ten minutes, I get up and go back to work. How weird to just carry on with normal life.

And carrying on with normal life is exactly what I have to do for the next two weeks while I wait for the pregnancy test. Infertility is all about hurry up and wait. Wait, wait, wait. Wait to get started, wait for your eggs to grow, wait for the insemination, wait for the pregnancy test, wait for the results. Wait, wait, wait.

I spend these two weeks wondering, dreaming, thinking. Hop-ing. I spend hours online, searching for all things infertility. I study reams of information about ovulation, about inseminations, about pregnancy symptoms.

Finally, I go for the pregnancy test and wait for Dr H to call me with the results. I'm so excited. So nervous. I try to tell myself not to expect anything, but of course I'm hopeful. An IUI cycle has around a ten to 20 percent success rate per cycle. Most people suc-ceed after about three cycles; by the third cycle, about 70 percent of patients will be pregnant.

Dr H calls. His voice is so soft I have to strain to hear. He gives me the result. It's negative. It hasn't worked. I am not pregnant.

Even though I told myself not to expect anything, I weep. I call Marko to give him the news and he shouts at me for weeping; he can't handle my tears. He feels helpless, powerless. He hates seeing me so hurt, but because he doesn't know how to deal with my tears, he shouts. I force the tears down again. I paste a smile on my face.

I'll just try again.

The second insemination cycle follows the pattern of the first, except this time we combine Clomid with the injections from the beginning. Again Clomid does nothing except turn me into an unstable raging bitch. This time I use 20 vials of the hormone injections. At R200 a vial.

I wait for the results, this time with less excitement and more trepidation.

Negative.

Again I weep. Again he shouts. Again I force the tears down.

I'll just try again.

I've now given up any hope of falling pregnant naturally. I just don't see it happening. In order to get pregnant you need an egg and some sperm. At the right time. I'm not ovulating at all. There is no egg. It just isn't going to happen. And as much as I'm trying not to let it be that way, I can't help but think of sex as a means to an end. I'm finding it so hard to divorce the sex from the reproduction. It just seems pointless, fruitless. Literally. I know this is bad for my relationship with Marko, but it's hard not to think like this. Everything about sex and about feeling sexy is just so fucked up in my mind. Sex is not going to work. I need more infertility procedures.

I try again, my third attempt at artificial insemination. Again it's negative. Marko stops shouting. He gets better at handling my tears, softer. Perhaps because I cry less – at least on the outside. Inside, the tears are damming up. I'm running out of space.

We've been unsuccessfully trying to have a baby for 12 months now. We're no closer to achieving that goal, but we're a lot poorer. I'm a lot sadder. My despair is growing larger and my world smaller.

FRIENDS WHO LIVE IN THE COMPUTER

I can feel myself getting more and more insular, more obsessed. I can think of nothing else. The yearning for a child is consuming me; it is all I do, all I think about. Suddenly the big world outside is fraught with potential for hurt – pregnant women and babies are everywhere, all daily reminders of my failing.

My friends and family, much as they love me, don't understand what is going on inside me. They also don't know how to handle this Tertia – this Tertia who cries little on the outside, who stores her tears inside her chest. A sad Tertia, an angry Tertia. The world of infertility is foreign to them. My mother is unbelievably fertile, my sister even more so. They don't understand the world in which I live; they don't recognise the person I've become. I don't want to socialise, not with anyone. I just want to stay at home. I can't bear to be around anyone but my husband. He is the only one I allow into my world.

The only time I feel even remotely happy is when I'm on the Internet, winding my way through the networked spider web of the cyber world. I find solace and information in the computer. I spend hours online, searching, researching, looking for stories, miracles or miracle cures, for stories of hope and inspiration. And on my travels in cyberspace, I discover the wonderful, fabulous, life-saving world of online infertility support groups and bulletin boards. There I find a safe haven, a best friend, people who understand, people who are just like me. At last! People to talk to.

Infertility bulletin boards are the coffee shops of cyber space. It's a place where you can hang out with like-minded people, people in the same boat as you. These people get where you're at. They can relate. They understand your pain. Suddenly you feel less lonely, less alone. You have a fabulous time bonding with your new best friends, swearing undying love and friendship for one another and forming little friendship groups. You laugh, you commiserate, you virtually hold one another's hands. It's you and your cyber friends against the rest of the world and all you want to do is spend every possible moment with your new family – the ones who understand, the ones just like you: infertile.

The first bulletin board I find is The Clomid Club. I find it by Googling 'Clomid success rates'. It's a group of 15 women, 13 of whom live in America. We chat, we swap stories, we share all sorts of intimate details. We're all embarking on the journey to have a child. There is something about the Internet that creates a sense of community. You meet the most amazing people. You form such close bonds with people whom you will never meet, people whose last names you may never find out.

The Internet is a funny place. It allows you to be whoever you want to be – just ask the 55-year-old perve pretending to be a 15-year-old girl in a chat room. Thank goodness my infertility bulletin boards are not invaded by too many 55-year-old perves pretending to be 15-year-old girls. Instead, they're made up of women from all walks of life – all backgrounds, social standing, class, race, ethnicity, nationality. In real life, I would choose to be friends with probably only 20 percent of all the people I meet along the way, if I had to meet them face to face. But that doesn't matter. We're all women and we have something in common, something that makes us different, alienated from the real world. Our infertility. So we share our lives.

Every morning, I wake up at five, grab a cup of decaff and settle down in front of my computer, excited and full of anticipation to read who has said what, what's happened at Kristen's scan, how Laura's egg retrieval went, whether Jessica is pregnant. I feel like I know these women personally. They are my best friends. I remember driving home from Hermanus once, so anxious to get home to find out whether Laura's IUI had worked, whether she was pregnant or not. The minute I got home I logged on, and yes, she was pregnant!

Sometimes we chat in private chat rooms – you type something your friend can see in real time and get the response in real time. Back and forth you chat, like a telephone conversation, only typed. It's wonderful. It's so immediate, it really does make the world seem like a village.

Because of the time difference, I don't manage to chat online too much. Sometimes I wake up at four in the morning, or stay up until midnight, just to join the chat sessions with my friends in the computer. I am that desperate for the support, the friendship. I'm that hooked.

Even though I spend hours and hours on the computer, holed away in my study, Marko never complains. In fact, I think he is secretly relieved. He knows it is either them or him to whom I am going to pour my heart out, to whom I am going to obsess. And talking, especially about emotional stuff, has never been his strong suit. So he leaves me alone to spend my days and nights on the computer. He watches TV. I spend my time online. It works for us.

Then, slowly, one by one, my Best Friends in the Whole Wide World start to get pregnant. And I don't. And suddenly there is distance between us. I feel like I'm on the outside looking in – the class dunce. I begin to feel increasingly isolated. There's nothing like having your fellow infertiles get pregnant on you to make you feel like a real failure. See, even infertile people can get pregnant and I can't.

And so I move on, to another bulletin board, another new home made up of people who are more like me. People for whom Clomid hasn't worked, people who need to move on to harder drugs, more invasive procedures. New friends, old feeling. I've come home again.

Then they get pregnant, too. The first during the first month of trying, the next few over the following months. One by one. And I don't. So I move around the Internet until I find a home that suits me, where the people are at the same stage as I am. There are plenty of us out there. I make amazing friends along the way. Friends I'd be friends with in real life. Funny, witty, clever people. Friends from all over the world. Janey in New Zealand, Bianca in Australia, Tess in Hong Kong, Nick in England, Mollie and Andrea in Canada, Julie, Bridgette, Charmaine, Sandra and many others in America. Friends whom I adore and whom I will never meet in real life but if I did, I'd choose them to be my friends anyway.

These women become my rock, my life raft. As do many other women I meet along the way. And I really need them, because Marko and I are leaving the relatively easy world of IUIs behind. We're about to enter the big, scary world of IVF.

IVF 101

In vitro fertilisation, or IVF, is artificial insemination on steroids. IVF is what people mean when they speak about test tube babies. IVF, in its various guises (GIFT, ZIFT, IVF with ICSI, etc.), is the big daddy of infertility treatment. It is the most invasive, the most expensive, and the most taxing, from every point of view. It is also the most frightening, because unlike injections and IUI, after IVF, there is nothing to upgrade to. You've reached the ceiling of fertility treatment.

Very simplistically, this is how a normal IVF cycle works:

Firstly, through a course of hormone suppression treatments, the fertility doctor shuts the woman's own reproductive system down, putting her into a state of pseudo-menopause, with all its horrible side effects. This is done so that the doctor has total control over the timing of your cycle. He then artificially starts a cycle by administrating various forms of hormone therapy designed to stimulate the ovaries into producing a whole lot more eggs than the usual one. This is the ovulation stimulation part of the process.

During this part of the process, the woman will undergo several scans and blood tests to determine how the eggs are growing, how the uterine lining is looking and whether or not she has blood on her hands from murdering husbands/co-workers/stupid people. OK, not really the last one. But you can imagine, all those hormones do not a happy woman make.

THE SCIENCE

Once the eggs are at the optimal size, a trigger shot is administered in order to mature or ripen the eggs. Thirty-six hours later the woman is sedated in a clinic and the eggs are collected from her ovaries with the use of an ultra-sound guided vaginal probe (that is a long bloody needle through the wall of your fanny!). Luckily you (hopefully) don't feel this part because you're under sedation, although I know women who felt the entire procedure. Ouch!

Meanwhile, husband dearest does his bit by producing a sample into the collection jar. The sperm is washed and spun and prepared to be either injected directly into the retrieved eggs through a process called ICSI (intracytoplasmic sperm injection), or mixed with the eggs in a test tube (actually a Petrie dish) and left to fertilise the eggs on their own. 'In vitro' literally means 'in glass' in Latin. It also means 'outside the living organism' – in this case, outside you.

Twenty-four hours later the embryologist inspects the Petrie dish to see how many embryos have resulted from the fertilisation. The embryos, now at a two-cell stage, are then transferred to a new dish. They then grow to four cells the next day and eight the day after, on day three. The best one, two or three embryos are placed back into the woman's womb either on day three, or grown a further two days in the lab and transferred back on day five, depending on the clinic and how the embryos look on day three.

The woman, in the meantime, has started injecting herself with progesterone for the second half of her cycle. Once transferred, the embryo will hopefully implant itself into the uterine lining within the next few days. However, you will only know this has happened two weeks later when you have the pregnancy test done.

Infertility specialists have done truly amazing things. They can help a woman who has never ovulated before produce eggs, they can harvest sperm from a man who is unable to get an erection, they can join together one tiny egg and one minute sperm cell. Yet they're unable to influence or control the one last, final, vital stage in the reproductive process – implantation.

Once these dear little ones are back on board the mothership, it is up to God/fate/nature/the embryos themselves to facilitate implantation. Without implantation, there can be no baby.

WHY IT'S SO STRESSFUL

IVF is incredibly stressful, and for so many reasons. In the first place, it usually follows a long, hard road of trying to conceive. No one goes into IVF lightly. So plenty of history, tears, trying and years of sadness precede an IVF.

It is also exceptionally taxing on both the woman and the man, but especially the woman – from a mental, emotional and physical point of view. Those hormones! They make you feel like shit. They make you fat. They can turn you into a total bitch.

Then, of course, there is the whole financial aspect. IVF is fucking expensive. As in at least R15 000 an attempt. And medical aid covers not one single cent, even if your infertility is the result of a medical condition. Apparently, medical aids consider having a baby cosmetic and infertility an unworthy diagnosis.

Lastly, there is the psychology behind IVF – the fact that it represents the end of the fertility treatment road. You see, when you're trying to conceive through sex, there is the thought at the back of your mind that if that doesn't work, there are other procedures to try. There is Clomid (not invasive and hardly expensive), or if that doesn't work, you could try artificial insemination. There's always a plan B. Of course, not everyone can afford to go even this far, so good old-fashioned baby-making sex may represent the end of the road for many.

Artificial insemination ups the ante. The stakes are far higher and the disappointments more crushing. It is invasive. There is the monitoring, the injections. It's also a lot more expensive. Yet, for me, there was always the thought that if the IUIs didn't work, there was the all-powerful panacea, IVF. IVF represents the big guns. Surely it will work – IVF, the big back-up plan, the ultimate fail-safe. And that is why IVF *has* to work; if it doesn't, there's nothing behind that last curtain. That's it. It is IVF or bust.

Of course, IVF doesn't always work the first time, or even the second. You know that. You accept that. Perhaps you fail your first IVF. Very sad, yet understandable. Almost to be expected – everyone knows the first IVF is a test case, a check on how you respond to medication and so on.

Then you might just fail your second IVF, too. You start to feel a little worried. But OK, most people conceive within three IVF cycles. There's still hope. Maybe you're just at the wrong end of the stats. With around a 40 percent success rate per attempt, three IVFs to achieve a pregnancy are realistic. Surely the next one will work?

Then you fail your third IVF. And your next. And maybe your next. Suddenly you're staring down the barrel of a gun and the end of the road looms. What lies beyond IVF? There is no Next Big Thing. This is it. And that's an absolutely terrifying feeling. That sense of despair, of abject terror, is something the lucky ones who succeed without IVF, or who succeed on their first or second IVF don't have to face.

Of course, IVF is not the absolute end of the road. There are alternatives you may never have considered: adoption, surrogacy, donor eggs. All wonderful options that could lead to a happy ending. Still, those are not options one normally considers when starting out. These decisions are made after much soul searching, many failed cycles and usually more than one's fair share of heartache. No one *just* adopts, or *just* does donor eggs.

What makes IVF an absolute mind fuck is that there are so many pass/fail points along the way. Will the medication suppress your body's functioning enough to start an IVF cycle? Will your womb be free of cysts? On and on. If you fail one or more of these points, you don't even get to start.

Then, once you start the follicle stimulating medication, each scan, each blood test represents another pass/fail point. Do you have enough eggs? If you have too few the doctor will cancel the cycle. Are your hormone levels as they should be? Is your uterine lining what it should be? Then there's retrieval – how many eggs did they get? How many were mature? Then fertilisation – do we go for ICSI or for normal fertilisation? How many fertilised? Then, in anxious anticipation, you watch and wait as the embryos hopefully grow and divide – how many cells are there now? What grade are they? Will they make it or will they die? Then the transfer – how many embryos do we have to work with? How many do we put back? Will the transfer go smoothly?

Then you have the long, terrifying two-week wait – the time between transfer and the pregnancy test. After all the frenetic activity of injections, blood tests, scans, procedures, monitoring, you sit and do nothing. Wait. Hope. Overanalyse every tweak and twinge. And then the ultimate pass/fail point – the pregnancy blood test.

Sigh. Can you see why it's so emotionally charged? So exhausting? So all-consuming? Add to that the financial burden and the end-of-the-road fears and you get a picture of why IVF is such an all-consuming experience.

It is for these reasons that the stakes are so enormously high when doing IVF. And it is for these reasons that I approach my first IVF with something akin to terror.

IVF #1

After I get the news of my third negative pregnancy test, I've had enough of the artificial insemination cycles; they're clearly not doing anything for me at all.

Remember that conversation with Dr H during my first cycle, when I asked him how many injections I'd need and he said some women needed as many as 30? And I felt so sorry for those poor, faceless wretches? Well, let's hear it for self-pity, because with my last artificial insemination cycle I went up to – you guessed it – 30 injections. What a waste of money for a ten to 20 percent chance of success! I'd far rather do a cycle that gave me a 40 to 50 percent chance at success, which IVF does.

Dr Heylen's general rule before moving on to IVF is three artificial inseminations. If a positive pregnancy test has not resulted after three attempts, it is most likely not going to happen. So, after my third artificial insemination fails, Dr H and I have a chat. He asks me what I want to do next. I ask him what he suggests. He says he would recommend moving on to IVF. It is what I hoped he'd say. I am so ready to move on to IVF. I just want a baby – now – and I want to do whatever it takes to get there. Scary or not.

Dr Heylen suggests I take a break before the first IVF. I want to hear nothing of it. I don't want a break. I want a baby. By this time, my whole world revolves around infertility and my quest for a child. I'm addicted to the procedures, the treatments. I hate them. They make me feel terrible, they break my heart and my bank balance, but without them I feel powerless, helpless, hopeless. At least with the treatments I feel as if we're doing something; doing nothing is just terrible. I'm at work physically, but my mind, soul and heart are not. I know I should take a break. I know my body, my mind, my soul, my relationships all need it. But I can't. Every day doing nothing feels like a day wasted.

I go straight into my first IVF cycle. There's no turning back now; I've crossed the line. This is the end of the road in terms of high-tech infertility procedures.

In the meantime, Marko and I have moved into our first owned home. It's a good feeling. It feels like a fresh start. The new house has three bedrooms, one for us, one to be used as a study and the other for the baby's room. Marko wants to use it as a guest room in the meantime, but I don't want to do this. It's going to be the baby's room, come hell or high water. It can stand empty until the baby arrives. We're doing IVF now. Surely it won't be such a long wait?

I'm charged up for my first IVF, almost frenetic in my approach to the cycle. I start with two different injections every day, one to suppress my own hormones, the other to artificially stimulate my ovaries into producing eggs. This time Marko does the injections, the ones in the bum. I do the stomach jabs – they're easy. But the ones in the butt he has to do. He hates it. But he does it.

My first scan is only on Cycle Day Ten – an age away. I'm dying to know what's happening inside. I wish I had my own ultrasound machine at home. What the hell is going on inside? Are my useless, lazy ovaries actually doing anything? How many eggs will they make? I try not to think about how much money I am injecting into myself every day. Hundreds of rands.

Cycle Day Ten arrives and I'm beyond nervous. Terrified. This had better fucking work. I am now somewhat of a regular at my clinic. I know all the staff by name. They know me. I wait my turn. I hurry past the pleasantries. I'm dying to know how many eggs I have. Dr H scans me.

I can see some eggs – they look like dark blotches on the screen –

one, two, three … *Yay!* Nine! *Nine!* I have nine eggs brewing. Fan-fuckingtastic! But before leaving the clinic, I have to have my oestrogen levels, progesterone levels and levels of luteinising hormone tested. These will tell the doctor whether my body is doing what it's supposed to be doing. The one should be high, the others low.

I leave Dr H's room on a high – *nine* eggs. How great is that! It's fantastic! I SMS everyone – my mom, my sister, my friends. This is going to work. I can feel it.

I later call Dr Heylen to find out my blood test results. It's not good. Something doesn't look right. The results don't correlate with what we saw on the screen – the levels look too low. Dr H thinks things are maybe just moving along a bit slower than usual. I think he's just trying to reassure me, make me less paranoid. It doesn't work.

Shit. What now? What the fuck is happening? Will my body ever work as it should? Dr H tells me to carry on with the injections, to increase the dose to three ampoules a day and to come back in two days for another scan. I return two days later. No growth in the follicle size. What the fuck?

Dr H seems less confident, less reassuring. Perhaps my body is just more resistant to the drugs than we thought. More injections, more waiting. Back again two days later. My eggs have started collapsing and my hormone levels have dropped. Dr H looks up from the ultrasound monitor and says, 'I don't understand this. In ten years of doing IVF, I've never seen a result like this.'

Oh God, no! Please don't tell me that. I'm relying on you, on the medical profession, to fix me up, sort me out. Please, please, dear God, let me not be some anomaly that can't be fixed.

Dr H tells me to stop all the injections; he's cancelling the cycle. Do not pass go, do not collect R200.

It's over.

I cannot fucking believe it. I can't believe that I just went through all those injections, those blood tests, *all that money*! All for nothing. I never even had a fucking chance. I am terrified. What does this mean? Am I beyond help? Does this mean IVF won't work for me? Oh God, no! It has to work; there isn't anything beyond IVF. You don't understand – it *has* to work.

Dr H suggests we take a break before trying anything else. Every fibre of my being screams, 'No! I can't stop now. Don't make me stop!'

But I know I must. I'm about to snap, I can feel it. I'm stretched so thin, the tears I've been shoving down are pushing their way up. If I start screaming now, I don't think I will ever stop. I have never felt so small, so broken, so desolate. My future stretches before me – empty, bleak, lonely. Broken, broken, broken.

Poor Marko, what a shit deal he got, this broken wife. I feel so guilty. I feel like he married a dud. What a useless woman I am. If he married someone else, he wouldn't be going through all of this. I tell him I'd understand if he wanted to leave me. He gets cross with me for saying so. I can't help it. I'm so broken.

I want to curl up in my bed and never get up again. But I can't. I have to carry on. I have a husband, a family, a job.

What not to say

I look like shit. I feel like shit. And I'm crying in the work toilet. A colleague has followed me in and talks to me while I'm trying to clean the mascara that has run down my cheeks from all the tears.

'What's wrong?' she asks, her voice full of concern. I need a shoulder to cry on, somebody to listen and to care, so I tell her the whole story.

She nods sympathetically, rubs my arm, and says, 'Have you considered going to see a psychologist? Because, you know, maybe you don't really want to have a child and there is something in your mind that is blocking your ability to conceive.'

What the fuck?

No, dearie, I'm spending thousands of rands and having my heart ripped in two because, actually I don't really want a child. If you have an infertile friend, don't ever say something as insensitive as this to her. Here is a list of what *not* to say to an infertile person.

'JUST RELAX'

As in, 'Just relax and you'll get pregnant.' Ooohhhwa! If anything will make an infertile's blood pressure rise to murderous proportions it is hearing

FROM THE HEART

that statement. This helpful piece of advice also sometimes presents itself in the form of, 'Just don't think about it and it will happen.'

When you have a medical reason for not getting pregnant (Polycystic Ovarian Syndrome, endometriosis, tubal issues, uterus issues, endocrine issues, thyroid issues – the list is endless), no amount of relaxing will get you pregnant. Seriously. Promise. But don't take my word for it, read the scientific studies. If I was any more relaxed while having sex, I'd fall asleep on the job.

This is not a good thing to say to an infertile. It drives us crazy. You may as well be saying that (a) we're causing our own infertility problems by being tense (a silly thing to say in the face of a medical diagnosis – remember, the cause of infertility is *medical* for 90 percent of people), and (b) it is a simple thing to cure.

'JUST BE POSITIVE'

People just love saying this. If they ask me how I am, or how it is going, I'm usually honest enough to say I'm terrified, or nervous that the cycle won't work. The stock answer? 'Just be positive. It will be fine.' Now, unless all of these people are psychic, or crystal ball gazers, or tarot card readers, I'm not quite sure how they can so easily predict my future. And what happens if it's not fine? What then? Was I not positive enough? Oh, so it's actually my fault? Again?

It makes me cross, because it's such a glib, throwaway comment. Be positive? You be positive, OK? How about I be realistic. It's easy enough for you to say – you're not the one going through hell. And that's exactly what I tell them. 'You be positive for me; forgive me if I'm just a little scared.' It *doesn't* always work. I have the scars to prove it.

'JUST HAVE FAITH'

I find this the hardest to deal with. Have faith? So, if it's negative it's because I didn't have enough faith? Faith in what, exactly? That everything will be all right? Oh goody, does that mean God always answers prayers? That if I believe it will happen? Yay! What's that you say? Oh, sometimes it doesn't happen? That it could also *not* work out? Part of God's plan, you say? So what am I having faith in then? That it may be OK, but it also may not? Bit confusing, don't you think?

True believers will acknowledge my fear and pray for me anyway. They will pray for inner peace and strength, not blind faith.

WHAT YOU CAN SAY TO AN INFERTILE PERSON

All I actually ask is that people *think* before they speak. Don't make glib statements, verbal 'there ... there ...' pats on the head. Because, know what? It may make you feel better, but it makes me feel worse. As if you're brushing my woes aside, as if what I'm going through is inconsequential.

HOW ABOUT SAYING THIS?

'I can't possibly fully understand what you're going through, but I can imagine how hard it must be. Know that I'm here for you, in whatever way you need me. If you want to talk, I'll listen. If you don't want to talk, that is also fine. Please tell me how to be a good friend to you.'

GOING HERBAL

I'm on a break from the treatments. I don't want to take a break, but I know I must. I can feel that my body is exhausted. So is my wallet. And apparently, according to my doctor and my family, I need a mental break. Yeah, right! As if I'm not going to be thinking about it all the time. As if the yearning gets switched off. But yes, they're right. I need a break from the treatments, the hormones, the injections. The angst of, 'Did it work?'

But no one has told me to take a break from trying other methods of conceiving, right? Apparently there's this quaint old method called 'sex' that gets some people pregnant. No shit.

I've decided to combine that whole s. e. x. thing with the herbal/homeopathic option. A friend of a friend who knows someone who knows someone else who got pregnant by this homeopath in Panorama told me about it. Apparently he is *the* guy to see if you're struggling to conceive. Has an excellent success rate. May as well give it a shot.

I'm kind of nervous to see him. I almost feel as if I'm going behind Dr H's back. But I can't sit around and do nothing. So I make the appointment and go to see the guy.

The homeopath lives right on the top of the hill in Panorama, where the rich people stay. His house is massive, a mansion. Either this guy is the biggest con artist ever, or he is really good at what he does. Being a total cynic, I lean towards the former. I can feel my BS antennae rise. He'd better not be a touchy-feely bullshit artist.

He has about four women working for him in little offices –

accounts people, receptionists, you know. As far as I can see, he is the only homeopath there. Must be doing well. The women seem to be responsible for protecting the good doctor from fanatical, adoring patients. He is spoken about in reverent, hushed whispers.

'Doctor is running a little late. Just take a seat and He will be with you shortly.'

Doctor Hocus-Pocus had better hurry the fuck up, or I am outta here.

It's my turn. Oh my God. The man looks like Elvis reincarnated as a TV evangelist. Gold chains everywhere. He gives me a greasy smile and offers his hand. You can*not* be serious.

My BS antennae are going ballistic, but I persevere. Towards the end of the appointment I feel a little better about him. I still think he is, by and large, a quack but I'll give it a shot. Hell, I'll do whatever it takes and this is a whole lot cheaper than IVF. Besides, I may as well do something while I wait for my next IVF.

He gives me some homeopathic pills that are supposed to help me ovulate, and tells me to have sex when I do. We'll see.

Amazingly, the pills *do* make me ovulate. Which is more than I can say for Clomid! I'm amazed. Perhaps not a total quack, after all?

Marko and I have sex at the right time, but in my heart of hearts I don't really believe it will work. I can't see how the herbal route can do for me what high-tech science has failed to do. And time proves me right. The herbs don't work. I don't get pregnant. It wasn't a total waste of effort, because … well … the sex was fun, but mostly because what it does is reaffirm my belief that science is the route to go. This 'trying naturally' shit won't work for me.

Anyway, sex is for pussies. Bring on the science!

THE LONG-SUFFERING HUSBAND

Let me properly introduce you to my darling husband. Marko is five years younger than me, but I swear he was born mature and responsible. He is tall, dark and handsome. He is one of the most principled people I know. He is also the most hard-working, dedicated, loyal employee ever. If I ever had my own business, I'd employ him.

They say be careful what you wish for. How very true. I wished for the strong, silent type. I got it, times ten.

Marko is *not* a big chatter. Apparently, men speak something like 1 500 words a day versus a woman's 2 500. Well, I think some guy out there has an extra 1 000 words, because Marko speaks only about 500 a day – most of those barked orders at work. Actually, he's not that bad – just not big on chats. Especially chats about emotional stuff. In fact, his most hated sentence ever is, 'Sweetheart, we need to chat.' I can see the man visibly droop when he hears that.

Much as I adore Marko, he is not without a few minor flaws. He's not very patient. He hates not being in control of things. The problem, of course, is that infertility is a process fraught with detail, with lots of hurry-up-and-wait, with irritations, with unknowns, with best-effort guesses. You need patience and perseverance to cope with it all. There is so much that you have no control over. Plus, of course, there is the whole emotional side to it. It is a highly emotional experience, with incredible highs and devastating lows. Mostly lows.

And so, because of who Marko is and because of what infertility does, I keep a lot of how I feel away from him. I try not to let him see how obsessed I am, how much this shit affects me. How I think about it all the time, how it threatens to totally destroy me sometimes. I pretend, I fake feeling happy, normal. I'm so scared that if he sees how much this affects me, the depth of my despair, he'll say he doesn't want to carry on down this road. And that would be unbearable. Of course, I can't hide everything. He lives with me, he has to see how down I get. I live in fear that he will say he doesn't want to try anymore.

We have an unspoken agreement. I'm in charge of all the infertility stuff. I plan, schedule, research, go to the doctor's appointments. I manage the details. I decide when we take a break; I decide when we do another IVF. If a big decision needs to be made, I consult him. Otherwise, I pretty much do it alone. I prefer it this way. This way, I get to carry on trying. It works for us.

I wonder sometimes, do I want this much more than he does? It's different for men, I know. They don't have the same primal urge, that instinctual drive to have children. We don't speak about it a lot and, when we do, he says he wants children, but if we don't ever have any, it will be OK. I wish I could be like him. If we never have children I think I will die of heartache.

One afternoon – it is a weekend, after some particularly horrible event, a failed cycle, or a fail at some or other pass/fail point – we're out walking the dogs. It's a good time to chat when we're walking the dogs. There is less pressure. I need to sound him out, to see how committed he is to this process. It is hard on both of us – financially, emotionally, in every sense. I am prepared to carry on trying until I have a baby, or die trying, whichever comes first. But I need to know how far he is prepared to go. If he says he doesn't want to carry on trying, then … well. Then I don't know what.

I tell him how I feel, that I'm frightened of what our future holds. I'm scared we may never succeed, never have a child.

In his quiet, strong way he says, 'Sweetheart, we *will* have a child one day. And do you know why? Because we will do whatever it takes. Maybe our child won't come to us through the usual channels, but *we will* have a child one day. Of that I have no doubt.'

I can't begin to tell you how much that means to me. It is as if a weight has been lifted off my shoulders. That simple sentence tells me so much, that he is behind me all the way, and that he is committed to carrying on trying. Even better, he believes that we will have a child one day. Something that in my darker moments, of which there are many, I am beginning to doubt. We will have a child one day. We *will* have a child one day.

And that is how Marko is. He is my rock, my foundation, my strength. He may not be the most romantic husband in the world – he's most certainly not the chattiest. He may not be like some other husbands who go to every appointment or who spend hours on the Internet researching stuff, who know all the details about eggs and retrievals and stuff. He may not be like some husbands, but he is exactly what I need. He is perfect for me.

IVF #2

After the great Sex-and-Herbs-and-Elvis Caper I decide to get back in the saddle, so to speak. God clearly has a sense of humour when it comes to my life plans, because amid the drama of my last IVF cycle a whole bunch of us were retrenched from the start-up company I was working for. I liked working there, one of the many reasons being that it brought home a decent salary – enough to make infertility treatment possible. Losing my job scares the hell out of me. Where am I going to get money to do more treatments? Luckily, it's not long before I find a fairly decent job with a salary that, while lower than previously, is enough to do one more IVF.

My new job is situated directly across the road from the fertility clinic. I take that as a good sign. I look for good signs everywhere. Where I can't find them, I make them up.

Dr H says that this time we're going to try a different hormone treatment as my body responded so poorly to the first lot. He suspects I might have Polycystic Ovarian Syndrome, or PCOS, as it is commonly known. It's a fairly common condition and relatively easy to treat. Even Posh Spice has it. I find this out after hours of Googling: 'PCOS and success rates', 'Getting pregnant with PCOS', 'PCOS and IVF'.

I feel a lot calmer about this cycle. Getting off the roller-coaster for a while has helped. The whole herbal experiment has also made me realise that high-tech is the way to go. That naïve optimism of the first cycle is long gone. I realise I'm in for the long haul; I'll do whatever it takes.

I start with the suppression hormones again, the follicle stimulating hormone, the aspirin to thin my blood to increase flow to the uterus and prevent clotting in the lining. Now we also add medication to deal with the suspected PCOS condition. Another few thousand rands spent on medication, syringes and whatnot. Same drill: I inject myself in the morning, Marko does it in the evening. I have bruises and track marks all over my body.

I am nervous for the first scan, the first of the many pass/fail points. I'm so scared there will be no eggs. That I'll be cancelled again. This time, the scan reveals plenty of eggs. Thank God.

'How many?' I ask Dr H.

'Many,' he answers with a smile.

I leave feeling a little more hopeful than when I arrived. We have eggs – so far so good. But I can't be happy. Not yet. I need the blood test results first. Everyone is waiting to hear how the scan went, but I don't want to say anything yet. I'll tell them after I get the hormone blood test results back. This was where I 'failed' last time. But, thank God, the tests come back fine. Perfect. What they need to be.

I get to move on to the next stage in the journey, the next pass/fail point – egg retrieval. This means I have to go into theatre. It is a day procedure, but because you are sedated you aren't allowed to drive afterwards. My mother comes with me for the retrieval. I'm so glad she is with me – she gives me strength. Much as I love Marko, he's not the ideal person to have around for these kinds of things.

I go through the admissions procedure, pay my money and the two of us are taken to the ward. I put on the hospital gown and climb into bed. I am so excited to have reached this point, a stage closer than I was at the last IVF. It feels real; it feels positive. Stuff is happening.

A few of us are in the ward. I crane my neck to read the boards above the heads of the other patients, trying to see who is treated by what doctor. I look at the other women, trying to guess whether they're old-timers or newbies like me.

Why doesn't anyone want to talk? We're in this together, after all. I've never understood why some women seem to feel embarrassed about their infertility. In my mind, there is absolutely nothing to be embarrassed about. We should be bonding in our sisterhood, not avoiding eye contact. Ah, the woman in the bed across from me has made the fatal mistake of meeting my searching eyes.

I beam at her and whisper, 'Are you also here for egg retrieval?' I'm like an excited schoolgirl on her first day at big school.

'Yes,' she answers quietly.

'Have you done this before?' I ask.

'Yes,' she replies with a smile. Good, someone who is prepared to talk to me, to bond with me.

'Oh, how many times?' I ask.

'This is my seventh IVF,' she whispers. *Seventh IVF!* Oh my God. Seven IVFs. Please, dear God, let me not have to do this seven times! I swallow the fear that bubbles up into my throat. I think she can see my fear.

She smiles sweetly and says, 'But this one is *going* to work, I just know it.'

She closes her eyes, a soft smile playing on her lips. I've never forgotten that woman. The clinic won't give out information about their patients, but I asked after her a few years later and Dr H said she had her happy ending. I'm so pleased for her, whatever form that happy ending took.

Then it's my turn to be wheeled into theatre. My mother stays behind. I wave goodbye. I am so excited.

The fertility clinic has this quaint protocol: once your eggs have been retrieved and cleaned up, the embryologist writes the number of eggs retrieved on your hand with a black khoki pen. This is done because they know it's the first thing you're going to want to know when you come around. And because you're so zonked after the anaesthetic, you won't remember what they tell you anyway, so they write it on your hand. It's sweet. And I adore Kimenthra, the embryologist at the fertility clinic. She has the perfect temperament for the job. Quiet, dedicated, professional, yet totally compassionate, kind and caring.

I wake up from the retrieval and I strain my eyes to stare at my hand, willing the numbers to come into focus.

Twenty-five eggs!!! Woooo-hooooo!! Thank God! Fuck. Thank bloody goodness. We have eggs! One step closer. My mother and I practically skip out of there. OK, more of a hobble than a skip for me, but we are elated.

I am sore, my ovaries ache and I feel bloated, but I'm on such a high, I don't care. Twenty-five eggs. Wooo-fucking-hoooo! I know this is only one of many pass/fail points, but at least I've passed it.

Next big one: fertilisation. The normal fertilisation rate is about 70 percent. So if things run to norm, I should hopefully have about 17 embryos to work with. Seventeen embryos would be fantastic.

I wake up at five, grab a cup of decaff and head for my computer to scour the Internet for stuff. Info. Anything. I Google 'eggs', 'IVF', 'possible success rates, 25 eggs retrieved'. Whatever. Anything to keep busy while I wait for the lab to open.

They only open at nine. Nine feels like years away. Eventually it rolls around. I phone. Kimenthra answers.

'Hi, this is Tertia Albertyn. I'm phoning to find out how many of my eggs fertilised.'

Kim says, 'Oh, Mrs Albertyn, I was just about to call you. There seems to be a problem; none of your eggs fertilised, but don't worry, we're going to try to rescue them by injecting the sperm directly into them ...'

I can't hear. The blood is pounding in my ears. Noneofyour-eggsfertilisednoneofyoureggsfertilisednoneofyoureggsfertilised-noneofyoureggsfertilisednoneofyoureggsfertilised.

It can't be true. Oh, for fucksake! It can't be true – please, God, tell me it's not true. How can it be? How can *none* have fertilised? It isn't possible; this is not supposed to happen.

I call Dr H. He has no answer for me. He is very sorry. He says this just happens sometimes – not often, but sometimes. It's difficult to say why. It could just be bad luck. It could be an infection in the sperm. He doesn't know. They're going to try what is called rescue ICSI on the eggs, in other words, inject the eggs with the sperm manually. But I know it's too late. I've Googled myself into a stupor. I know that the chance of a positive pregnancy result after rescue ICSI is very low.

Crack. The sound of my heart breaking. Again. I lie on my bed and sob.

The embryologist does the rescue ICSI and manages to salvage a few embryos. A few days later I return to hospital to have three of them put back in my womb. But in my heart I know the cycle is a bust. The pregnancy test proves me right. Negative. Even though I was expecting it, I am still heartbroken. All that fucking money down the drain.

It is getting increasingly difficult for me to paste that happy smile on my face. I don't want to go out. I don't want to socialise. Every social event is met with dread – will it turn out to be a mommy fest? Will I be the only one there without kids, the only broken one? I guard my fragile, bruised soul with terrified vigilance. I am so raw, so scared that something might sneak through and hurt me more. Every time I hear someone say, 'Oh, guess what!' or 'I have news', my heart sinks and I steel myself for yet another pregnancy announcement. I feel prickly, outside and in. And I can sense people getting impatient with me. I don't blame them. I find it hard to love myself; I can imagine how hard it must be for them.

My best friend Mel invites me to a braai. Her sister will be there with her baby, as well as another woman with her newborn. I tell Mel I won't be coming; I can't be around little babies right now. Mel is hurt and annoyed that I keep rejecting her invitations.

'When?' she asks. 'When will you be able to be around other people and their kids?'

'I don't know, Mel,' I say quietly. While I'm in this horrible, sad place I just can't do it. I'm angry at her for getting impatient with me.

'But what if this takes two years, or five years, or longer?' she asks.

I hate Mel in that moment. Does she think I *like* being like this? Does she think it is easy for me? Oh my God, what if it *does* take two years, or five years, or longer? What then? Is there an expiry date on our friendship? On her patience? God knows, there is an expiry date on my sanity. I can't fucking do this for five fucking years or longer.

And then, just to complete the happy picture, I find out my sister, also Melanie, is pregnant with an oops! baby. What makes it even harder to deal with is that I am the last to know. We braai at my place for my birthday. My whole family is there. They all know Melanie is pregnant, but poor-old, barren-old, fucked-up Tertia hasn't been told. I have never been so angry before in my life. I feel so betrayed.

Everyone knew, except me. Everyone sat at my birthday party knowing Melanie was pregnant, except me. There I was, obliviously going about my social duties with everyone anxiously watching me, whispering to each other, wondering how I would react to the news when they eventually fucking tell me.

I find out afterwards that my sister kept it from me to protect my feelings. She thought she was doing the right thing, but at the time it was the worst betrayal imaginable. It makes me feel like a leper, pathetic, as if I am insane and everyone has to be careful not to trigger a mad outburst.

Melanie and I have always been very close, best friends. We're so alike in many ways. Except for the fertility thing. My sister is very, *very* fertile – about as fertile as I am infertile, which is a lot. I think she collected the fertility genes I missed. She's so fertile that she gets pregnant after having unprotected sex with her boyfriend. She ovulates only two days *after* sex and still gets pregnant. I spend thousands and go through all this shit and … nothing. She has an oops! and gets pregnant. Life can be such a bitch.

I know none of this is her fault. She's having a baby – good for her. Why shouldn't she? It isn't her fault she's so fertile. It isn't her fault I'm so infertile. I don't want *her* baby. I want my own. I know all of this logically, but on an emotional, visceral level I hate her for her fertility. I envy her. I can't bear to be around her. It's so unfair of me; Melanie loves me. She wants nothing more than for me to be happy.

I know this, of course; it doesn't matter, I still don't want to be around her. Her happy, swollen, pregnant belly. My barren, empty, screaming soul.

It's time for another mental and physical break. I can feel myself stretching, snapping. I'm going to take three months off. I'll do another IVF in January. A new year, a new start. Hopefully things will be better in 2002; 2001 has been a fucking terrible year. I feel as if I have aged ten years. I am poorer, fatter, older and as barren as ever. I came close, but nowhere near close enough.

How to be a Good Friend to an infertile person

Being infertile in a predominantly fertile world is not easy. It's an alien state of being. You're constantly reminded of your empty arms, the hole in your heart. They're everywhere – beautiful babies, pregnant women dreamily rubbing their swollen bellies, baby shower announcements, pregnant sisters-in-law, births. You're surrounded. There's no escaping.

It hurts. And you can't say or do anything. What would you say or do anyway? You don't want them *not* to have babies, you don't want them *not* to be happy and excited. You want your own baby. But seeing it all, living with it every single day in every single place is a constant reminder of the very thing you long for so deeply. There's no getting away from it – at the mall, among your family, at church, at work – babies, bellies, prams. It makes you prickly, it makes you heartsore, it makes you want to withdraw from your social life and family. It also makes it hard to be friends with you.

In desperation, my dear friend Meriel asks, 'How do I become a Good Friend to an infertile person?' This makes me realise how hard that can be. Merely by asking this question, Meriel has shown herself to be a Good Friend, because for the most part, all we really want is acknowledgement of how hard it is to be infertile in a very fertile world.

So, from an infertile person's point of view, some advice:

Firstly, it ain't easy. Being a Good Friend to an infertile person is a thankless job with fluid parameters. It may appear that no matter how hard you try, you never seem to get it right. At times you will be extremely busy and

FROM THE HEART

the job becomes demanding. At others, you'll be benched, forced to sit on the outside looking in. Frequently, there will be no logic to the pattern. So, be aware of the volatility of work pressure when applying for the job. It's not a decision to be taken lightly.

Secondly, there is no universal job description. Worst of all, your job description will change from time to time. Infertiles come in different flavours. One can pigeonhole the flavours to some extent, but exceptions will always exist.

- Your eternal optimist/newly diagnosed/completely uninvolved infertile doesn't need too much in the way of special friendship; she believes the problem is temporary and will get resolved soon. She doesn't feel broken, different or an outcast.
- Your longer term/highly involved/high-tech infertile is a tricky beast – one to be handled with great caution and kid gloves. She feels alienated from society and carries great pain and angst in her soul. She may not show it all the time, but she has a very sensitive, raw spot that is easily bruised.
- Then you get the hardcore veteran (aka the good-humoured veteran), who's been at it for so long, it's become part of who she is. The hardcore vet has gone through the great angst and intense pain of the dark years and has come out realising that while infertility is unbelievably hard, it doesn't have to be all-consuming. Instead of crying, she laughs. Because infertility can actually be a comedy of errors.

An infertile will tend to move through these stages at her own pace. Which makes it hard to be a Good Friend. What is expected of you is so different at each stage.

She may be stuck in the dark stage – a very painful place. There is no hope, just a great deep, dark sense of despair. She feels totally alienated from the rest of the world and is consumed by her situation. Everything hurts and everything has the power to hurt. Her world shrinks to that of infertility and she fights tooth and nail to protect her fragile hold on sanity.

At this stage, all you can do is offer friendship and support from a distance. Say to her, 'I am here for you if you want to talk, or not talk – or drink, or swear, or shop. But if you don't want to do any of those things, that's perfectly OK. I'll be here, waiting, when you are ready to come out of the cave.'

If you can bear it, hang in there – your friendship should return to some semblance of normality once your infertile has worked her way through the dark despair. It has nothing to do with you or your ability to be a friend; it has everything to do with her coping with the horrible reality of her situation.

Being a Good Friend to the eternal optimist or the good-humoured veteran is a lot easier.

Survival tips

1. A Good Friend never judges. Unless you've walked in your friend's shoes, you can't say, 'Well, I would never do IVF/try for so long/spend so much money ...' Who likes judgmental people, anyway?

2. A Good Friend will educate herself about what her infertile is going through. (*Huge* proviso – see point three below.) Read up about infertility to get a high level of understanding of the intricacies involved in the process, so that when your infertile does share some of her world with you, you get it.

3. Never offer flippant advice, or hot-off-the-press, latest-research tidbits about a fantastic new procedure that is sure to work. Most of what appears in your local paper is stuff your infertile did in Infertility 101. Been there, failed that.

   Which goes back to point two. Educate yourself about your friend's diagnosis to avoid offering pointless advice. Whatever you do, never, ever say, 'Just relax.' Would you tell a diabetic to just relax? Would you tell someone who can't see to just relax? Of course not. Just relaxing will not change the medical diagnosis causing infertility. Do enough reading to carry on an intelligent conversation, should your infertile decide to engage you in one.

4. Never, ever offer platitudes. Platitudes will make you feel better but your infertile worse. Saying, 'Maybe you're not meant to have children,'

is an incredibly hurtful thing to say. You wouldn't tell a diabetic that maybe she isn't meant to have insulin, would you? Infertility is a medical condition. Not some factor in the bigger plan of the universe.

Then there is this beauty: 'Are you sure you want kids?' Spoken while she looks lovingly at her own screaming kids. No dear, I am spending thousands and enduring physical, emotional and mental anguish just because I am bored and there's nothing on TV. And also please don't tell me about your friend/cousin/colleague who got pregnant naturally after eight years of trying. It doesn't make me feel better – it depresses me. *Eight years?* I have to endure this pain for eight years?

5. The tricky one. Announcing pregnancies, baby showers, births and other kid things. You're just going to have to trust your infertile to know what she can or cannot handle. Don't hide things from her, but respect her wishes when she says, 'I don't think I'm going to be able to handle that.'

   Your infertile knows her good days and bad days, what she can or cannot handle. By all means invite her, but give her the choice to say no. Don't tell her in front of other people. Broach the subject privately first, so that she has time to compose herself and put on a brave face. If any tears are shed, remember that it is not because she isn't happy for you; she is. It's just another little knock on an already very bruised and battered soul.

6. The level of involvement. Infertiles differ in this. Some, like me, are pretty open about the whole thing. Others prefer to keep their infertility private. Find out what your infertile prefers and operate at a level with which she feels comfortable.

7. Which brings to me to my final point. If you don't know how to act, ask. I love that my friends ask me how I want them to act around me. They also know that if they ask the question, 'How is it going with your infertility treatment?' I will either tell them or I will say, 'Not great. I don't want to talk about it now.' They totally respect that and don't push. I have great friends.

Much has been written on the web about this topic and how to act around an infertile. If you're a Good Friend, you will have done a little web surfing and read those things.

I thank my Good Friends who have stuck with me. I know it hasn't been easy. I appreciate your friendship, I really do.

IVF #3

It's a new year, a new start. January 2002. On to IVF #3.

This time we tweak the medication even more. I say we, because by now I'm fully involved in my own treatment. Dr H is divine like that. He treats me as an equal, an intelligent, thinking adult. He knows I Google ferociously. The poor man is endlessly patient with all my questions, all my Internet printouts about the Latest and Greatest New Thing to get me pregnant. He patiently explains why the latest miracle won't work, or why it may just work.

Dr H and I review my history. It seems we have the egg-making side right, the last haul of 25 eggs being a good one in anyone's book. The fertilisation part is where it all went wrong last time. And this time, we're not leaving that to chance; those sperm cells of Marko's have clearly inherited his stubborn streak. This time, we're going to force the little buggers to do their thing through a process called ICSI (Intracytoplasmic Sperm Injection). ICSI is the process in which a high powered microscope is used to inject specially prepared single spermatozoa into a mature egg in order to effect fertilisation.

Around we go again, I start the shooting up, the suppression hormones, the ovarian stimulation injections, the blood thinners, the thousands of rands to be given as a deposit. The whole shebang.

Dr H has taken leave (selfish bastard!) and I see Dr K in his absence. Dr K makes me laugh. He is the archetypal nutty professor. I swear, he even looks the part. He's very clever; nothing like my darling Dr H, but he knows what he's doing.

Once again, I approach the first scan with nervous trepidation. The first IVF has left a huge mental scar. So has the second. I know now that nothing is ever a given, that I can't take any pass/fail point as a fait accompli – that I'm so far out of range of 'normal' that I'm practically a category on my own. A category called un-fucking-believably unlucky.

Dr K scans me. First stage seems OK. I can see for myself that we have eggs. Lots of them. I ask Dr K how many eggs he thinks I have. He replies, 'Enough for an entire football team, plus the referee and some reserves.' We like that. A lot.

I kind of guessed I had quite a few eggs inside because my tummy is hugely swollen and bloated, and my poor lazy-arse ovaries have been complaining like crazy. I don't think they've ever worked so hard in their lives before. The scans and the blood tests all go well; everything is happening as it should.

Time for egg retrieval, once again with my divine mother at my side.

I come around from the operation and immediately force my eyes to focus on the number written on my hand. What the fuck! Thirty-five eggs! I shut my eyes tightly and open them again, forcing the haze of the anaesthetic away. Still there. Thirty-five eggs. No wonder I was so bloody sore and swollen!

Yay!!!!! Have eggs! Have *lots* of eggs, a fabulous haul. Surely I'll get some embryos out of them. All we need now is good fertilisation results; with the ICSI, which 'forces' fertilisation, we should hopefully get at least a few.

Why don't they do ICSI every time, you ask? Firstly, it is expensive (as if none of this other shit is expensive!), and secondly, because some form of 'natural selection' is supposed to take place during fertilisation – only those eggs that should be fertilised will be fertilised during the process of unassisted/natural fertilisation. Whatever. I've never been big on natural.

I lie awake the whole night and call the lab at one minute after nine on the dot.

Kim is not there. Instead, the head embryologist, Ms Battle-axe, barks into the phone, '*Hello!*' Friendly customer service is clearly not her strong suit. Bitch.

'Tertia Albertyn here. I'm calling to find out how many of my eggs fertilised,' I stutter. I'm so, so, sooo bloody nervous, I can hardly talk. Oh, dear God, please let there be at least some embryos.

She barks, 'It's nine o'clock now. We only open at nine. I'll phone you back in a while. Bye.'

Fucking *cow!* It is fucking one minute after nine. What the fuck have you been doing for the last minute, you fucking slacker? I can't believe it. I'm sick with nerves and she says she will call me in a while?

I call back after 15 minutes. I literally cannot wait a second longer – my head will explode. Does this woman have any bloody idea how much emotion is vested in this process? How much anxiety?

She comes on the line and seems to have thawed by ten degrees to -50 °C. Fucking battle-axe.

'You have 34 embryos,' she barks in a slightly friendlier tone. *What?*

'Thirty-four. You have 34 embryos. We retrieved 35 eggs from you and 34 fertilised with ICSI. Well done.'

Oh hallelujah, praise the Lord!!! Skippidy-skip-skip. Thirty-four embryos! That is bloody excellent. I have so many embryos I could have a million kids! I am so bloody happy. See, the reason you want lots of embryos is, first and foremost, because it allows you the choice to select the best ones to return to the uterus. Embryos go through a natural attrition process as they grow from one to three to five days old. By day five only the strongest few remain – perhaps around 50 percent of what you started with. Then the rest, those embryos that are not transferred back into your womb, can be frozen for future IVF attempts – a process known as Frozen Embryo Transfers, or FETs.

The success rate with FET is lower than with a 'fresh' cycle, because handling the embryo during the freezing and thawing process creates the risk of damaging it, thereby either severely reducing the chance of implantation, or losing it completely. Some fertility clinics in the United States claim success rates of around 50 percent with frozen embryo transfers. Rates at my clinic are far lower. But because a frozen cycle is so much cheaper than a fresh cycle, people want to have enough embryos left over to freeze.

Thirty-four embryos is a fabulous number to work with. In fact, I'm told it's one of the highest fertilisation percentages attained at the clinic – it's, like, a 98 percent fertilisation rate. Bloody excellent! Of course, not all will survive the attrition process. Remember, only about half do.

But for now, for today, I'm on top of the world – we have 34 embryos. I'm a veritable chicken. Cluck-cluck.

Day three arrives and it is time to check on how the embryos are doing, how many are still alive. By this stage, it is common for about 40 percent of the embryos to have perished.

I call the lab. Thank goodness Kim is on duty, She tells me all 34 embryos have survived and are dividing. This is just fantastic news. I ask that half of them be frozen at this stage, as freezing on day three yields the best results for FET, at least at this clinic – and that the rest be left to grow to day five.

So, we have eggs, we have fertilisation, now we have embryos – good embryos, lots of embryos. Another step closer. I'm feeling really good about this cycle.

Day five is transfer time. It's a Saturday and the clinic is quiet. Being a day hospital, most procedures are done from Monday to Friday. The wards are empty. Dr K and Kim arrive at my hospital bed. As usual, they draw the curtain and get busy with the preparations. The catheter is ready and loaded with my precious embryos – three of them. The best three. My little babies. By this stage, day five of the embryo's life, it has all the cells it needs to create a whole baby. It is even genetically recognisable as male or female. All the genetic markers are there – for eye colour, height, whether the child will be short, athletic, artistic – all there. It is weird, the thought that if all goes well, one, two or three of my children are sitting in the tube of that catheter.

I'm quietly confident. We seem to have all the bits needed to make a baby – good embryos and a willing uterus. Now all we need to do is transfer the embryos into my womb and wait patiently for them to nestle into my uterine lining and hang around there for the next nine months or so. Easy, huh? Transfer should be a breeze – I've had it done before and it was quick and painless. The usual procedure is that the doctor threads the catheter through your cervix and slowly, gently, ejects the embryos from the catheter into a determined spot in your uterus. It is usually over and done with in minutes.

Of course, this time it doesn't work like that at all. This time, the transfer is hell. For some reason or another, Dr K can't thread the catheter through my cervix. He tries and tries again. It is getting painful and I can feel my uterus starting to cramp in protest to the pushing and prodding of the catheter.

Dr K is trying to stay calm and positive, but I can sense trouble. He says he has to reload the embryos into a firmer catheter, as my cervix seems to have a kink in it. He can't get the catheter through my cervix into my uterus, which means he can't get the embryos into the right spot. The longer he tries, the harder he battles, the lower my heart sinks, the heavier the weight on my chest.

I turn my head to the side, slow tears rolling down my cheeks. I know the cycle is a bust. All that trauma to my cervix caused by trying to get the catheter through, not to mention reloading the embryos, can only mean bad things. I can't believe it. Traumatic, difficult transfers are statistically so uncommon, they hardly ever happen.

Why, oh why, does it always happen to me? Why?

We had eggs, we had fertilisation, we even had good embryos. We were so close. So bloody close.

IT TURNS OUT YOU CAN BE A LITTLE PREGNANT, AFTER ALL

Back home, I Google myself into a coma. The University of Google doesn't have good news for me. Traumatic transfers (the official term for when your transfer is a royal fuck-up, like mine was) mean significantly reduced odds on a successful outcome. And we all know how I fare with the whole statistical odds thing.

Once again, like so many stages in the infertility cycle, I'm in the hurry-up-and-wait phase, the two-week period until the pregnancy test. Time is dragging. To pass the time, I decide to join my parents at their beach house in Hermanus. My very pregnant sister is there. It's hard seeing her swollen belly. Very hard. I try to avoid her as much as I can without being rude or hurtful. I try not to look at her belly.

My nephew tells me with pride, 'Do you know what, Aunty Tertia? My mommy is special, she has a baby in her tummy.'

Oh God, yes! She is very special indeed.

Everyone is having fun, on the boat, skiing, riding on the motorbike. I can't do any of that shit, just in case I am, in fact, pregnant. The part I absolutely hate about the two-week wait is that you have to act pregnant, just in case you are. It always makes me feel like a fraud. It also makes the whole experience all the more consuming. You can't just forget about it and act normal. You can't drink wine, you can't have sex, you can't eat sushi, you can't do this, you can't do that.

I lounge around, trying my best not to drive myself crazy, obsessing over every sign or lack thereof. I sneak glances at my sister's belly.

I fantasise about what it would feel like. I wish it was me who was pregnant – with all my heart. I go to the loo a million times and pull down my pants, looking for telltale blood spots on my panties. And voila! Three days before the pregnancy test, there it is – the all too familiar, much dreaded red smear.

Fuck.

I pull up my pants, my shoulders drooping under the weight of my whole family's hope and impending disappointment. I get a sanitary pad from the cupboard, sit down on the toilet seat and put my head in my hands. I sit for a long time, tears plopping onto my shorts. I look at the marks they leave on the material – big, fat, watery stains. I feel so empty, yet at the same time so heavy. I get up, wipe my nose, leave the bathroom and tell everyone. As expected, they're heartbroken for me. Weighty disappointment, collective disappointment. A heavy burden.

My parents don't have Internet access at their beach house and I feel panicky and lost without my friends in the computer. I need to speak to them. They need to talk me down, off the ledge. I need to Google, 'bleeding three days before pregnancy test, chances of a positive pregnancy test', to see whether I can find stories of hope, of miracles, of other people who bled three days before their pregnancy test and still had a child nine months later. I need my friends in the computer.

I make Marko take me into town to look for an Internet café. I log into my bulletin board and post my sad news. I wait a while and soon enough I get some replies. They all tell me not to give up hope – lots of people bleed a little in early pregnancy, so I could still be pregnant. I appreciate their support, I appreciate their wanting to be positive for me, but I know it's over. I just need to accept the fact. I need to give up on the hope.

At least I can stop acting pregnant. Fuck this, I decide, and go skiing and swimming in the lagoon the next day. My mom asks whether I shouldn't rather wait for the test to be sure that I'm not pregnant. I tell her I know I'm not. It's just a case of waiting for my period to come in full.

It is also the weekend of my sister's baby shower. I will not be there. There is absolutely no way in hell I can sit in a room full of mothers and babies and pregnant women and ooh-and-ah over baby stuff. It would kill me, everyone talking about their birth stories, their cute babies. What do I have to say? Nothing. Baby showers reek of all that is fertile. I have no place there. My sister is probably upset with me for not being there, but to be quite honest, I care more about protecting myself right now than about manners and social niceties.

I don't even bother to go for the pregnancy test scheduled for Monday. What's the point of wasting a hundred bucks on hearing someone tell you it's negative? I know it is. Well, except for the fact that my period hasn't actually started. I'm still spotting, but it has got less. Which makes me wonder what the hell is going on.

I schedule a follow-up appointment with Dr H for the next day. This time I want Marko to come with me. I want to have a full and frank discussion with Dr H about what we should do next – three IVFs and nothing to show for it. Perhaps it is time to look at other options. I need to have a plan in place, something to look forward to, work towards. Staring down a tunnel of nothingness freaks me out; goals are what focus me.

Given the fact that I haven't fully started my period, I decide to do a blood test just before the appointment – just to make double, triple sure that I'm not pregnant.

Dr H is kind and caring, as usual. He says he's so sorry the cycle didn't work. I ask him about donor eggs, whether using donor eggs instead of my own will give us a better chance. I ask him whether surrogacy will help. I have an offer from a friend, a real earthy, wonderful, beautiful-inside-and-out friend who is willing to surrogate for me. Dr H says he doesn't think surrogacy will help; there is nothing wrong with my womb. He doesn't believe there is anything wrong with my eggs either. But at this stage, I'm tired. I just want a baby. I'll do whatever it takes, but I want to get off this roller coaster ride from hell.

I. Just. Want. A. Baby.

I almost wish there was something wrong. At least, if something is wrong we'd know and our decision would be made for us. Problem A means treatment option X, problem B means treatment option Y, and so on.

Dr H says he hasn't received the results for the pregnancy test scheduled for the day before. I tell him that I only went this morning. He phones his assistant and asks her to get the results. I listen dispassionately, thinking ahead to the conversation I am about to have with him, the discussions about our plan B.

'Have Mrs Albertyn's results come through yet? What? Thirty-seven? Are you sure?'

Thirty-seven?? Anything over five is considered a positive pregnancy result. *What the fuck!!* The test is positive? But! But! I'm spotting, what does this mean? I am flabbergasted.

'Yes, the result is positive,' says Dr H. 'But the number is low. That combined with the spotting could mean it is a non-viable pregnancy. Or it could mean that the embryo implanted late and the pregnancy is fine.'

The only thing we can do is carry on with the hormone injections, wait the requisite 48 hours and do another blood test. The 'score' or number that results from the blood test is a measure of the amount of pregnancy hormone given off by the embryo. It indicates the viability of the pregnancy, among other things. It is supposed to double every 48 hours. A doubling number indicates a good, healthy, viable pregnancy.

The next 48 hours pass in a stupefied haze. I don't know what to think. I don't know what to tell people. What do I tell them? I am pregnant, but I am also possibly not pregnant? Or, I was pregnant but am no longer pregnant? Or, I'm pregnant but the pregnancy is doomed?

I am willing myself like crazy not to get my hopes up. This pregnancy can't work; it's impossible. Dr Google says the number should be at least greater than 100. Thirty-seven is a piss-willy number in comparison. But ... Dr Google also says healthy babies have been born from pregnancies that have started with numbers as low as 37.

My mind, my emotions are all over the show: Am I pregnant? Am I not? If I am, what will happen? Will it last? Will I miscarry? Oh my God, this not knowing is worse than a definite no. I drive myself crazy. It's all I can think about. It's killing me.

Two days later I arrive at the pathologists' at eight in the morning to have my blood drawn again. (If they opened their doors at four, I would have been waiting there!) By this time I know the drill and mark the form urgent myself.

And I wait.

And wait.

I phone the receptionist at the clinic.

Nothing yet.

I phone again.

The results are in, but only the doctor is allowed to give them to the patient.

Fuck! Hurry up, please! I'm dying here!

Dr H calls me. Fifty-seven. The number should be around 70. But not all numbers double exactly every 48 hours. Some take a little longer. Shit, fuck, shit. What the fuck does that mean? Am I or am I not? The pregnancy could still be viable, but it could also not be viable. It's not looking great, but the embryo is clearly growing, since the number is going up.

Hope is a terrible thing. While there is a fraction of hope, I can't give up. I wait another 48 hours, carry on with the hormone injections, act pregnant, even though I may not be. Try not to lose my mind totally. Try not to think about the fact that I may just have a baby inside me.

The results come back – 75. Not good. Still pregnant – the embryo is growing – but it is looking increasingly less like a viable pregnancy.

Dr H now believes it could be an ectopic pregnancy. In other words, the embryo has implanted itself in a place it shouldn't – in my tubes or somewhere else; not in my womb, where it belongs. The embryo is perfectly healthy, it is just in a place where it can't survive. And unfortunately there is no way of moving it to where it should be. What's more, leaving it where it is could be, at worst, life-threatening for me; at best, it could rupture my tube.

More waiting, more blood tests, more uncertainty. The number keeps going up by just enough to force me to wait another 48 hours for another blood test. At work, in meetings, it's all I can think about. In a moment of complete irony, I attend a presentation where the speaker, in trying to get his point across, makes a joke.

He says, 'It's like saying you're a little pregnant – you either are, or you aren't.'

I have to restrain myself from laughing bitterly and telling him, 'Oh yeah, Mr Fucking Smart-Arse, what would you call what I am?' I've hated that expression ever since.

Fifteen blood tests later, I have scars from the continuous drawing of blood. They struggle to force the needles through the scar tissue; my arms are full of bruises. Three weeks of slowly losing my mind. I am pregnant, yet the pregnancy is doomed; I am, and at the same time, am not pregnant. It turns out you can be a little pregnant, after all.

It is clear that my little embryo is not going to make it, even though it is growing and the numbers keep going up. A scan reveals it is indeed an ectopic (tubal) pregnancy. Which means we have to terminate the pregnancy before my tubes rupture and I risk internal bleeding.

There are two ways of terminating the pregnancy. Either by having an operation to remove the embryo, or by using the drug Methotrexate. Methotrexate is a chemotherapeutical drug used to kill cancer cells. It will now be used to kill my embryo. Dr H faxes me a script and tells me to get the drug and have someone inject it. Then to go home and rest.

I'm at work. My world is crumbling and no one around me knows. My heart is so heavy. This feels so wrong. I have to kill my baby today. Sorry folks, can't stay, have to go kill my baby. I know it's only an embryo, only a few cells big. I know it can't survive. I know I have to do something about it or else I might die, but it feels so fucking wrong to do this. This embryo is my child, my baby.

I phone the pharmacy down the road. They don't stock Methotrexate; it's a rare, very specific drug. I phone a few more. No one has it. I start to feel a little panicky. I want to just get this over and done with. I don't want to think about it anymore. I can feel myself starting to get quietly hysterical inside. I need to fight that hysteria. I can't let the people at work see. I can't let Marko hear.

Eventually I track down some Methotrexate in Wynberg, in some godforsaken pharmacy down some side alley. I drive there in a daze. I park my car. A self-appointed car guard comes up to me to ask for money. I stare at him blankly. I can't talk. He is part of reality; I am in a nightmare. He looks at me strangely and walks away. I walk down the road. My feet are so heavy; every step an enormous effort. I place my hand on my belly. I whisper to my little embryo to forgive me for what I am about to do. I have to keep fighting the hysteria, the urge to run back to my car. I want to get in my car and drive and drive and drive. No one even knows where I am. I haven't told anyone what I'm about to do, where I'm going. I am going through this big thing, and no one knows. No one. The world feels fuzzy, blurry.

Three people in white coats are standing behind the high counter in the pharmacy. Everything seems surreal. I ask for the drug. They hand it over. I ask them to inject me. They refuse. They say they can't inject this scheduled drug without a doctor's note. I look at the three of them in turn. I beg them to help me. They refuse. They shrug and say no. I cannot believe I'm begging people to kill my embryo.

Somebody, please just help me! Can't you see this is killing me? Please just help me! Somebody? Don't panic, don't panic. Deep breaths. Swallow. Keep swallowing. Keep it down.

I call Dr H from the pharmacy, my voice thick with tears and hysteria. He tells me to come in straightaway – he will help me.

I love Dr H, I really do.

I'LL HAVE MY EMBRYOS ON THE ROCKS,
THANK YOU: IVFS #4, #5 AND #6

Well, that was fun. Not.

It is still not over, as my pregnancy blood count has to drop to zero before we can do another procedure. Which means more blood tests, every second day. My poor veins! It takes about a week for it to drop down back to zero. Fun, fun, fun.

Even more fun is Dr H's suggestion that we do a kind of cervix stretching procedure in preparation for the next cycle, to prevent a repeat of the last IVF disaster. Yes. Cervix stretching. Sounds fabulous, doesn't it? Thank God they knock you out for it, because there's no way in hell someone is going to stretch my poor cervix while I'm awake. It's a simple procedure, but I have to go to hospital and it will take me a week or two to fully recover. Nice.

It also means yet another day off work. And no work means no pay. And no pay means less money for IVF. Dr H, the absolute honey, says he will do it on a Saturday.

After this procedure I decide to take another, shorter break before my next IVF. This will be my first frozen embryo IVF cycle, known as FET. I have 17 usable embryos on ice. A frozen embryo cycle is much less stressful, much less expensive. It is also, in my case, much less successful.

It is February, my sister's wedding and I'm a bridesmaid. I'm looking gorgeous in my pink frock, or at least I think so. I am thin, very thin. My family is worried about how skinny I am. I love

---

FET

Frozen Embryo Transfer is when leftover frozen embryos from a previous IVF cycle are transferred to you during a natural or medicated cycle. FET is a relatively new type of fertility treatment. Introduced in the 1980s, this procedure takes embryos that have been frozen for a period of time and replaces them in your uterus after they have been thawed. FET is a relatively non-invasive procedure, which is why many couples choose to have it performed.

From http://sharedjourney.com/ivf/fet.html

THE SCIENCE

---

being skinny. I know it's psychological, but if I can't make my body do what it is supposed to do when it comes to making babies and staying pregnant, then I'll control it some other way. I will control it through weight. Look, Ma! I can control it, punish it, make it do what I want by denying it food. I love being thin; it makes me feel in control. And secretly I like punishing my body – punishing it for all its failings.

The wedding is lovely. I decide to let my hair down completely, even though I'm in the middle of a frozen IVF cycle. I don't care; I'm going to get merrily drunk. I've packed my medication and injections in a Tupperware lunch box, ready for Marko to do the honours at the predetermined hour. He is my designated driver, my appointed injector.

It is time for the jab. I'm on a roll, dancing up a storm. There is something about wine that magically turns me into a really funky, hip dancer. Amazing, huh! I tell Marko it's time and skip off to the loo, Tupperware box in hand. The loo is tiny with both of us in there, especially with one of us drunk and in a pink bridesmaid's frock. I mix the meds, draw it up into the syringe, hitch up my dress, drop my knickers and bend over the basin. Marko is in position behind me, one hand on my ass, grabbing a solid piece of butt cheek, the other at the ready with the syringe, when the door suddenly opens. In my tipsy – OK, shickered – state, I'd forgotten to lock the door.

'Oops!' I shout drunkenly. The intruder beats a hasty retreat. I wonder what she thought.

And so we move through the hurry-up-and-wait. The pregnancy test. The negative result. I'm not surprised; I just don't have much faith in these frozen cycles, although I know of many people who have succeeded with it. Even though I don't think it will work for me, I have to try at least. I have the frozen embryos, and frozen IVFs are so much cheaper than the fresh ones. As in about R12 000 cheaper.

To add a little extra stress into the mix, I get retrenched again; just because, you know, my life is so incredibly uneventful and boring. Turns out to be a blessing in disguise, because I get a fabulous new job, a much better one. A better paid one! More money means more IVF attempts.

A month into the new job I try another frozen embryo IVF cycle, IVF #5. The embryo transfer takes place over the Easter weekend. I promise Dr H Easter eggs in return for good embryos. The hospital is quiet; I've brought each of the staff on duty some Easter eggs, as well as some for Dr H's kids. Easter is supposed to be a time of fertility and abundance. A time for good eggs. Perhaps that bodes well for this IVF. I foolishly allow myself to get hopeful about it. It fails.

That's it! I'm going to try this frozen IVF thing one more time. Even though it's much less stressful on the body, and even though it's a far less invasive procedure, and even though, at R5 000 a shot, it's a lot cheaper than a fresh IVF, it is still a fair amount of money.

I have 11 embryos left. This time, I mean business. I tell Dr H I want to thaw them all and put back whichever embryos survive the thaw. I'm tired of pissing around.

And this time, I'm going to get spiritual about the cycle. I've been distant from God for a while. This time, I'm going to try prayer. I've tried everything else and it hasn't worked. May as well try prayer.

And I pray: 'God, I am putting this cycle in your hands. Only you can give life. I'm placing my embryos in your hands – please bless them with life.'

It feels a little strange trusting God again – He's let me down so badly up until now. But as I say, nothing else has worked – it really does seem to be in the hands of a higher power.

I can't help but be attached to those embryos. They are my future babies; they have Marko's and my DNA, all the DNA they need to be our child. To some people they may be just embryos in a Petrie dish; for me, they're my future children. When I drive past the clinic I send my embryos some mother love.

Embryo transfer is scheduled for lunchtime and I'm working half-day. The plan is to work in the morning, then drive to the clinic, lie down for a few hours afterwards, then go home and start praying some more. As I start packing up my things at noon, my phone rings. It is Dr H. His voice is soft, apologetic. I don't want to hear what he has to say – it can only be bad news. Of course, it's bad news. How could it possibly be anything else? Story of my fucking life.

None of my embryos have survived the thaw; they have all died. I slump down at my desk and lower my head on my arms. I lie, unmoving, until someone walks in and asks if I'm OK. No, I am not OK.

How much lower must I go? I am utterly desolate. So completely hopeless. So helpless. Are my embryos that bad that none of them survived? Will I never, ever get pregnant? I feel so betrayed by God. I've never been particularly religious in the traditional sense, but I've always been close to God. I pray every night. My prayer now is a bitter accusation: 'This time, God, I trusted you. Only you can give life and you chose not to. You chose to allow all of my embryos to die.'

I am furious with God. I can't pray anymore. I can't speak to God, I'm too angry. It's the start of my two-year break-up with God. I am just too infuriated.

This is a low point. The lowest. Somehow it's worse than the failed cycles and the ectopic pregnancy; maybe it's just an accumulation of all the hurt, the pain, the disappointment. I can hardly speak; I am so deeply, profoundly hurt, broken, angry. People around me are getting scared for me.

I am devastated and disgusted with myself and my pathetic body. Remember the room I've kept ready for my baby for so many long, lonely months? I've given up on it. I've put in a spare bed and made it a guest room. It stands empty. I am without hope. I'm an empty shell when my sister's baby is eventually born. Happy. Sad. Sad, mad, bad.

THE DEEP DARKNESS OF DEPRESSION

My dad urges me, gently, to see a psychologist. But what use is talking? Talking won't change reality. I'll walk into the appointment barren, I'll leave barren. What's the point? I don't want to see anyone; in fact, I don't want to leave my house. I want to stay inside and never come out. But my dad begs me to see someone.

'Please go,' he begs me. 'Do it for me, just once, and I won't ask you again.'

OK, I will go to see this shrink. Whatever. I have no strength left, anyway. Besides, I adore my father. I've never been able to refuse him anything.

I make the appointment, all the way in Stellenbosch. The guy comes highly recommended. He's very laid back, very chilled. None of the wishy-washy psychobabble and the 'tell me about your childhood' I was fearing. I like it that he is part of the university. It makes him seem less quackish, more knowledgeable.

The appointment starts off tense. I sit in the chair, arms folded across my chest. I feel defensive; I dare him to feed me a bullshit line. I'll be out of there so fast, his head will spin. But he is nice. Kind. Caring. Decent. We chat. I cry. Quietly, he asks me probing questions. I sob and choke out answers. I fill in a questionnaire. I have to come back again next week. Which is when he diagnoses me as being clinically depressed.

It's a shock to hear those words – initially I fight it. Clinically depressed? I know I am sad, but depressed? Don't clinically depressed people belong in special wards in special hospitals? I function. I go to work. How can I be depressed on top of everything else that is wrong? Fucked-up physically, fucked-up mentally. How much more broken can I get? And yet, it is a relief to hear the diagnosis. Infertility is so hard, I've been through so much, it's no wonder I am depressed.

Yet I can't show anyone. I dare not let anyone, especially Marko, see how depressed I am. I'm scared that if people know how I really feel, they will make me stop trying. I'm scared that Marko won't want to carry on trying if I let him see my bruised, battered, broken soul. I'm scared they will lock me up. So I act happy, I try to act normal. I keep it all inside.

The psychologist asks me to describe how I feel.

It's like I have this black, oily monster living inside my chest cavity, I explain. I can feel it, physically feel it. It's made up of all the pain and emotion I've felt since embarking on this journey, all the tears I turned inward instead of out. It is made up of hurt, fear, envy – of hopelessness and helplessness, of terror and tightly suppressed hysteria, of bitterness. But mostly it is made up of hot, dark, debilitating anger turned to ice-cold rage. Anger at the world, at God, at fate, at my body, my life, my circumstances. The worst thing about this rage is that I can't direct it at anyone; it's no one's fault. I can't let it out in case people see – so it festers inside, it boils and bubbles, rotting, destroying me. This monster lives inside my chest, alongside my broken heart and empty, barren, childless soul.

It started off small, this unwelcome tenant. But it's growing and it is consuming me. There are times when it gets so big it threatens to choke me. I can hardly breathe, I can't speak, my chest burns because the monster is choking me. I can't get air, my throat is burning. I keep swallowing, swallowing all the time, swallowing the monster back down again. I'm scared to open my throat in case the oily mess starts oozing out, in case I drown in it. Once I start to spew this monster out of my mouth, I fear it will never stop. I will disgorge this black, oily mess. It will just come exploding from my mouth and people will be horrified. People will be disgusted; they will know how the trying is affecting me. They will make me stop trying. I can't stop trying, ever – not until I have a child. I would rather die.

Um … well, yes … I think perhaps I am a tad depressed.

The psychologist suggests anti-depressants, but I'm reluctant. I have such an addictive personality, I'm scared I will get addicted and not be able to come off. He refers me to Dr P, a clinical psychiatrist. Dr P works at a government hospital, in a not-so-nice area.

I force myself to make the appointment; I force myself to go. Even the drive there is difficult. It feels as if by going there, getting the pills, I am finally admitting to being depressed. I hate that label – I don't want it on top of that other label I already have. Clinically depressed infertile. Pitiful. Pathetic.

The hospital is horrible. The area downstairs seems deserted, the décor is about a hundred years old. Everything feels surreal, like I'm in a bad movie. I walk up a horrible flight of grey stairs. God, what a depressing fucking place. Just being here makes you want to take anti-depressants.

I've come the wrong bloody way. I'm on the wrong side of the building. I have to walk down another long passageway. Everything is grey and institutional. As I walk down the seemingly endless passage, I look into the open doors. Why is everything so quiet? I see a group of six adults sitting on the floor around a brightly coloured plastic table, a kids' table. They are drawing pictures. Like kids.

Oh fuck, what the fuck is happening to me? How the hell did my life end up like this? I'm in a bad dream. A nightmare. Control the panic, don't freak out. Just breathe. Don't-freak-out-don't-freak-out-don't-freak-out.

Eventually I get to Dr P's waiting rooms. Thank fuck it looks normal, with normal people working there. There are a few people in the waiting room. I wonder why they are there. Are they also fucked up like me? Probably mad, but perhaps not quite as barren? I have to control the urge to run out of there, get in my car and drive home.

Dr P is very professional, very scientific. He asks me why I'm there. I try my best to tell him my story without crying. I last about three minutes. He gives me a tissue and quietly explains a few things about depression and treating depression. I like him. He reminds me of Dr H a little – he is also soft spoken, he also shares his knowledge with me. He explains the medical facts behind the medication. I like that. I feel calmer. What he says makes sense. I feel less like a freak.

He gives me a prescription for the anti-depressants. So, it's official. I am officially depressed. Who would have guessed I'd end up like this? Not me. Not in a million years. But my life can't get much worse, so I may as well try the pills. Apparently they take a few weeks to start working. I have time. I'm not going anywhere.

Hurry up and wait. The story of my life.

I *HEART* PROZAC!!!!

Oh. My. God!!! Oh my God! These pills fucking rock!

Wooo-hoooooooo!!!!

I am skipping all over the place. I am practically manic.

Sigh. I love drugs. Seriously, the Prozac kicks ass. I feel so, so, soooo much better. That black oily monster? Still there, but much, much smaller. It's about the size of my fist now. Much more manageable.

The old Tertia is back. I sleep better, I can concentrate at work, I don't snap at everyone. Oh, and big bonus, I lose weight. Got to love that! Of course, everyone around me is appalled by how much weight I have lost. My mother is worried sick. I don't help matters by saying, 'Mother, if I can't control my body in terms of its reproductive ability, I will control it through my weight.' My weight loss feels heady – I feel in charge, for the first time in a long time. Useless body, I'll show you.

For the first time in ages I want to socialise. I go out drinking and partying again. I also start smoking again. OK, that's not so good. But, you know what? Giving up smoking made bugger-all difference, so I may as well smoke, drink and enjoy myself. I'll stop when I do my next cycle.

I love life at the moment, I really do. I feel good, I look good – all in all, life is pretty good. Marko is smiling from ear to ear, because for the first time in a long time I feel like having sex again. Many people say that anti-depressants dampen your libido. Hell, no!

You want a dampened libido? Try infertility. It kills libido; and so does depression. The anti-depressants make me feel like myself again; I'm lighter, happier. And that makes me feel sexy. And when I feel sexy Marko gets sex – a win-win situation.

People think anti-depressants make you all spacy and *dof*. Not at all, they just take away those crushing lows. For me, they took away the rage. I'm not a spaced-out version of myself – I am like the old Tertia: me before I became so broken. I am still infertile, and it still hurts like mad; I still want a baby more than anything in the world, but the oily black monster is no longer choking me. I can breathe. God, what a relief!

In or out of the closet?

I've always been very open about my infertility and what I'm going through. When people ask me whether I have children, I say no and if they ask more questions I tell them we're trying. Depending on the person, I may say more. And if they have lots of time and I have lots of wine, they will hear about needles, retrieval, ICSI and any other gory details.

Along the spectrum of disclosure there are those on one end who are very private about their infertility. I think it's harder for them, in a way. No one in their social circle knows they're struggling to conceive. Sometimes their closest friends and family don't even know. The people in their lives just assume they don't want children. And the fact that they're going through assisted reproductive technologies like IVF is an even more closely guarded secret. I understand where they're coming from. After all, it's no one's business that they're infertile or getting help.

At the other end of the spectrum you get people like me. Everyone in my life knows I'm struggling to conceive and that I'm doing IVF. My whole family, my social circle, even the people I work with know. I've never hidden any of it. I believe I have nothing to be ashamed about. Infertility is a medical condition. If I had diabetes, I wouldn't hide it from people and I feel the same about infertility.

If you visit as many bulletin boards on the Internet as I do, the level of

disclosure becomes apparent very quickly. Some people remain anony-
mous. They post their messages under pseudonyms and don't reveal any
personal information. I, on the other hand, post messages under my first
name and most people know I'm from Cape Town.

I began to understand something about this after an interesting
conversation with a friend (gorgeous twin boys on her third IVF). She
said she was very private about her and her husband's infertility. She told
no one.

I asked her why she thought she was so closed about it and I wasn't.
Her answer took me by surprise. Their diagnosis was a male factor and she
didn't want anyone thinking any less of her husband. I can understand
that. Unfortunately, many dickheads in the world associate fertility with
sexuality. I can't tell you how many guys have offered to have sex with me
to 'help' me conceive. Just this week a so-called friend at work offered to
help me out with a shag.

'We can shag till the cows come home, darling, it's not going to get
me pregnant. I'm the one with the issue, not my husband. But thanks so
much for that unselfish offer,' I said. What is it with people (men?) that they
think fertility is related to sexuality? Perhaps men will just use any excuse
to get their end away?

So my friend's reservations about going public make sense. I suppose
I'd be far quieter about our situation if it were due to male infertility.
Because I'm the one with the problem and because I don't particularly
care what people think of me, I tell everyone. I know with absolute cer-
tainty that my infertility has nothing to do with my sexuality. Funnily
enough, society does not seem to judge an infertile woman as less sexy
or sexual. It seems to be accepted that a woman can be infertile and still
be sexy and attractive. But society has another set of norms for men.

I can't say which is better, but I guess it is easier to go public about it.
People seem to be more sympathetic, more understanding. And hopefully you get to field fewer questions that go, 'So, *when* are you guys going
to start thinking about having a family?' Then again, the downside is that
your private business becomes everyone else's business.

Each to her own, I guess.

IVF #7

Just because I'm on happy pills doesn't mean my desire for a child is any less. And, unfortunately, no amount of shagging is going to get me pregnant, so it is time for yet another IVF. I'm trying not to think about how much money we have already spent on infertility treatments. And how much this next IVF is going to cost us. So, back to Dr H to start the next cycle.

This time I decide to add acupuncture to the mix. All around the bulletin boards my infertility friends are speaking about it. One thing you can be sure of with an infertile: she will do absolutely anything, try anything, if she thinks it will improve her chances of success, no matter how painful, no matter how seemingly bizarre. In fact, research has shown that infertility patients are second only to cancer patients in what they will endure in order to find a 'cure' – in our case, a successful outcome.

So, if sticking needles into my body will help, I will stick needles into my body. Hell, I would stand in the middle of the highway during peak-hour traffic, stark bloody naked, if I thought it would help.

Acupuncture for infertility

German researchers said they have increased success rates by almost 50 percent in women having in vitro fertilisation (IVF).

The theory is that acupuncture can affect the autonomic nervous system, which is involved in the control of muscles and glands, and could therefore make the lining of the uterus more receptive to receiving an embryo.

From http://news.bbc.co.uk/1/hi/health/1933901.stm

Through a friend in the computer I hear about an acupuncturist called Vicky, who apparently specialises in infertility patients. Perfect. Her practice is also close to the clinic. Vicky is divine – young, clever, caring. And she's suffered losses of her own, so she knows how it feels. I expected a tree-hugger, an ethno-bongo type set-up; what I find is quite the contrary – very professional and reassuring. Vicky always starts off feeling my pulse or energy flows. She can tell with uncanny accuracy how I'm feeling. 'Your pulses are very weak – did you have a bad night?' Or, 'Is your throat sore? I can feel it from your pulse.' She can also tell whether I feel pregnant or not.

So, I go for scans, blood tests, and now acupuncture treatments as well. At a fee, of course. There is nothing cheap about infertility. This time I make it past each of the pass/fail points where I came short in my first three IVFs:

- ☑ *Retrieval:* 28 eggs (fail point for IVF #1)
- ☑ *Fertilisation:* 24 embryos (fail point for IVF #2)
- ☑ *Transfer:* No problem, transferred three healthy-looking embryos (fail point for IVF #3)

So far, so good. Then we wait again – the delightful two-week wait until the pregnancy test. I have acupuncture three times a week to hopefully help with implantation. I stop smoking again.

Vicky is hopeful. She says my pulses feel strong and everything points to a positive result. I must admit, I'm feeling hopeful, this time. Everything has gone well, so far – the eggs, the fertilisation, the transfer. Surely, this time, we will succeed?

It is three days before the scheduled pregnancy test. I'm not bleeding. I take this as a good sign and decide to do a home pregnancy test. I pee on the plastic stick. I stare at the results window, willing the second line to appear. It doesn't. It's negative. Fuck!

I rush to my study and post my news on the bulletin boards, crying to my friends in the computer. They chastise me.

'It's too early,' they say. 'Those home pregnancy tests are evil! Wait for the blood test.'

I hope they're right; I fear they're wrong. Damn, I am so nervous. Just before I leave for the blood test, I go to the bathroom and there it is, as regular as fucking clockwork. Blood on my panties. It's over.

I don't even cry this time. I just feel empty. I can't speak to anyone. It's enough of a burden dealing with my own pain; the thought of having to tell others and dealing with their disappointment is more than I can bear right now. I SMS the news. I e-mail Dr H:

Hi Doc
Bad news, I'm afraid – my period started this morning. I went for the blood test anyway, but expect it to be negative.
Please phone me when you get the results.
How soon can I do a frozen embryo IVF?
Tertia (very sad)

I like that Dr H lets me e-mail him. I much prefer it that way. I spend the rest of the day with a heavy heart.

That afternoon, I get a call from Dr H:

'It's positive – 137.'

'What? But how can that be? I'm bleeding,' I splutter.

'Well, 137 is a pretty strong number, and yes the bleeding is not good, but at the moment you are pregnant, so continue with the hormone support and go back for another blood test in 48 hours.'

Oh fuck, not again. I'm too scared to tell people. It doesn't seem real. I have to tell my mother, though. She says, 'What does this mean?' I don't know, Mom, I really do not know anymore.

A long, long 48 hours later, I go for another blood test, hoping to see a result of around 260ish, a nice, strong, doubling number to indicate a viable pregnancy. Of course, nothing is ever simple with me. I should know better by now. The number comes back at 167. What the fuck does that mean?

I don't know. Dr H doesn't know. Nobody knows. All that anybody knows is that this is not how it's supposed to be. The number should have been around 260, with a margin of about 30 either way. What we have is nowhere near that. Could have been a pregnancy that was initially growing but then the embryo died; it could be what is known as a vanishing twin – two embryos implanted, but one has since died. Who knows? As much as we know about IVF, there is equally much we don't know.

It's Friday. Dr H says I should go for another blood test on Saturday morning. If the number is going up, we may have hope, if going down, well, then we know it's over. The living in limbo, the not knowing, the could-be-but-could-also-not-be kills me. And people expect me to just not think about it? You fucking try not to think about it.

By this time I know the location of all the blood testing centres in the Western Cape. More importantly, I know which labs process results the fastest. I figure out that the lab at Kingsbury Hospital will turn the results around quickest. I drive all the way to Claremont to arrive as the doors open. I have the blood drawn and drive home slowly.

Wait, wait, wait. Time slows down to a crawl and the test is all I can think about. I wonder, I speculate, I hope, I despair. I imagine a million different scenarios, none of them hopeful – I'm too scared to hope.

The number should be around 250ish. The results come back 150. It's over. Fuck. I immediately light up a cigarette (I might have stopped, but I didn't throw away the box!) and pour myself a glass of wine. So what if it's only midday? I don't care. It's not every day you get to be pregnant for a whole four days. I proceed to get very drunk. The rest of the weekend goes by in a haze of cigarette smoke and wine.

By Monday I have some of my sanity back, thanks in no small way to my happy pills. Without them I'd be right back down there, in that black hole, unable to breathe. Of course, I have to go for one last blood test to make sure the number is going down properly, that it really is over.

Dr H calls me with the results. 410.

What the fucking fuck! How on earth can the number go up, then down, then up again? Is the universe trying to drive me fucking insane? I am going to completely lose my mind.

Dr H is as perplexed as I am; the number is supposed to go

either up or down, not up and down. He says to carry on with the hormone support and to go for a repeat blood test in four days' time. Hurry up and wait.

Four days later the number has doubled beautifully – it stands at a magnificent 1 800.

Oh my God, I'm pregnant!!! I am pregnant!! Thank you, God!

HANNAH

I'm ecstatic and terrified at the same time. I'm worried about the erratic blood test results in the beginning. What would that mean for the pregnancy? Dr Google doesn't seem to have much to say on the topic. I am scared it is another ectopic. Dr Google says once you've had one ectopic, you run a higher risk of another. But there is not much I can do until the first ultrasound.

I have to wait a whole two weeks until the first ultrasound. Two weeks of wondering what will happen. Is it finally my turn? Is this it? Is this my happy ending? This time I make Marko come with me. If this is going to be the first ultrasound of our future child, I want him to be there. We're both sick with nerves in the waiting room. We don't speak to each other. We can't. Our mouths are dry. We sit there, me wringing my hands and Marko with his legs bouncing up and down with nervous energy.

Eventually it is our turn. I hop on the exam table and Dr H starts the scan. Oh look! There it is – the most beautiful looking blob in the whole world. Even better, a beautiful, beating heart in the middle of the blob – my little baby, our baby. Our baby has a heart, and it is beating. Marko and I look at each and smile – this is what we've been waiting for for so long.

The scan also shows signs of another sac, an empty sac, from an embryo that implanted but then didn't make it. Our vanishing twin. Which explains the up and down numbers. The pregnancy started out as a twin pregnancy, and then the one little embryo died.

But we're pregnant. I can't believe it. It doesn't feel real. I'm too scared to believe it.

I go out and buy every single pregnancy magazine I can find. After years of staring at them longingly, it is finally my turn to buy them. I am pregnant! Marko suggests that we go to Killarney for the day, to watch motor racing. I happily agree because I can take my stack of pregnancy magazines and a blanket and read all day. I want to devour every single word, prepare for every stage, every pregnancy sign and symptom.

Of which I have none. Not one symptom. And it worries the hell out of me. Dr Google does not have good things to say about that. Well, Dr Google doesn't come out and say it directly, but he says morning sickness is a sign of a good, strong pregnancy. I have not one iota of morning sickness. Does this mean I don't have a good, strong pregnancy? Everyone tells me not to worry, that plenty of people don't have morning sickness and their pregnancies turn out just fine. But it worries me anyway.

In fact, I worry a lot. More than just worry – I am anxious, extremely anxious, horribly anxious. Thing is, I've stopped my antidepressants, even though Dr P, the psychiatrist, assures me that Prozac is perfectly fine to take while pregnant. Even Dr Google says it is perfectly fine to take while pregnant. But I want to do the right thing, the best thing for our baby. I don't want to take them, just in case. And of course, I am pregnant now; it's what I have wanted for so long. The root cause of my depression has been removed – I shouldn't need those pills anymore, I should be happy. Right?

Except I'm not. I'm happy to be pregnant, but it doesn't feel real. In fact, it feels extremely tenuous. Coming off the anti-depressants has left me anxious. It's a horrible, rushy, panicky, sick feeling. Unfortunately, not a morning-sickness feeling.

The anxiety is driving me crazy. I need to do something, so I send poor Dr H another e-mail:

Hi Doc
I'm driving myself absolutely crazy. I'm so scared that I am not pregnant because I don't feel any pregnancy symptoms – no morning sickness, nothing. Just feel like crying or getting angry. Should I be worried that I am not feeling pregnant yet?

I can't believe that after waiting for this for so long I'm too scared to enjoy it. I'm scared that I have such bad eggs that the embryo will stop growing and die. The only thing keeping me sane is that I have no spotting at all.

I don't know whether it is because I am off the Prozac or what, but I feel terrible. So I want to ask you some questions:

1. *Should I be worried that I am not having any pregnant symptoms yet?*
2. *If I miscarry now, will I start bleeding?*
3. *Will the scans affect the embryo if I have too many?*

I just want to know all is OK.
Thanks Doc – as soon as I'm past 12 weeks, I will be buying presents for all! I hope I will be happy then.
Rgds
Tertia

He e-mails me back to say that some people just do not have morning sickness, that a miscarriage is often, but not always, accompanied by immediate bleeding and that we will just have to wait until the next scan. And that I must do my best to relax a little. I know I won't be able to relax until my next scan, which will be at eight weeks and three days. I need to see that flashing heartbeat again.

As you know, I haven't been speaking to God for a while now. I've been pissed off with him. It's Sunday night, the night before the next scan, and I think I should start speaking to God again; I've missed him. I'm still angry, but I'd like to start speaking to him again. So, tonight I'm going to church with my mother for the first time in years. I sit in the pew, holding my flat belly and pray that the next day's scan will bring good news.

Marko comes with me for the scan and, sure enough, there is our blob. But where is the flashing heartbeat? Dr H moves the ultrasound probe around a bit. I can't see the flashing heartbeat. I can feel my own heart sink. The room goes quiet, heavy with our collective dread. Dr Heylen's voice drops. He can't find the heartbeat, but he wants to double-check on a more powerful machine. I feel like telling him not to bother – I know it is over. I get dressed and go to the radiologists across the passageway.

I look at Marko. 'I knew it, I just knew it,' I mutter. I'm not even surprised. I knew it; I knew it wouldn't last. I knew this was too good to be true. It was too easy. I feel numb. Dead.

I can see the pain on Marko's face. Oh God, my heart aches for him. I feel I've let him down. Dr H is devastated; he so wanted this to be my happy ending. I've let everyone down. I'm such a failure, such a broken, useless, worthless woman. I just can't seem to do this; I am too fucking useless. My useless, useless body.

Oh, my poor little baby, I am so sorry. You never even had a chance. I wanted you so very badly. I am so sorry.

The more powerful machine gives the final answer. The little embryo must have died in the last 24 hours. Dear God, is this a sick joke? I go to church for the first time in years and this happens? My baby probably died while I sat in church. I will never to talk to you again. Ever.

The dead embryo must be removed from my womb, so a D&C is scheduled for the next day. My wonderful, beautiful mother is with me as I lie waiting for them to scrape my little baby out of my womb. I wanted to come alone. I'm scared I'm going to lose it completely and I don't want anyone to see me totally unhinged. My mother won't let me. She begs me to allow her to come with me. She says she won't say a word; she just wants to be there for me. I say OK. I don't have any energy to fight, anyway.

Oh God, this feels so wrong. I reach for my mother's hand and sob. Great heaving sobs. I am so glad she is with me. I need her.

Dr H comes in. He pats my hand, tells me how sorry he is. I notice that his knuckles are raw and ask him what happened. I make a weak attempt at a joke and ask if he's been in a bar fight. He laughs and says no, he just had a particularly heavy session with the punching bag at the gym last night.

He looks into my eyes and says, 'Yesterday was a hard day.' God, I love this man. I know he really cares. I can see how much he is hurting for me.

The D&C is quick, painless. Just like that – the brief pregnancy is over, the baby is gone and the dream shattered. I immediately go back on the anti-depressants. I need them.

I've decided to name the baby. I've decided she was a girl. She just felt like a girl to me. Her name is Hannah. I make a little memory box of her things: the printout of her first scan, a pressed flower from the bouquet I got from her daddy when we received the happy news, a pair of knitted booties from an aunt. It is a small box – she was a small girl, here for a small time.

People differ in their views on whether to name a lost baby, a miscarried baby. Many people, especially those who have never lost a baby through miscarriage, don't even consider the foetus a real baby. That's their view. Hannah was real to me. She was my child. She was real. I saw her heartbeat; she carried all my dreams and hopes with her.

Dr H sends the foetal tissue away for testing to establish what happened. One of the hardest things is not knowing what went wrong with little Hannah. If you don't know what is wrong, how do you fix it?

Perhaps my eggs are just totally shit, useless. Maybe it is time to seriously consider donor eggs. I've asked my sister whether she would consider donating her eggs. I know that using a known donor, someone you know, carries enormous issues, not least of these the role that person will play in your child's future. How will the donor feel about the child? But here's the thing: I so badly want a child that is genetically related to my parents, my father especially. I don't know why, but it is important to me to have a child that carries some of my father's genes, so my sister would be the perfect donor. Plus, of course, she is super-fertile, which has to help.

The results come back – Trisomy 21. She had Down's Syndrome. What a relief. We have a reason for the loss. She was a special little baby, but she was genetically unable to survive. Of course, plenty of Down's babies survive and thrive, but she was obviously severely genetically broken. The body will often miscarry genetically imperfect embryos.

I am so relieved to have a medical reason, a known cause for the loss. Trisomy 21 can happen to anyone. It is quite common. It was just bad luck, a fluke. It means I can try another cycle with my own eggs. It means I don't have to deal with the complexities of donor eggs – for now, at least.

But first, a break. My body, mind and soul desperately need a break from the pregnancy and D&C. Some time off to smoke, drink, have gratuitous sex and not have to think about hormones, eggs, embryos, injections, dead babies or any of that other shit.

Closer and closer

FROM THE HEART

I have a theory. About my path. You know how people say that destiny/ fate/God (to whom I'm still not speaking) has a plan for everyone? Well, I have a theory about my plan. My theory is this:

I think that somehow, for some reason, I am destined to go through every single bloody thing that it is possible for an infertile person to go through. As if I need to personally experience each possible step, each possible fail point along the way. And with each IVF, I get closer and closer.

- IVF #1 – no eggs, got cancelled, didn't get to pass begin.
- IVF #2 – lots of eggs, but no embryos because of zero fertilisation.
- IVF #3 – had eggs, embryos, fertilisation plus a positive pregnancy, but unfortunately it turned out to be an ectopic pregnancy.
- IVF #4 and #5 – horrible, useless frozen embryo cycles that ended up being a big waste of time and money.
- IVF #6 – another frozen embryo cycle, but this time it was even worse – all the embryos died during the thawing process leaving nothing to transfer.
- IVF #7 – had eggs, embryos, a positive pregnancy test, even got to see a heartbeat, but never got to see a baby.

Closer and closer, one step at a time.

I wonder if the reason for my long, horrible, sad journey is not so that I can help other people? I love helping people and I've become somewhat of an expert in this infertility stuff. I'm the advice person on some of my bulletin boards.

This theory of mine helps me approach the next IVF with a fair amount of hope. It's as if the bad things are out of the way now. We've been through everything (well, besides one totally terrible thing – a thing so terrible I can't even articulate it), so surely, please God, the next one will give us a live baby?

It's been over two years now. Two years of non-stop stress, of angst and heartbreak. I can feel us getting closer. I can't stop now – we are so close.

I NEVER EVEN KNEW I HAD A
GLAND THERE, LET ALONE BARTHOLIN!

It's time for the next cycle. I've quit smoking. My acupuncture appointments are made. Mentally ready? Check! Emotionally ready? Check! Physically ready ... um ... what the fuck is that lump in my fanny?

There I am washing my bits, as one does, when I feel it. Not in my fanny as such, but kind of on the outside. I panic. Oh great! Now I have cancer. I am dying. Fabulous. I will die childless and barren. Not only have my completely fucking useless female bits not done their bloody job by producing a child, they are now going to cause my death. Can they do nothing right?

I e-mail Dr Heylen to tell him I'm worried the lump is cancer from all the fertility drugs. He e-mails back:

Dear Mrs A

It is not cancer. You are not dying. It's a blocked gland. See Dr C at Constantiaberg. She's the best.

Phew. I'm not dying. It would be terrible to die barren. Almost as bad as dying a virgin, except if you died a virgin you wouldn't know whether you're barren, now, would you?

What I have is a blocked Bartholin's Gland. Good Lord, I didn't even know I had a gland there. Apparently everyone has it. Two, actually. And in *one* percent of cases the gland gets blocked and needs to be treated. Oh, those impossible fucking odds. Lottery ticket, anyone?

I need to sort it out before my next cycle. The procedure is known as a Bartholin's Gland marsupialisation and, no, it's not the insertion of a kangaroo in your fanny, merely some kind of bypass – a quick and relatively painless procedure.

But! In a few cases the gland is so badly blocked it requires complete removal. And yes, you've guessed it – again I'm the lucky one-percenter. My gland is beyond saving and has to come out. Ouch!

I leave the hospital one Bartholin's Gland poorer and with one very sore fanny. Kind Doctor C gives me a few condoms to be filled with water and frozen – a personal icepack for my fanny. Recovery takes six to eight weeks, so my fanny and I are out of action for the next month or so. More waiting. Wait, wait, wait. *Hurry up!* I want to get on with it. I'm itching to get IVFing again.

I manage to pass the time in a haze of cigarette smoke and wine. I've just about totally abandoned my clean living protocol. It's got me nowhere and, to be perfectly honest, being bad is just so much more fun than being good. I refuse to be infertile *and* well-behaved.

IVF Barbie

When the product developers at Mattel were looking to design their new Barbie, IVF Barbie, they soon realised there was no universal Barbie that would accurately portray the spirit of IVF Barbie. So they came up with several variations.

FROM THE HIP

NEWBIE BARBIE

Also known as BabyDust Barbie, this is a bright and perky lass, filled with optimism and confidence that IVF Will Work. She is thinner and usually younger than the other IVF Barbies. Her accessories include rose-tinted spectacles, a positive bank balance, healthy medical-aid coverage and a million questions. Newbie Barbie has lots of other Newbie Barbie friends and they congratulate each other on a job well done. This Barbie only says pleasant, optimistic things and believes that Attitude is Everything. Her motto is 'Think Positive!'

PREGNANT NEWBIE BARBIE

Pregnant Newbie Barbie is the big sister to Newbie Barbie. She is still slim, but now has a cute little boep. She is proof that IVF Does Work, usually the first time. She also comes with rose-tinted spectacles, a positive bank balance (only very slightly depleted) and total confidence that All Will Be OK. She glows when pregnant and liberally uses baby dust (a glittery tub of ground-up positive attitude that apparently has hocus-pocus power to make one pregnant) when playing with her Newbie Barbie sisters. She comes with Very Cute maternity clothes, a double stroller, and a fully decorated nursery, even though she is only just a few weeks pregnant. Her motto is 'See! Thinking Positive Works!'. Newbie Barbie and Pregnant Newbie Barbie are great playmates and you can collect them as a set.

JOINER BARBIE

Joiner Barbie is cousin to Newbie Barbie and Pregnant Newbie Barbie. Joiner Barbie is to be found all over the bulletin boards on the Internet, and she comes with groups of friends just like her. These groups even have names. The name normally has a furry animal in it, or it may make reference to a season. Think Spring Blossoms or Bubbly Bunnies. Accessories include a chart or table of some sort, lots of smiley faces, baby dust, declarations of eternal friendship and love and lots of ((((hugs)))).

VETERAN BARBIE

Veteran Barbie is not at all related to any of the Barbies above. Veteran Barbie is the Anti-Barbie. She's a whole lot plumper than any of the Newbie Barbie range, less perky (in boobs and attitude), has greyer hair, a largely negative and overdrawn bank balance, plenty of bruises and marks and a slightly cynical attitude. She is dressed in comfy trackie pants with an elasticised waistband. Her accessories include a wealth of knowledge of reproductive procedures and protocol, the ability to practically do her own cycle, a snarky attitude, little tolerance for stupidity, a well-defined sense of humour, the ability to laugh at herself, a fondness for wine, beer or crack and a healthy distrust of rumoured sure-fire IVF success potions, positions and theories, baby dust and Newbie Barbies. This aversion in its more severe form can be allergic and acerbic. Veteran Barbie tends to swear like a trooper (especially when playing in the Barbie House with Newbie Barbies and Pregnant Newbie Barbies). Parental guidance is advised.

PREGNANT VETERAN BARBIE

Pregnant Veteran Barbie is very similar to Veteran Barbie, only in this incarnation she has an added baggage of neuroses and paranoia. She continuously and obsessively over-analyses every twinge, convinced that the end is nigh. She buys strollers and decorates the nursery only in her eighth month of pregnancy. Accessories include disbelief and a sense of not quite belonging, and ten home pregnancy test kits, just in case the first one was faulty or the clinic made a mistake with her blood test. Pregnant Veteran Barbie has been known to pee on sticks up until the day before giving birth just to see two lines forming.

CELEBRITY IVF BARBIE

Celeb Barbie comes in two versions: Denial Celeb Barbie and Out-of-the-Closet IVF Barbie. Denial Celeb Barbie does not play with the other Barbies and pretends not to be an IVF Barbie at all. She drops the IVF part of her name and thinks donor eggs is a swear word. She pretends that the birth of her twins at age 49 is Natural and she did it All On Her Own. She also claims her boobs are her own and that she's never had a face lift. Hence her credibility is shot to shit.

Out-of-the-Closet IVF Barbie has a firm grip on reality. She's the preferred Barbie. We like her.

IVF KEN

Ken is a wanker. Besides being a wanker, there is very little that Ken does in IVF land. Sometimes Ken administers shots, hands out tissues and occasionally accompanies Barbie on visits to Fertility Doctor Ken (normally during the first few cycles only). But mostly he is just a wanker. When choosing an IVF Ken, try to get one that also cooks and does DIY. Otherwise just sit him down in front of your Barbie TV and let him know when it's time for him to make his, um, contribution.

Mostly Barbie loves Ken, unless Ken is being particularly insensitive or obnoxious. Then he becomes a wanker in all senses of the word. Some

IVF Barbies don't have a Ken and they do just fine. If you find a good Ken, hang on to him – don't swap him with your friends.

FERTILITY DOCTOR KEN

Dr Ken is the all-knowing, all-seeing Ken. He may or may not be a wanker. In the figurative sense of the word, that is. He may be very nice. His accessories are many and wonderful. He comes with a zooty new car (normally very expensive), a smart house, a healthy bank balance and a holiday home or two. Dr Ken knows everything and is considered second only to God. Some are kind, some not. All are rich.

Dr Ken's office is filled with fun toys like ultra-sound machines, dildo-like probes, waiting rooms filled with a whole selection of Barbies (some there, annoyingly, with miniature Barbies or Kens in tow), medicines and procedure rooms. Dr Ken comes with a free Nurse Ratchet Barbie, who will not return your calls, will spout forth annoying platitudes and will generally add to your frustration levels. When purchasing Dr Ken you will also get Ultrasound Ken and BloodDrawer Ken.

Mattel foresees a big demand for its new range. For extra fun and lively interaction, they recommend you collect the full set of IVF Barbies, put them in the Barbie house together and watch the sparks fly.

IVF #8

In my worst nightmares I never, ever imagined I'd be doing eight IVFs. *Eight*. That's a lot of IVFs. A lot of money, time, tears and emotional energy spent. But, it's IVF or nothing, and nothing is not an option.

This time, I throw everything into the mix, all the different cocktails of drugs and hormones I've researched – acupuncture, blood thinners, everything. My stomach looks battered and bruised from the injections. I don't care, I'll do whatever it takes. Whatever.

We get only eight eggs. My smallest haul yet. I'm not too worried, because I have a theory. Yes, another one. This theory says that quantity compromises quality. 'Normal' IVF patients get around 12 eggs. That is considered a good haul. I've been averaging around 30 eggs – surely something is being compromised there? My entirely unproven, unsupported and probably completely crap theory says that the quality of my eggs is weakened by having so many. And, of course, the whole wanting to have some left over to freeze doesn't matter to me any longer. The frozen embryo transfers have been a complete non-event. So I am not displeased that we have eight.

By day three we have only four left. Hmm … not so happy now. Four don't give us much to work with. I tell Dr H that I think we should do a day three transfer. For my other cycles the embryologist has been letting the embryos grow to day five, at which point Dr H returns the strongest looking ones. I want to try something different. Besides, I don't want to risk losing any more embryos through the natural attrition process.

Two of the embryos look good (eight cells), two OK (six cells). I have a chat with Dr H. I've had enough of this IVF shit – I want to go for broke

Tertia: 'Doc, I want to suggest something.'

Dr H *(nervously)*: 'Ja …?'

Tertia: 'Let's chuck all four back.'

Dr H: 'Hmm … I'm not sure that's a good idea.'

Tertia: 'Come on, Doc, we only have four. You know I usually have *lots* more at this stage. Plus, this is my *eighth* IVF! It's not like I'm a newbie at this. I mean, really, what are the chances *all four* will take? Especially since only two are good, and the other two just OK.'

Dr H: 'OK, Mrs A. I'll do it, but only because we've had that chat about the dangers of a multiple pregnancy and what your options are.'

You know, Dr H and I are practically Best Friends. We have each other's mobile and home numbers saved on our cell phones; we send each other e-mails. OK, I bombard him with e-mails; he replies dutifully. We've known each other for some time, now. He has seen my fanny on numerous occasions, he has worked on my insides. Yet, he insists on calling me Mrs Albertyn or Mrs A. I guess it's good doctor-patient protocol.

He agrees to a day three transfer and puts all four embryos back. See, the thing he was speaking about – that more-than-two thing – is a discussion doctors have with many of their IVF patients. It's the talk you get when you're pregnant with more than one baby. It concerns selective reduction – terminating one, two or more of the foetuses.

Carrying more than one baby is risky. It means a higher risk to the mother (some women are unable to carry a multiple pregnancy to term safely, or at all), and a higher risk to the babies. The pregnancy is often lost altogether, or the babies are born prematurely, which could lead to neonatal death or long-term problems and disabilities for the surviving baby or babies.

Because IVF patients routinely return more than one embryo to the uterus, there is a much higher risk of multiples. The rate for multiples is one in four. Doctors in Australia will put back only one embryo, for exactly the reasons mentioned above.

Doctor and patient must decide what to do in a case where more than one embryo implants. It is a conversation all IVF patients should have with their doctors where more than one embryo is transferred. Will you, the patient, take the risk and carry all the babies, or will you reduce them to twins or a singleton? Opting for selective reduction means going to see a specialist who will terminate one or more of the foetuses. The procedure itself carries risks. So, all in all, the medical profession is anti-multiple pregnancies.

But try telling that to an infertile person who's been trying for a long time. Firstly, most of us actually want twins so that we never have to do another IVF again, and secondly, we'd rather deal with being *too* pregnant than not pregnant at all.

Transfer is a breeze and the two-week wait goes smoothly. No spotting, no bleeding. I don't know why, but I'm feeling very confident about this one. Not sure whether it's my quality-versus-quantity theory, or my so-close-and-getting-closer theory. I go to acupuncture three times a week and Vicky tells me my pulse is exceptionally strong. She says, 'If you're not pregnant, I'll be very surprised.' Damn, I'm close.

Two days before the scheduled blood test, I do a home pregnancy test. It's five in the morning. I'm excited. I have a very, very strong feeling that this IVF has worked. I pee on the test stick and wait.

Thank you, God! There, right before my eyes, the second line appears. It's faint, but it's there! Pregnant! I feel like I'm going to burst. I knew it!

'OK, calm down. Think logically,' I tell myself. It could be left-over hormones from the trigger shot. The trigger shot that makes you ovulate has the same hormones as the pregnancy hormones, so if you do a pregnancy test straight afterwards, you will get a false positive. But! It's normally out of your system anything from a week to ten days after receiving the shot. So, it could be from the trigger shot … but it could also be because I am P. R. E. G. N. A. N. T!

I can't keep it to myself a second longer. I jump on the bed and wake Marko by shoving the still-wet-from-my-pee stick in his face. He looks at me as if I'm mad.

'What the fuck?'

'A positive test, arsehole,' I giggle. He is fully awake now. I tell him about the trigger shot possibility. We make a deal not to get too excited. Yeah, right.

I count the minutes until eight o'clock and call Dr H with the news. I ask whether it could be leftover hormones from the trigger shot. He says maybe, maybe not. Probably not, but to make sure, I should go for an early blood test. It is a Saturday morning and I wait outside in my car for the pathologist to open at half past eight. Hurry up, already! I mark the form *urgent*. I ask them to speed courier the sample to the lab at Louis Leipoldt, which does testing on a Saturday – a four-hour wait.

The average result for a positive pregnancy test on day 12 (which is where I am) is 48. Forty-eight is a good number to have on day 12. I get my results – 156! Oh. My. God. Am I pregnant, or what?! *Very* pregnant. Three times the average pregnant!

I'm bursting to tell people. I want to shout it from the rooftops, tell the whole world, but after the last few debacles, I will only truly believe it when I get my 48-hours-later, nicely-doubled result back.

Which is 365! I am *very, very* pregnant!

I can now tell everyone. Everyone is so happy for me. Hell, I'm ecstatic for myself! My mother says she knew it, my sister says she knew it. Everyone is on a high. The only person who is not happy is Dr H.

He says, 'That number is very high – too high.' See, the higher the number (usually), the more babies you have inside. Based on these very high results, it looks like we may have more than one baby, and this worries Dr H – a lot. But I am on cloud nine. I am happy-skippy-*pregnant*!

Vicky is convinced I am carrying more than one baby. She says my pulses are unbelievably strong. She thinks there are three. *Three!*

Um ... three is not such a good idea. I hope she's wrong, although she hasn't been up until now.

This time Marko and I decide that it is better that my mother accompanies me to the first scan. We're both a little gun-shy after the last scan. My mother and I meet downstairs in the parking lot. She gives my hand a squeeze. I lie on the exam table and Dr H scans me.

There's the yolk sac, the foetal pole, and a beautiful, wondrous, beating heart. But wait ... there's another. We have twins. Twins! First prize. My mother holds my hand tightly. We are both grinning from ear to ear. We get a printout of the two little sacs. Two little blobs, two gorgeous little blobs. Dr H appears somewhat placated. Twins are not too bad. We, Dr H and I, can handle twins. I have to come back in two weeks for another scan.

My mother and I are beside ourselves with excitement. We manage to restrain ourselves until we get outside and there, in the sunshine, we throw our arms around each other and hug – you know, one of those deep, hard hugs that speak volumes about all the pain and anguish that has gone before.

Twins! Life is so great.

SEEING DOUBLE DOUBLED

God, I feel fucking awful. Well, divinely awful. I have nausea from hell. Why the fuck they call it *morning* sickness I'll never know. It's all-bloody-day sickness.

Secretly, I'm over-bloody-joyed to be feeling so ill. Remember? Morning sickness is a sign of a healthy pregnancy. And I am sick to the gills. Dr Google says one is more prone to morning sickness in a twin pregnancy, so that's why I'm so damn sick. Everything makes me feel like puking, even the car radio. I can't put it on, it makes me want to puke. The good thing is that the constant nausea tells me that I'm still pregnant, which helps to pass the time until the next scan. My mother comes with me to the second scan. I am nervous, but not as nervous as before. I am too sick not to be pregnant.

Up on the bed, ultrasound probe in. There is our beautiful blob with its beautiful, beating heart. It's starting to look more like an alien, with a big head and small arm buds, and less like a blob. Which is a good thing. And there is our other, beautiful alien blob.

Um … hold on a moment … what the hell is that? There appears to be another alien-like blob with a beating heart.

Oh fuck. And another.

Oops.

Four!

What was it I said to Dr H? 'I mean, really, what are the chances *all four* will take?' Well, in my case, the answer is clearly 'very fucking excellent!' I should learn to bear in mind just how often I hit the statistically fucking improbable one percent!

Dr H is grave. This is serious. A quad pregnancy is dangerous, for mother and babies. And yet, you know what? At this stage, I couldn't care less. I am actually overjoyed. I am very, very pregnant. Pregnant-pregnant-pregnant-pregnant! I feel like hugging myself. No bloody wonder I'm as sick as a dog.

Dr H is having none of that. We need to have a serious talk. My mother and I sit across from his desk. We discuss our options. The best we can hope for is that one or, hopefully, two of the embryos don't make it – that they naturally stop growing. If they don't, we will have to face selective reduction. The other option is to keep all four and try to carry them for as long as possible. That is not an option for me – it is too risky. I can't risk losing all of them. Dr H sends us off with a warning that if things don't happen naturally within the next few weeks, we will have to decide where and when to schedule the reduction.

Of course, now Vicky is saying, 'I told you so!' That woman is amazing. How the hell does she know exactly what is going on in my body? I'm almost more nervous to see her than to go for a scan. Just by feeling my wrist she can tell what's happening inside my body. Vicky rocks!

You know what? Secretly I'm glad there are four. As horrible as this sounds, it is as if I have babies in reserve. So if (when) something happens to one, two or even three of them, like has happened so often in the past, we have enough babies to ensure I end up with at least one at the end. But of course, I know that carrying four babies is dangerous, so I'm hoping nature will help me out here.

The eight-week scan reveals that all four are still there and growing – hanging in there, becoming increasingly more human looking. The ten-week scan reveals the same.

It's time to schedule the reduction. It's a risky operation, and Dr H wants to make sure I go to the best foetal ultrasound specialist. He recommends Dr G, who has worked in a fertility clinic in London; she knows her stuff. She and Dr H go back a way. The only crappy thing is that Dr G works at Tygerberg Hospital, which is a government hospital and not ideal. It's a horrible place – a dive. But if Dr H says she's the best, I'll take his word for it.

I'm still as sick as a dog. The only way I can stop myself from being sick is to eat, all the time. My stomach can never be empty. The moment it's empty, I start retching. I wake up every two hours at night to eat – it's the only way to get through the night. I'm enormous. At three months, I look six months pregnant.

Happy as I am to be pregnant, I don't allow myself to get too attached to the babies. How can I when I'm going to be aborting two of them? What a terrible thought. I don't allow myself to think about it. I hate that word – abort.

The plan is to schedule the reduction for when I am 12 weeks pregnant – after the nuchal scan. This is the big one – the one where they measure the nuchal fold at the back of the baby's neck and do all sorts of other measurements and tests to see whether everything is OK with the baby. It is at this scan that problems like Down's Syndrome are picked up. Because of my age, and because I've had a Down's baby before, I am considered fairly high risk for another Down's baby.

The way a reduction usually works is that the babies are first thoroughly scanned to see whether they all look 'normal'. If any of the babies look ill or genetically abnormal, they are reduced, leaving behind the healthy babies – those with the best chance of survival. If all the babies look OK, the decision is made based on the position of the embryos in the womb.

Much as I'm dreading the procedure, I also just want it to be over with. I want to start bonding with my babies. I want to enjoy my pregnancy. At 12 weeks, nature has not decided to take any of the four. We have to do the reduction. Marko will come with me to the nuchal scan – this is a big one. Based on the results of that scan, the four will be reduced to twins.

Tygerberg Hospital is disgusting – dirty, depressing. The doctors are amazing. They do a wonderful job and the level of expertise is first class, but the hospital itself is an absolute dive. Thank goodness the foetal assessment centre is clean, but everything else looks grimy – walls, floors, everything. I'm too scared even to touch the door handles. The lift doesn't go to the floor we need to go to, so we have to walk up the stairs. The staircase stinks of pee.

We find the waiting area – hard wooden benches, no cushions. Swollen, pregnant women. There is a young girl – she can't be older than 13 – belly swollen. I feel so sorry for her. The receptionist behind an ancient wooden desk instructs us to fill in some forms. Back to the waiting room to wait. We are then called to wait in the passage, on wooden chairs lining the one side, just outside the door of the foetal assessment unit. Marko and I. Anxious. Quiet. Some men in overalls push a trolley past us.

Marko whispers, 'Do you know what that was?'

'No,' I answer.

'A dead body.'

Oh great.

Dr G is lovely – a small woman with a tiny voice. She speaks so softly in her accented voice, you have to strain to hear. She's very thorough and good at what she does. I climb on the bed and Dr G starts the scan. Her machine is a million times better than the one Dr H uses. You can see everything so clearly. Little arms and legs, the head. You can even see their fingers. The babies are all bouncing around, waving. Doesn't seem real that there are four babies inside me. For a moment Marko and I forget why we're there, we are just so thrilled to see jumping babies on the screen.

Dr G measures and calls out measurements to her assistant. She looks, she measures, she calls. She's very thorough. She takes ages. After an hour-and-a-half she is finished. My back is killing me. I'm glad to get up.

She asks some questions and tells us to go and sit in the private waiting room. She wants to enter the results into a programme on her computer and will discuss the results with us afterwards. We sit in the waiting room. It's more like an unused office, with a table and some chairs. There are medical posters on the walls. Stuff about trisomies, about genetic defects. I decide not to read them. I'm feeling sick again; it's been a long afternoon. I'm way past my two-hourly feed, but luckily I brought a banana and some crackers. I offer some to Marko, but he doesn't want any. Thank goodness – more for me.

After what feels like hours, but in reality is only 15 minutes, Dr G comes back. She has a computer printout in her hand; her face looks grave.

Marko and I look at her expectantly.

SELECTIVE REDUCTION, *NOT FOR SENSITIVE READERS*

Dr G starts talking, 'Based on the results, it is difficult to know what to do ...'

I knew this would happen. That they'd all look so perfect that it is making it difficult to decide which ones to reduce.

'... because there seems to be something potentially wrong with each one of them.'

Marko and I stare at her blankly. Her words are fighting with the sound of the blood rushing to my head. It just can't be possible. It *cannot* be possible that something is wrong with each one of them. Have I not been through enough? Is my body so fucked-up that I can't produce a healthy child at all? Am I doomed never to have my own biological children?

It's noisy in my head. Very noisy. The thoughts. The words. The blood. Dr G's voice penetrates the noise.

'Are you OK?'

'What do you mean Doctor? What is wrong with them?'

Based on my age, and based on the fact that I have had a previous Down's baby, and based on the thickness of the nuchal fold, the computer programme that draws parallels from thousands of cases worldwide, has given me the following odds for my babies:

- Baby One has a one in 15 chance of having Down's Syndrome.
- Baby Two has a one in 55 chance of having Down's Syndrome.
- Baby Three has a one in 25 chance of having Down's Syndrome.
- Baby Four, who has the best odds, has only a one in 200 chance

of having Down's Syndrome. But it has what looks like a fatal heart defect.

The normal range for someone my age to have a baby with Down's Syndrome is around one in 500. Anything under one in 100 is considered high risk. The results are shockingly bad.

My world collapses again. I feel small, frightened, lost.

'What do you recommend, Doctor?' I ask.

She answers, 'There is so little statistical data from which to draw, that it is extremely difficult for me to give you an informed medical recommendation.'

I am so fucking sick and tired of being in the statistically minute percentage, sick to death of it. I ask her what she would do in my situation.

She lowers her printout slowly and looks at us intently. She talks us through the various scenarios and the risks attached to each. The risk of a reduction, versus the risk of premature labour, versus the risk of a baby with a developmental problem. It makes me feel better. I like numbers, I'm a logical person. I prefer dealing with numbers and logic. Between the three of us we make the following decision:

She will reduce baby number two straightaway; a baby with such high markers for Down's usually doesn't have a very long life expectancy at all.

Then she will do a CVS (a type of amniocentesis, but done at 12 weeks instead of 16 to 20) on Babies One and Three. We will then make a decision based on whether Babies One and Three are 'normal'. Meanwhile we will wait until Friday to see whether she can get a clearer reading of Baby Four's heart.

We all agree. I sign the consent forms. I get back on the exam table. Suddenly everything becomes brisk and businesslike.

The CVS is a horrible procedure – it hurts and it's scary. Dr G sticks a long needle through my belly, through all the layers of skin, muscle and into the womb, into the placenta of each baby. Some of the placenta is then drawn into a waiting vial, using a pumping motion. These cells are then rushed off to the lab for testing.

Dr G explains what happens with the reduction. She will place the ultrasound paddle on my belly and make sure everything is out of the way. A chemical solution will be injected into the sac of the baby, causing it to die instantly. The foetal material is reabsorbed into the mother's body.

This sounds truly horrific and the experience lives up to the expectation. I turn my head away from the screen. I can't look. I don't want to see. Marko is holding my hand.

In a quiet voice, Dr G explains that I will feel some pain as the needle goes in. I do feel some pain, but nothing compared with the pain I feel in my heart. I start sobbing. I try not to sob too hard, because I am so scared the needle will go into the other babies' sacs by mistake. Marko squeezes my hand tighter.

It's over. The sobs subside, but the tears keep rolling down my cheek. Dr G asks if I'm OK. I can't reply. I can't talk. I just nod my head. I get up and get dressed.

Dr G rubs my arm. 'I'm so sorry. You will hear from me within 48 hours with the results. We'll decide what to do then.'

We walk back to the car. Stunned. I'm supposed to be going to hospital for bed rest, but all I want to do is crawl into my own bed and not get up until 48 hours have passed.

I drive myself crazy with 'what ifs'. What will we do if something is wrong with Baby One and Baby Three? What if there is nothing wrong with Babies One, Three or Four? I decide that I can't go through another reduction. If there is nothing wrong with Baby Four, I will take my chances and have a triplet pregnancy.

For once, I don't go on the Internet, I don't speak to my friends in the computer. My world is tiny – it's just me, Marko and my mom.

Forty-eight hours later, I am tightly wound, like a spring. I don't want to move away from my phone in case it rings. I'm at work when the phone rings. I recognise Dr G's gentle voice before she even introduces herself. I ask her to hold while I close my office door. I don't want people to see my inevitable breakdown.

'The results have come back. Two normal males.'

Two normal boys!

But I have to come back for her to have another look at Baby Four's heart. I thank her and say goodbye. I put the phone down as gut-wrenching sobs rip through my body. I lean my head against my desk, trying to get my breath back. I hold my belly.

Two normal boys. My boys. Normal. Normal boys. Normal.

I dial my mother's number. I have to tell her, just quickly. I know I should phone Marko first, but somehow this is a mom moment. She is overjoyed. I can hear how much the news means to her, how worried she's been. I phone Marko and sob some more.

We are having two boys. Sons. We still have a way to go; we still don't know what will happen with Baby Four. And of course the next two weeks will be critical in monitoring any possible fallout after the reduction of Baby Two. But for now – for this moment – life is beautiful.

We return to Tygerberg Hospital. I hate that place now. It will always hold horrible memories. Dr G looks at Baby Four again. It doesn't look good. It doesn't look like the foetus will survive outside the womb. We need to reduce again.

This time the procedure is not as traumatic. It feels like the right thing to do. Then I make the stupid mistake of asking Dr G whether she can see what sex Baby Four was. She asks me if I am sure I want to know. I say yes. I wish I hadn't. It was a girl. It wouldn't have made a difference to our decision, but it does cause a pang in my heart. It seems that I'm destined never to have a girl.

The next few weeks will be scary, because if I am going to miscarry as a result of the procedures, it will most likely be within the two weeks following.

And so, with that last procedure we are now pregnant with twins. Hopefully from now on we can have a relatively normal pregnancy. At last I can start to bond with the babies. I can start being happy. Surely the worst is behind us.

THE PREGNANCY

At about 16 weeks I eventually stop feeling sick. This is a little disconcerting; at least the sickness reassured me that I was still pregnant. It is a terrible period, that time between the morning sickness and until you feel the baby move. I constantly have Dead Baby Thoughts. I live from scan to scan. The day of the scan and for a few days after, I'm on a high. Then the anxiety starts creeping back. By the time of the next scan I'm convinced the babies have died. It's horrible.

I start keeping a diary. It's a bold move, but 17 weeks seem like a reasonably safe place to start.

Week 17

Can't believe I'm only starting this journal now. Typical me, procrastinator of note. Just been too scared to jinx it all.

Good week, good scan with Dr H. Not many complaints, besides sore ribs – have terrible rib pain as my chest expands to accommodate the pregnancy. Everything else OK. Feel a little paranoid because have not yet felt the babies kick. Trying not to be paranoid. Impossible.

I've decided to wean myself off the anti-depressants. So far, so good. Much better than last time.

DEAR DIARY

We decide to name the babies. Luke and Ben. We like strong, simple names.

My sister calls to tell me that she's been to see her gynae; she's worried because she's been off the pill for a month and nothing has happened. She wonders whether she will struggle to get pregnant again. The gynae believes she may have a problem with secondary infertility.

What the fuck!

You don't get pregnant in the first month and you think you have fertility issues? Oh, do me a favour and *fuck off*. After I put down the phone I feel sick. A month. How the fuck must I feel? It is insulting. Don't you dare call yourself infertile or suggest that you have infertility issues because you aren't pregnant *one month* after going off the pill.

The doctor sends her for blood tests and I get a call from my sister. Oops. It appears secondary infertility is not the cause of her messed up cycle. No, my dears – she is, in fact, pregnant. Life is crazy isn't it? I hate that my first thought was, 'Oh well, I bet this means something will happen to my pregnancy.' I wouldn't wish infertility on anyone, but my goodness, how about sharing some of the fertile stuff around?

Week 18: The week of the kidney!

DEAR DIARY

Started on the weekend – thought I had a bladder infection as my bladder and left side hurt like hell. Did a pee test and Dr H calls me in. Panic stations, of course – me imagining the worse. They've picked up a terrible disease – what if it's Aids? Ridiculous, I know.

Pee test shows no infection. Meantime I am in agony. Dr H does a scan and sees that my urethra is blocked. The weight of the babies is pressing on the flow of pee between kidney and bladder. *Ouch!* There is nothing we can do but hope the little buggers move and it gets better. Sigh. I can feel I'm not 25 anymore and that I'm pregnant with more than one baby!

The babies start moving at about 19 weeks. At least, that's when I start to feel them. At last! It feels amazing. I sit with my hand on my belly all the time. I *love* feeling them move. Little Luke is my active baby. That's because his placenta is behind him, whereas Ben's placenta is in front of him, cushioning his movements somewhat.

Work has started on the new house we're building. We're moving to Durbanville, just down the road from my parents. I need to be near my mom. I don't think I will cope without her, especially with twins. It's a wonderful area – perfect for kids. Quiet, almost rural. We visit the building site every weekend. I spend hours fantasising about laughing babies, happy families. I plan where I'm going to put the cots, where the change table will go; I rearrange things a million times in my mind. I make Marko participate. I love it. It feels so good. At last, I will have a baby's room with a baby in it.

Our new neighbour is also pregnant with twins! She is a month behind me. The young couple across the road are also pregnant. My cousin lives up the road and she is pregnant too. Our children can all play together – we'll have play dates. How cool will that be! I am so happy. This is so perfect. Finally! Finally I get to be part of the mommy world, a world I've been denied for so long – a world I've avoided for so long.

Week 19

Felt a kick! Eventually! Everyone says to expect flutters. I felt no flutters, just good hard jabs. It's fantastic feeling them kick.

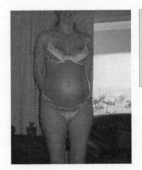

Big scan this week. Mom came with me. It took ages – my back was killing me. At least my kidney is a bit better. Although now I have a growth in my mouth – apparently it's called a pregnancy tumour. Great. Not much they can do. My gums are sore. I'm really taking strain!! Feel ancient!

Hot Mamma!

I am enormous! My belly is huge and I *love* it. I'm so proud. I make Marko take a photo of me in my bikini – don't I look gorgeously pregnant? Pretty huge for 19 weeks, huh?

DEAR DIARY

I sit and watch TV, eating (I eat *a lot*), one hand on my belly. I make Marko feel. When he puts his hand there, the little buggers stop moving. But eventually he feels them. What a divine moment! I think to myself, 'This is what it's all about.'

I'm excited to be having twins. I join the twins and triplets society. It feels bold and very brave to do so. I'm too paranoid to actually buy anything, just in case it all goes wrong. I want to order a twin pram from the UK so that my brother can bring it with him from London, but I'm too scared I will jinx the pregnancy. And it will break my heart to stare at the empty twin pram if something goes wrong. As if that will be the worst of my problems!

But I don't buy a thing: A friend in the computer, Lauren, was pregnant with twin boys. She lost them at 20 weeks. All I want to do is get to 21 weeks, so that I can pass that scary mark.

Week 20

This has been a significant week for me, a milestone (yet another) because this is where Lauren lost her Zachary and Spencer. I just wanted to get past this point. It is Sunday, I am 20 weeks and six days – almost there. One day shy!

Been feeling Luke kicking strongly. Ben not so much. Think it's because of his placenta placing. Marko felt two strong kicks tonight: was v. cool.

Kidney much better, nearly totally fine. Ribs still flipping sore, makes me so uncomfortable all the time. My bladder also aches. Had Braxton Hicks for the first time on Saturday, was *not* happy – petrified it was pre-term labour, of course. Feels weird having your uterus go hard like that.

DEAR DIARY

I'll never forget the day I 'turn' 21 weeks. Such a good day. It feels like I can stop being scared. I start to imagine what my life will be like as a mom to two boys. I picture myself at soccer games, shouting from the sidelines. I picture camping trips, fishing trips. I'm sad that I will probably never have a daughter, but I'm now totally into the idea of being a mom to boys.

It's a glorious day. For the first time in my pregnancy I relax. Life is good. Things are going to be fine.

THE DOCTOR'S APPOINTMENT I DON'T RETURN FROM

One whole day. I have one whole day to enjoy my pregnancy.

On Tuesday, 3 December 2003, I wake up with damp panties. I don't know what to make of it, but I'm paranoid, super vigilant about signs of pre-term labour. An unexplained wetness is one of the danger signs. It's hard to tell what a normal discharge is, as there is so much of that in a pregnancy. My heart plummets. This doesn't feel right.

The whole morning I wrestle with myself: Should I call Dr H and make an emergency appointment or should I just leave it until my scheduled appointment the next day? Wait till tomorrow or go today? What if there is nothing wrong and I waste his time? What if there is something wrong and I could have prevented a terrible tragedy by going in today? Back and forth, back and forth. I decide if there's any more fluidy stuff I will go for a peace-of-mind check up.

There is a little more. I call Dr H and he squeezes me in for a quick check up. I know how fully booked he is, so I really appreciate his helping me. Dr H has never, ever refused to see me. And I have made many, many emergency appointments. Have I told you how much I love that man? I pack up my laptop, tidy my desk and drive to his rooms.

Dr H and I joke around, as we usually do. I tell him what has happened. He says it's probably nothing. I hop (OK, by now I don't hop, I'm too big – I clamber) onto the table and he has a look down below. He can see some fluid and tests it with litmus paper to establish whether it is amniotic fluid. Which would be Bad. Very, Very Bad.

I am feeling a whole lot less jokey.

It doesn't appear to be amniotic fluid, but Dr H wants me to stay in the hospital on bed rest for a few days, so that he can check up on me.

'Why?' I ask.

'Because your cervix is starting to open a little, and I just want to make sure everything is OK.'

Fuck. *Fuck!* Not good.

He does a quick scan of the babies. Both are fine. OK. Deep breaths. Dr H has warned me that I may have to go on bed rest from about 26 weeks. He places nearly all his twin pregnancies on bed rest at that stage. I haven't been keen to do this, as I'm a contractor, which means no work, no pay. But of course, I will do whatever is required.

So, here I am, all dressed up in work clothes, my car downstairs in the parking lot, my laptop in the car, thinking I'm popping into the doctor's office for a quick visit and then going home. But no – it's straight into the hospital for me. Dr H walks me to the ward and speaks to the ward Matron.

'This is Mrs Albertyn. Look after her, please. She's my very special patient.' I smile. I'm sure he says that to all the women, but it makes me feel good anyway. His words must carry some weight around there, because they put me in a private room. Good. I don't feel like chatting to anyone else. I have to make a few calls. I call the medical aid to get authorisation. I call Marko to tell him I'm not coming home and that he has to drive all the way home from town, pack a bag with my toiletries, PJs and panties and drive all the way back to Claremont. He sounds worried. I try to reassure him. I act a lot jollier than I feel. In truth, I am scared, very scared.

LOSING LUKE

I have to go for a full scan on the babies and Dr H wants the hospital to check my cervix, the amniotic fluid, everything. Because I am now officially on bed rest, I get fetched in a wheelchair and driven to the radiologists at another hospital. I feel silly being pushed in a wheelchair, but I'm fearful enough to do whatever they tell me. The whole cervix opening thing has scared me into not wanting to stand up at all.

A sweet young woman does the scan. I climb on the bed and she blobs the freezing cold jelly on my swollen belly. Why is that stuff always so damn freezing? I crane my neck to see the screen. It is turned mostly towards her. I am desperate to see my babies again.

'There is Baby A and there is Baby B,' she points out. They call them Baby A and Baby B, the A baby being the one closest to the cervix. That's Luke. She does a few measurements on both.

'Look, there's his head, there are his fingers,' she says, pointing to Baby B – Ben. She keeps talking, almost babbling.

Why hasn't she said any thing about Baby A, Luke? She turns the screen to face her and says she wants to do a few measurements on Baby A, then she will turn it back to face me again. I'm starting to feel nervous. Something doesn't feel right. What is going on? She stands up.

'I'm going to call the duty doctor to confirm my measurements.' Something is definitely wrong. I can feel it. What is going on? My heart starts racing.

She comes back with a middle-aged man. He has a kind face.

He greets me with a soft voice. With the screen still turned towards him, he starts measuring. I can't take it anymore.

'Doctor, what is going on?' I can hear the hysteria creeping into my voice. He turns his head from the screen and looks at me.

'I'm sorry, Mrs Albertyn. There is no heartbeat for Baby A.'

Oh God no! No, no, no, nooooo!!!

'Are you sure?' I plead. 'Please check again. Please, please. It can't be. Please check again. Are you sure?'

He shakes his head gravely. 'I've checked and double-checked. I am so sorry.'

'No, no, no, no, no, no! It can't be … it can't be … noooo …' I roll over on my side, clutching my belly, sobs tearing my body apart.

No-no-no-no … I can't stop saying it. I can't stop sobbing. The doctor and his assistant keep patting my leg, both whispering, 'I'm so sorry.'

I spin around. 'Are you *sure*? Please check again. It was all fine yesterday. Please check again.'

They check again. Of course there is nothing. My little baby, my little Luke. Dead. Oh God, no! Don't do this to me. Please, God, no! Please, please, please. Not my baby, please God, I am begging you.

Through this fog of sorrow I realise the doctor is talking to me.

'We need to finish the measurements. Then we'll call Dr H. Are you OK?'

I look away. I try to hold it together until I'm back at the hospital. One look at the nurses' faces tells me they know. They wheel me into my room and I lie on the bed, facing away from the nurse. She asks if I am OK. I nod. She leaves.

I start sobbing again. I'm trying not to cry – I'm scared all the weeping will cause me to go into labour and lose Ben, too. I force myself to stop. My heart is going to break. My little boy, my active, happy little Luke, I felt you move just yesterday. What happened?

'How could this happen, Doctor? How? He was fine. What went wrong?' I want to know when Dr H comes by. Dr H doesn't know; it could be many things. But I need to know why. If I don't know the reason I will go crazy. I need to understand what went wrong, so that we can do our best not to have it happen to Ben.

'Give me three possibilities,' I beg Dr H.

He says it could have been an infection, or membranes that ruptured, or it could have been placenta failure. If it was placenta failure (which does happen, though not often), then the chances of the same thing happening to Ben are slim. If it was ruptured membranes, then hopefully the same thing won't happen to Ben. But if it was an infection, then it is quite possible for the same thing to happen again. I ask Dr H what Ben's chances are of making it.

Fifty-fifty, he says.

I can't believe it. How can I go from being wonderfully, blissfully pregnant with two healthy, normal boys, to having one die in utero and the other at 50 percent risk of dying, too?

Luke will have to stay inside my belly. They can't take him out, as this will jeopardise Ben's chances of survival. Everything is now focused on saving Ben.

I call Marko. I hate having to tell him over the phone. He knows me so well, there is no way I can disguise the tears in my voice. Crack. I hear his heart break over the phone.

My mother is devastated. At last week's big scan, she, like me, saw the two boys somersaulting in my womb.

I curl up into a ball on my bed, my hand on my belly. Both my sons are in there – one brother dead, the other alive, side by side. I pull the blanket over my head and weep without sound.

That is where I lie, where I spend my tears, for the next five weeks.

BED REST

My world is now confined to my hospital bed and my private room. I know the privacy can't last; I will have to move to a general ward soon and I'm dreading it. I love having my own room. It is filled with flowers from my mother's garden.

Our goal is to keep Ben inside me until at least 26 weeks, the age of viability – then to stay inside till 28 weeks, even better, 30 weeks, 32 weeks … I have to stay in hospital until at least 36 weeks, if he doesn't arrive sooner. Obviously, the longer he stays inside, the better his chances of survival. As tedious and horrible as it is, I'll do whatever it takes and hope I'm still on hospital bed rest in February, which would mean we've passed the 30-week mark, a massive milestone.

My mother visits every second day. She sits on the chair and tells me stories – about the past, about my sister and her kids, about my father, about stuff. She brings a taste of the outside world to my small hospital world. She takes my dirty laundry and brings back freshly laundered underwear. She brings me homemade food and snacks. I so look forward to her visits. She accompanies me to all my scans.

I feel so desperately sorry for Marko. He has to do all the household chores. Feed the pets, do the washing, everything. Not to mention keep an eye on the builders. Our new house is set to be ready for the arrival of our baby in late March. Sigh. He has to choose all the finishes, negotiate with the builder, go to the site every day. But maybe this is a blessing in disguise. It keeps him busy.

I miss Marko. The hardest part about being here is how much I miss him. One day, after he leaves, I sit by the window and watch him drive away. I will never do that again. I just want to lie in my own bed with my husband. Not in a hospital ward with machines and nurses around. The prenatal observa-

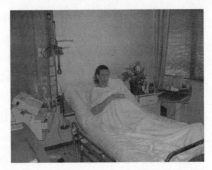

My bed, my world

tion ward is in the maternity section of the hospital in Claremont. It is so very far from home.

I live by, and for, the grind of the daily routine.

05:00: Get woken up with tea.

05:30: Blood pressure and temperature check.

06:00: Check Ben's heartbeat and for possible contractions.

08:00: Breakfast.

10:00: Visitors, usually my mom.

11:00: Visitors gone. I read, have a glass of milk and a cookie.

12:00: Lunch, then a nap.

15:00: Visitors again – sometimes my dad, sometimes friends. Not a day goes by without at least one person visiting me.

16:00: Visitors gone.

17:00: Supper.

20:00: Lights out.

I live by this routine – it becomes my universe. I get very upset if anything disrupts it – late visitors or people who don't leave on time make me anxious.

The parking lot, the one that services Pick 'n Pay downstairs, becomes hectic the week before Christmas. I sit on the window-sill, looking down at the frenetic activity. I marvel at how the simplest things, like being able to go Christmas shopping as and when you want, seem such a luxury when you're bedridden. People are laughing – happy and suntanned. Do they even know how lucky they are?

My colleagues have been absolutely amazing. They've sent flowers, gifts, books. They SMS, telling me not to worry about anything at work, to just look after myself and my baby. Several have been to see me, even my boss. It was a little weird receiving him in my hospital gown. But I really appreciate that he made the effort. I work for an excellent company; they really do care about people.

Meanwhile, little Ben continues to hang in there. Some days are bad – others better. When we're doing well, I'm ecstatic; when not – when there's the slightest hint of a problem – I'm completely paranoid. In a way the bed rest is a good thing, because it's just him and me. I spend all my time with my hand on my belly, feeling his movements, talking to him, telling him how much I love him. I sing to him, softly, stroking his limbs as they bulge against my skin. He is my whole world and I love him immensely – more than I ever imagined I could love someone that I have yet to meet in person.

Christmas Day is no big deal to me. To my mind, it's just another day to cross off the calendar. The hospital is so quiet, just myself and one other patient. And, of course, the poor nurses on duty. But my family makes it special. My sister, Nina, and my brother, Paul, are down from London. My mom brings me delicious Christmas lunch. So much better than the boring hospital food. The problem with a maternity hospital is that the menu consists of only four dishes, which are rotated. No one really stays longer than three nights. You arrive, have a (hopefully live, healthy) baby and go home. No need for a complex, varied menu. Except when you're doing time on bed-rest row. Because I'm here for so long, they do me special favours like making simple bread-rolls for lunch, or soup.

Paul calls while I'm wearing the monitoring belt, sound turned up, all the better to hear Ben's heartbeat. I love listening to it – so loud and fast. Paul wants to know what that sound is and I tell him it's Ben's heartbeat. He can't believe it. Doo-doof, doo-doof, doo-doof – what a wondrous sound, my little boy's beating heart.

Big party for New Year's Eve. *Not*. Marko is not coming through. What's the point? And I don't want him driving on New Year's Eve – too many drunk arseholes on the road. I go to bed early, though not before I have a small celebration with my darling mother, who's smuggled in half a glass of wine in a Tupperware bakkie. Delicious. I sip on it slowly, savouring every mouthful.

Bad news! I've been moved from the private room into the general prenatal observation ward. It has four beds and *one* bathroom. *Horrors!* Do you have any idea how much I hate sharing a bathroom? I've been on my own for a while, but now a woman with bad gestational diabetes has joined me. She's much further along than me. I'm jealous.

My new neighbour watches TV all day long. It's driving me crazy. It's on from the minute she wakes up until she goes to sleep. I fucking *hate* TV. Now I have to listen to her soapies all day. And can you believe it? She actually watches the Teletubbies. A grown woman voluntarily watching the Tubbies? Hope she leaves soon. Thank God for cricket. Feels weird lying here, right next to the stadium, watching the cricket on TV and looking at the stadium from my window.

I am pleased to be in January. A whole month is out of the way and we are very close to the magic 26 week mark. Almost there.

WELCOME TO THE WORLD, LITTLE BEN!

I wake up with a start from a hard, painful cramp. It's Sunday morning, 4 January 2004, and the cramp is so sharp, so vicious, I literally jump out of bed, hunched over, clutching my tummy. Ouch! I wonder what it is – these days I am full of aches and pains, my bladder particularly. So this pain could be courtesy of my bladder. I'm a little concerned about the pain, but I'm half asleep.

I get up to pee. Out of habit, I look down at my panties and notice more of the same brown mucousy stuff that has been there for the past day or so. I hate seeing it there. When it first appeared, I showed the nurse on duty, but she said it could be many things. It could even be Luke's sac breaking down. It worries me.

But the discharge, combined with the distinctly uncomfortable, crampy feeling, is worrying. I ask for the CTG machine, which monitors contractions, to be placed on my belly. Even though they don't seem to mind, I hate asking – it makes me feel like a paranoid, pain-in-the-arse patient.

Good news. Ben's heartbeat is fine. There are signs of uterine irritability, but I have those all the time. My uterus is so irritable, anything sets it off. Marko comes to visit, but we hardly talk. He knows by now that if I admit to being worried, things must be bad. We sit there in silence – me anxious and off kilter, Marko helpless. I tell him to go home and he leaves.

I ask the nurses to put the monitoring belt back on and to check again for contractions. The CTG machine shows signs of irregular contractions. I've had those before, but I sense these are different.

I seem to be the only one who is worried – the nurses seem unconcerned. I hate being a pain but things just do not feel right. I make the nurses call Dr L, who is looking after me while Dr H is on holiday.

Dr L instructs the nurses to give me a muscle relaxant to try to calm my uterus. It doesn't work. I now sense something is horribly wrong. I make the nurses call the doctor back. The belt goes back on. The contractions are still there. Dr L arrives and checks my cervix. I am five centimetres dilated. Ben is coming today, and soon. Now.

It is too early! I am not yet 26 weeks! But there's no stopping labour. Ben is arriving, ready or not.

A strange calm descends on me as everyone else jumps into action. I am in slow motion as the world around me goes into overdrive. I call Marko and tell him to come back right away. He does the 30-minute trip in 12 minutes. I don't think the car has ever been the same again. I call my mother and ask her to come to the hospital. I need her here. I won't be able to do this unless I know she is here.

I am scared, yet not too scared. I think I am a little numb, in denial. I lie there rubbing my stomach, whispering to Ben. I look up and see that Dr H has arrived. I am overjoyed to see him. He is wearing shorts and a T-shirt. He has interrupted his holiday. I don't know who called him, but I am so glad they did. He takes my hand and squeezes it hard. I hold his hand for a while, looking into his eyes. No words are said, but I can feel his strength and concern for me.

My mother arrives as the nurses are prepping me for surgery. Everything seems surreal – I feel as if I am in a play, or a dream. They have found an anaesthetist and a paediatrician. Everyone is ready.

An epidural is administered, then I lie down with Marko in his green scrubs by my head. This is it. My baby is about to be born. Instead of excitement, there is fear in the air. This is not how it should be.

Then I hear the sound that makes me cry every time I think about it – the tiniest mewling, a barely audible whimper. I hear, for the first time, the sound of my son's voice.

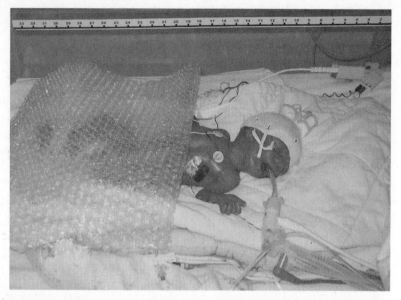

Little Ben Albertyn was born at 17:00 on 4 January 2004, weighing 920 grams – less even than two tubs of margarine or a packet of sugar. Tiny, fragile. Perfect and absolutely beautiful in every way.

As they lift him to cut the cord, I catch a glimpse of him – he is so very, so painfully tiny. The sight of Ben's small body makes me cry. Marko, too, starts sobbing. I've never seen him cry before and it breaks my heart. It makes me cry even more. We cling to each other, Marko and I, sobbing into each other's arms. Oh God, it isn't supposed to be like this. My poor little baby boy – he is so tiny. So very, very tiny.

He is whisked away immediately by the paediatrician, who starts working on him frantically – pumping, wiping, checking. I can't see what is going on. They take him away with pipes and tubes all over his body and rush him up to the neonatal intensive care unit.

THE FIRST 24 HOURS

I'm drugged to the gills and high as a kite. Everything feels surreal. I can't believe I have just given birth. I haven't seen Ben yet, but Marko has and he looks extremely anxious. He says Ben is so tiny and they're working on him all the time. He can't get near him for the doctor and nurses who are frantically trying to intubate him, to get some oxygen into his miniscule, immature lungs. I hear what Marko is saying, but being still spaced out, I don't feel the panic – just a drugged calm.

The paediatrician returns after about two hours. He looks exhausted. Marko and I hang on to his every word as we learn how our son is doing. He has managed to stabilise Ben, but he suggests we transfer him to a better hospital, one with a better NICU. The paramedics are called in.

I am still completely bed-bound. Marko is going back and forth between my room and the NICU. He is sick with worry. He says he's not sure it's such a good idea to move Ben – he looks so fragile. But it is too late – the ambulance is already on its way to Constantiaberg Hospital, where there is a better NICU. I will be transferred there the next day, to be with Ben.

We're all exhausted, emotionally and physically, but I'm still on my drug high and feeling calm. Everyone is worried, but I'm optimistic. It will be fine – of course it will be fine. I'm on too much of a high to believe otherwise.

Every single fibre of my being aches to be with my son as we arrive at Constantiaberg Hospital the next evening. I feel incomplete

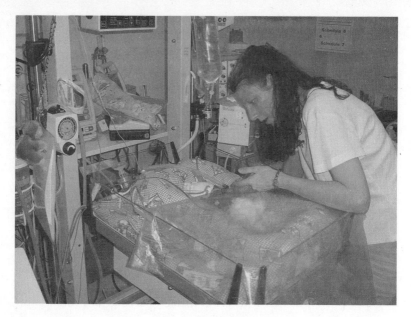

Ben, three days old

without Ben. The ache in my body has nothing to do with the Caesarean. I ache for my child. At the same time, I'm nervous to see him, to find out for myself just how sick he is.

The NICU at Constantiaberg is attached to the normal nursery. To get to your tiny, very ill, premature baby, you have to walk through the nursery full of fat, happy, healthy, *big* babies. It's a terrible, dreadful set up. A very, very bad idea.

My movements are still very slow and painful and it is tempting to stay in bed, but I must go to meet my son. I hobble into the NICU. It is a small room with lots of equipment, monitors, alarms, screens and special beds, beds that look more like tables or serving trays.

And there on one of the beds, under the warming lights, is the tiniest creature I have ever seen. He looks like a tiny baby bird. Full of pipes and tubes and plasters. This is my son, Ben. My child, my flesh, my hope, my love, my life. Oh my God, he is so tiny, so painfully, scarily tiny. I start weeping. It is such a shock to see him.

I feel a rush of love and guilt.

I sob to him, 'Oh my baby, my little boy, Mommy is so sorry, so sorry.' Marko rubs my arm.

'Sshh,' he consoles me. 'Don't get yourself so upset.'

I can't help it. My poor baby – he doesn't deserve to be lying here, with pipes and tubes everywhere. He should be happy and safe in my tummy – warm, protected. Reality hits me with force, all my naïve optimism gone. The protective haze of the post-op meds have worn off. I have a dangerously ill baby.

Dr HH, the paediatrician, is a big man. He looks like a giant among the monitors and tiny babies. He explains that the immediate objective is to stabilise Ben. The ventilators are breathing for him. Because he is so premature his skin is paper-thin. It blisters to the touch, so we can't touch him at all. And all I want to do is hold him, press him against my skin. I ache for him.

I have a million questions. Right now, there are no answers, only hopes and guesses. They will do whatever they can, but we literally have to take it one hour at a time, one minute at a time. So many questions, the burning one being: Will my son live? That is the answer I desperately need, and the question no one will answer.

THIRD-DAY BLUES

The nurses at Constantiaberg don't know how to handle me. I'm a pariah; they avoid me as if my pain is contagious. My baby is very sick; they can't bring him to me. I don't have millions of happy visitors, there are no cards or flowers that say 'congratulations' in my room. So I am basically left alone. They've put me in a private room, at the end of the passage, far away from everyone. For that I am grateful. It kills me to see the happy, normal families with their smiling, cheery visitors and their fat, healthy babies. It breaks my heart. At the same time, it just increases my isolation, my feeling of being so alone – so different.

I wake up on the third day after the birth, my second day at Constantiaberg. The full weight of reality hits me like a punch in the gut. Third-day blues have set in. Badly. The birth high and morphine having worn off, I am utterly overwhelmed by everything. I have a very sick son; he could die.

I get up and stagger forward. I am so exhausted, so desolate, so helpless, so scared. I fall into the chair next to my bed and slump forward. I want to get up to go to Ben, but I can't move. It's as if, when they took Ben out, they removed my insides and I am slowly dying. I know I must get up, shower, put on a new gown and go to my son. I look up – there are no clean towels in my room, no clean hospital gown – no one has bothered to replace them. Everyone has forgotten about me. I don't count – I don't have a healthy baby. I want to get up and tell someone, call someone, but I can't move. I wait for someone to come, but no one does.

My milk is coming in. My boobs ache. I need someone to help me. I need to express milk for my little boy – he needs me. This thought gives me the strength to get up, stumble to the telephone and ask for a nurse to come and help me. Eventually someone arrives and I ask her for a breast pump so that I can express.

'Oh, I didn't think you'd need one,' the bitch says.

Why? Because my baby is going to die? You callous, unfeeling, heartless cow. She leaves. I sit on my chair, in yesterday's gown – dirty, numb. And I cry and cry and cry.

I don't know how long I sit there. Hours, maybe. My phone rings, but I can't move. I have never felt so much like dying, so dead. Eventually I answer a call. It is Melanie. My voice is so twisted with tears and pain, she doesn't recognise it. She wants to know what is going on.

'I don't have any clean towels,' I sob. She realises how bad things are. She instructs me to wait right there – she is on her way. I couldn't move even if I wanted to. It's as if my body broke when my heart did. She gets on the phone and raises all sorts of hell with the staff. She gets in her car and practically flies all the way from Somerset West to Constantia, making phone calls all along the way. She calls Marko and tells him to get to the hospital. She calls Dr H and tells him that I'm in a bad way and need help. She calls the hospital and threatens the worst kind of exposé possible if they don't help me immediately. It seems to work. Suddenly several nurses are rushing in with clean towels, helping me with the breast pump, showing me how to express.

Dr H arrives. I start weeping again when I see him.

'I want to go home, Doctor. Please, I have to get out of here.' Dr H will not let me go in this state. I am too upset. He is worried about me.

I force myself to calm down. He says if I'm OK, I can leave the next day, but only after seeing someone from the Postnatal Depression Society. I force myself to calm down. In due time the PND lady arrives. She is sweet enough, though I think she is out of her depth.

In the meantime, Ben is stabilised. In the preemie world, after your baby is born and stabilised, the first 24 hours are generally regarded as a honeymoon period. Nothing too terrible happens, mainly because no testing is done, so no one knows if anything threatening is happening inside. The focus is on the basic functions of breathing. After the honeymoon period, tests on the brain and organs are performed, and you start to get an idea of how your tiny child is responding to life in the real world.

The first results come back from his head X-rays. The news is not great. Ben has a grade II brain bleed. It could mean no problems; it could mean a few developmental problems later on in life. It could also mean Cerebral Palsy. But that's for later. Right now we have to focus on getting him and keeping him stable.

On the fourth day I go home. Much as I want to be near my son, I cannot spend one more night in the hospital. Each time I see the happy mothers and their normal, healthy babies, my heart threatens to shatter into a million pieces. I need to go home.

It is just so wrong, so very, very wrong to leave the maternity hospital without your baby. Every fibre in my being is screaming out that something is missing. My every maternal instinct is saying *wrong, wrong, wrong*. I left my baby behind: *wrong, wrong, wrong*.

It's a long drive home. I look at the cars driving by. I want to tell the drivers about my baby. Ask them to pray or something. How can the world be carrying on as normal when my little son's life is hanging in the balance?

Five weeks after leaving home for the office with my two boys in my tummy I am returning, a shadow of myself. One baby dead, the other critically ill.

THE NICU

Home, for now, is the rented house. It feels strange to walk into the house. I can't believe I walked out of there five weeks earlier, my life so normal, so different. Still in pain from the C-section, I go straight to bed. I want to cry, but I don't want Marko to see my tears. I don't want to cause him any more heartache.

For the next week or so, our lives fall into a type of routine. I wake every morning at about three. I lie and think. And cry. And pray. I beg God to look after Ben, to make him well. I drop off to sleep again at about five. As I open my eyes an hour or so later, I think of Ben and worry about his night.

My first thought is always, 'Please, God, let him still be alive.' I call the NICU with sick dread, 'Hello, it's Mrs Albertyn. How is my son doing? How was his night?' If the answer is 'stable', I'm elated. If he hasn't had a good night, my heart stays in my throat the entire day.

I can't drive yet, so my mother fetches me in the mornings to do things. I need to find a breastfeeding clinic to get help with the milk in my boobs. The first one we find just depresses us further. The woman is unhelpful, dismissive. She saps what little internal reserves I have left. I want to go home and crawl into bed. My mother begs me to try one more clinic. This time, Melanie phones ahead and arranges that I go at a separate time, on my own, so that I don't have to sit among the happy ladies with their bouncing babies. The breastfeeding consultant is kind. She asks for our story. My mother and I are so grateful, we both start crying.

Marko works half-day. We go to spend time with Ben in the afternoons. We talk to him. I bend over so that my face is near his head and I whisper to him.

'Hello, my boy. Mommy's here. I love you, my boy.' We can't touch him or hold him. Sometimes we're just in the way. Mostly, we feel completely helpless and out of control. We're totally reliant on the doctor and the nurses. We live for the scraps of information they give us. We have a million questions and there are so few answers.

We sit on high chairs placed on either side of his bed, looking at him impotently. There are pipes and wires everywhere. He is connected to a million machines and every now and then an alarm goes off as his oxygen saturation levels or his heart rate plummets. Each time an alarm sounds, it is as if Marko and I receive an electric shock. We jump and our hearts race. We whip our heads around frantically looking for the nurse. It seems to take hours rather than seconds for her to come over and read the alarm, turn something up or turn something down. I hate those alarms.

I express my breast milk every four hours. I've hired a mechanical pump. I sit in the study and listen to the whir of the pump. I try not to think that this should be my son suckling at my breast, not some machine. I don't get much milk, but I know every drop helps and, really, he's not taking more than just a few drops a day. It makes me feel as if I'm doing something for my son. There seems to be so little I can do. I freeze the milk in sterile containers and take it with me to the NICU every day.

Dr HH says we shouldn't expect Ben to stay at the NICU for less than three months. *Three months!* It seems like forever, but that will take us to his due date, around 10 April.

Dr HH calls to say Ben has been taken off the vent and is breathing on his own! But standing at his bedside that afternoon, the alarms go off again. Those alarms pierce my heart. They ring in my ears for weeks afterwards. Ben is having an apnoea attack. He has stopped breathing and his heart rate is dropping. The NICU springs into action. Marko and I are asked to leave immediately. We have to wait outside while they intubate him.

We sit in the waiting room, shocked. I start crying, my head is in my hands. Is this the end? Is our boy going to die? Marko tries to console me, but he is scared himself.

After what feels like hours, Dr HH explains that taking him off the vent was a gamble, and that Ben just got too tired from trying to breath on his own. Apparently they have to gamble like that, to see when and if a baby is ready to come off the vent. I'm not sure I like the idea of gambling with my son's life.

You know, my biggest fear is Ben dying, but I am also petrified of the trauma leaving him severely disabled. The fact that he has had one brain bleed is worrying in itself. It sounds shallow, to be thinking like that now, when he is so critically ill, but I can't help it. I'm scared. Not so much for Marko and me, but for him. What kind of life can he expect to have?

Oh my little boy, I am so sorry. You were perfect, if you'd stayed inside you would have been healthy, strong. Now you have to face a future that is less than perfect, I am so, so sorry.

I get a lot support from the SA Preemie society, but no one can give me what I need – the reassurance that my boy will make it and will be OK. I can't help dwelling on the negative possibilities. I want to be positive and have faith, but my fear keeps the bad thoughts festering. And I miss him so very, very much. I feel so incomplete.

Throughout this time, Marko is amazing. He refuses to give up. I tell him I am scared to love Ben too much, in case he dies. Marko says he refuses to contemplate that. Besides, even if he doesn't make it, he, Marko, doesn't want to regret not loving him completely. He wants to love him 100 percent every single day of his life. Oh, how it breaks my heart to hear him say that. My most incredible husband, how I underestimate you sometimes. You put me to shame.

I am so emotionally charged whenever I speak to Dr HH on the phone that I forget to ask all the questions churning over in my mind, so I make a list.

Questions to ask

1. What are the goals for this week?
2. How do you feel about this week? Is he where you would expect him to be?
3. What is the plan re his PDA*?
4. What is the plan re the vent?
5. How is he doing with the breast milk?
6. You gave us 50 percent chance at survival for Ben last week – what are the chances now that he has survived his first week?
7. Glucose levels – if reduced, how will he get his nutrients?
8. Will he be growing and gaining weight at the moment?
9. What are your thoughts on the brain bleed?
10. When will we know if there has been permanent damage? What are the chances of this?

---

*Patent ductus arteriosus (PDA)

The unborn child has a blood vessel called the ductus arteriosus, which takes blood from the heart and bypasses the idle lungs. In healthy full-term babies, the vessel closes shortly after birth. But in preemies and some other, sick newborns, the ductus remains open (or, in Latin, patent). Once a baby is born and the lungs begin to work, the PDA floods the lungs with too much blood, which can cause respiratory problems and other ailments. In otherwise healthy preemies, PDAs can close spontaneously. Sicker and smaller babies require drug treatment to help the body close the PDA, and some require surgery called a PDA ligation, in which the ductus is tied off by the surgeon.

From ... [INSERT SOURCE]

THE SCIENCE

And then we nearly lose him. Dr HH is worried – Ben is very lethargic. I'm living in constant fear. When we visit Ben, he looks terrible – pale, puffy, his oxygen requirements sky-high. The biggest concern is his kidneys. He hasn't peed for nine hours. Dr HH fears kidney failure. If the test results show kidney failure, we have a decision to make: Whether to continue life support or not.

And so, just like that, we are staring our son's death in the face.

I have to get out of that hospital – every second there feels like I'm choking, as if there is too little oxygen in the air. We drive around until we find a little mall with a coffee shop. We move as if in a dream – as if we're in a movie with fuzzy edges and no sound. Hollow. Slow.

We sit and drink coffee. We don't talk much. What is there to say? Out of nowhere, in the middle of the biggest tragedy of my life, an old acquaintance walks past.

'What are you doing here?' he asks.

'Oh, it's a long, sad story,' I answer. Ask me, please ask me, I think. I need to tell someone about my son. The more people I tell, the more real he will be.

'Oh well, then rather don't tell me. I'm in a happy space right now,' replies the acquaintance. Fuck you, arsehole!

After a strong diuretic, Ben finally passes urine, thank God. Things are not great, but he's still alive. Still with us.

The next morning I am awakened at six o'clock by a telephone call. It is Dr HH. He is very worried. Ben does not look good. He is very lethargic and still. Dr HH suspects Ben may be in a coma.

Crack. The sound of my heart finally shattering.

'What now, Doctor?' I ask. My heart is aching – the pain is unbearable. It is taking every single ounce of strength to hold myself together.

There is nothing to do but wait for the results of further tests and Dr HH's final diagnosis. Marko suggests we do something – anything – to pass the time. We have the wheels of the car balanced. My son is dying and I'm sitting at Tiger Wheel and Tyre. I sit in the reception area and I look at the people around me. I get up and walk out. I am on the verge of totally losing it. My son is dying. My son is dying and there is nothing I can do about it.

Marko and I sit facing Dr HH. He is such a lovely man – a large, gentle man. Even though he is a paediatrician and there to look after my son, he is always concerned about how Marko and I are coping.

'Your son is in a coma. I don't think he's going to come out of it. Based on the test results, it appears that he no longer has any normal brain function. We need to talk about what we're going to do. I am so sorry.'

Marko and I start crying. Oh God, please, please don't take my boy. Oh God, please! *I hate you world … I hate you!* How can life be so cruel? Seeing my husband cry breaks me.

We have to make a decision, but what kind of a decision is that? Ben is effectively brain dead – a second brain haemorrhage ended any hope for him. We can leave him on the machines, but what kind of a life is that? I want my boy to be free. I want to hold him to my chest and never let him go. I want him to be free. Enough pain, enough needle pricks.

Dr HH says that some parents ask to switch the machines off themselves. I recoil in horror. Oh, God, no! I can't do that.

Dr HH quietly suggests that we hold him once the pipes have been removed and he is taken off life support. At first I say no. I don't know whether I can handle holding my dying baby – my dead baby. But he gently persuades me that it will be good for me, for us. Thank God he did.

The decision is made. We will take Ben off life support. Today my son will die.

Marko and I wait while they get him ready. The nurse on duty is our favourite – Samantha. She is young and always kind. She always gives us information, tells us how he is doing. One day, she tells me something I will always treasure. She says, 'Oh look, he has your thumb.' I have a funny thumb on my one hand, and my son inherited it. It was such a gift from Samantha.

Slowly, gently, she removes all the pipes and tubes and needles. She gently wipes him down and dresses him in a tiny yellow baby-grow. She wraps him in a blanket and then removes the last of the pipes – the breathing tube. For the first time since he was born he is free of cables, needles, tubes.

They close off a section of the NICU for us. I sit down in a blue leather armchair and they place my son in my arms for the first time.

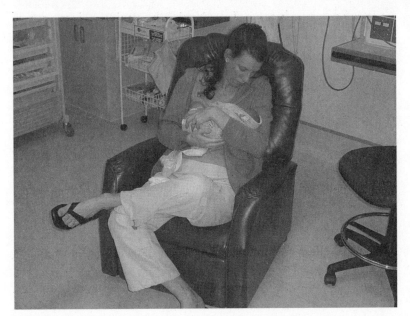

I hold my son for the first time. And the last.

Oh God, my darling son – my boy, my child, my heart. Mommy gets to hold you for the first time. I love you, my boy, I love you, I love you, I love you. I kiss his face, his eyes, his nose, his forehead, his lips. I can't stop kissing him. I can hear his faint breaths. I drink him in, I brush my lips against his mouth, absorbing his sweet breath into my soul.

Marko can't keep it in any longer. He walks away from us and breaks down in the corner. I'm not crying – not yet. I am just so grateful to hold my son. I hold him against my chest, my heart. I can feel the love pouring from my spirit into his.

I whisper to him over and over how much I love him. I tell him his daddy loves him, too, and so does his granny and his pops. I tell him his aunties love him; his whole family loves him. I kiss him again and again. I can't stop kissing him. I love him so much. I ask Marko if he wants to hold him. He says no, he can't. He is weeping.

As I hold Ben close to my heart, his breathing gets slower and slower. It takes 30 minutes for my baby to die, 30 minutes in which

I feel the most intense love of my life. I hold him tightly against my chest. Then he dies – in my arms, against my chest. I feel his spirit leave his tiny body and go straight into my waiting, aching heart, where it lives on forever.

THE AFTERMATH

Samantha helps us with the horrible details that follow a death. We have to appoint undertakers, we have to decide what to do with the body. We pack his few things up – his wristband, the teddy bear his daddy bought him. Oh God, look what we're taking home with us! It should have been our son, not a lonely little teddy bear.

Samantha hands us an envelope – in it is a memory keepsake. It has his handprint and footprint on it, plus a lock of his hair. I clutch it to my chest – it's all I have left of my son. Look, he was real! I had a son.

We drive home. It is early evening, the sunlight muted. The world looks soft around me. Fuzzy. I call my mom to tell her it is all over. I'm strangely calm after leaving the hospital. Apparently this is normal in grief – your body almost goes into a protective zone; you function just enough to get through the first few days of arranging undertakers, cremations and the like.

I want Ben's body cremated as soon as possible. I'm almost panicky about it. I don't want my son lying in an icy morgue. The thought of his body lying there, cold, alone, is driving me insane. I need him to be set free. I want his ashes with me.

My little boy is cremated two days later. We make up a memory box with all the things we've collected in his short life. The teddy bear, a star the nurse put up on his NICU bed, his wristband, the cards and letters, the scan of him and Luke, the lock of his hair and his hand- and footprints. We put his ashes inside and close the box. It is all I have left of my beautiful son. Ashes to ashes …

BEN ALBERTYN,

BRAVE LITTLE BOY

4 JANUARY 2004 TO 14 JANUARY 2004

Forever in my heart. Oh God, how I miss him!

Little Footsteps

How very softly you
tiptoed into my world
Almost silently, only for a
moment you stayed
But what an imprint your footsteps
have left upon my heart

— D FERGUSON

We should have taken our son home with us, not a lonely little teddy bear.

Naam: Ben Albertyn
Datum: 14 January 2004

Haarlok

Foto

Voetdruk

Handruk

All I have left of my son

THE GRIEF – RAW STUFF

The initial numbness, the shocked disbelief wears off. The pain is unbearable – overwhelming. I can't handle it. I am suffocating from it. I miss him so much. I think I'm scaring the people around me, but I don't have anything left inside to pretend to be OK. I am not OK; I just want to die. I drive in the car and fantasise about dying. It would be so easy to just carry on driving, to never stop. I lie awake at night and dream about dying; death feels so free, so wonderful. No more pain. I want to be free of this pain; I want to be with my son. I think of ways to persuade Marko and my family to let me go; it is only for them that I am here, and I need to be with my son. If I die, I get to be with Ben again.

Marko doesn't know what to do with me. I am hysterical with anguish. He calls my mom; she fetches me. I spend the day at her house. I am either lying on the bed, staring into space or sobbing my heart out. Marko tries to talk to me, tries to make it better, but it doesn't work. I try my best to stay calm, not to scare him, but I can't hide it anymore.

The pain overshadows everything. I can't even lie down anymore – it is choking me, suffocating me. I need to do something, or else I will go mad. Everyone is very concerned about me. I am concerned about myself. I just miss him, so very much. I feel so empty, so broken, so incomplete. So raw. Oh God, I miss him. I can't do this.

I go to see a grief counsellor, a wonderful woman called Sheila. She is exactly what I need – soft, kind, sensible, smart. She holds my hand through the next weeks and months.

Thank God for my mother. She is grieving herself, but she is always there for me. She talks about Ben, and I need to talk about him. I am absolutely useless, pathetic, lifeless, broken. It takes so much effort to pretend to be sane around Marko that I prefer to be at my mother's house. I feel so close to completely losing it, so close to cracking. I somehow feel that if I do crack, it had better be in front of my mother, not my husband. I don't want him to see me undone. I don't think he'll be able to handle it.

See, the thing is, I'm secretly scared I'm going mad – mad with grief. I know grieving is normal, but I feel as if I'm slipping into insanity, and that if I let go, I will slip into madness and never, ever come back. It terrifies me. It stalks me. It is waiting for me.

I go with my mother to my nephew's school sports day. There are happy families and babies and kids everywhere. This is a bad idea, a very bad idea. I can feel the hysteria creeping in. I can feel my fragile, desperate grasp on sanity slipping. I get up and walk a little, trying to take deep breaths to ward off the panic, but it is not helping. I can't breathe. My eyes start to roll back. I feel the madness coming. It is coming to take me. I try to call Sheila; I need her. My hand fumbles with the phone. I can't talk. I start hyperventilating. I fall. My mother grabs the phone and Sheila tells her to take me to the closest emergency clinic.

I don't want to go to hospital – they will lock me up. They will find out I'm insane. I try to fight it, I try to tell them I'm OK, but I am slipping away. My mother bundles me in the car and drives me to the hospital. I am sobbing hysterically.

I try to talk. 'No, no, no! I don't want to go. I … I …' But I don't know what I want. I want the pain to stop – please, someone, take the pain away. I am so broken, broken, broken. I am going mad with pain and grief.

We arrive at the hospital. I walk in and smell that hospital smell. The memories of the day Ben died come crashing over me – that smell, that horrible, horrible hospital smell. I have to get out of here! I try to stand up, but the nurse gently pushes me back onto the bed. The doctor on call gives me a sedative.

I slowly calm down and the wild terror recedes. Now I'm just empty. Exhausted. That was terrifying. I came close to losing it – I stared insanity in the face.

I now understand how people can commit suicide. I've never understood before. I suppose because I approached it from a scientific, logical point of view. The instinct for self-preservation is one of the strongest human drives there is. How can anyone go against such a strong instinct?

Well, I completely understand now. The pain – oh, my God, the pain. It is just too much, too crushing. You'd do anything to stop it.

But I know I can't do it. I can't do to my parents what life has done to me – robbed me of my child. I can't do it to Marko. So, I continue to dream about death – fantasise about it.

Two weeks after Ben dies, I return to work. I know it is very soon, too soon, but I need the money. It is all about money, now. I need money to do another IVF. If I don't do another IVF, I will … I don't know what I will do. So I go back. It is too early, way too early. I am nowhere near ready, emotionally, mentally, or physically.

The days blur into each other. I carry on seeing Sheila. I am desperate to get better. I'm so scared I will be this broken, sad person forever. I want to rush through the grieving process. The old Tertia was a cool, flirty, witty person, fun to be around. I'm desperate to get her back. What if she never comes back? Who will I be then? People liked the old Tertia; they seem to be avoiding the new Tertia – the raw, grieving Tertia.

People at work don't look at me, can't look at me. They stay away from me. As if grief is contagious. When they see me in the passage, they walk the other way. It makes me feel lonelier – panicky, isolated. It makes me frenzied in my attempt to get better. I need to get better. I need to stop grieving. I need to stop crying.

Sheila, in her wonderful, calm, intelligent way tells me that this is a very real fear, the loss of self. I am fearing that I have lost who I am, and it is this fear that is making me so anxious to get 'better'.

Fuck this. I'm not going to allow them to make me disappear. I'm not going to be turned into a sad, pitiful person, a shadow of who I was. They can't just keep running away from me, pretending I'm not there. I send an e-mail to everyone in my company:

To all my colleagues
Thank you to those of you who have expressed your condolences to me this past week that I have been back at work. Coming back to work after such a terrible tragedy has not been easy, and I really appreciate those who have spared me a kind word or gesture. I know it is hard facing someone who is so obviously in pain. I appreciate those who were brave enough to do that. For those of you who do not know what to say, I suppose there are few words one can say, other than 'I'm sorry'.

Losing a child is a tragedy that no one should ever have to go through. These past few weeks have been unbearably painful for my husband and me. As some of you know, we have been trying to have a child for four years and have endured much heartache, procedures, IVFs, etc., so it makes this loss a double blow.

What I have realised during this tragedy is that people who are grieving need their loss acknowledged – they need kindness and nurturing more than ever before. But mostly we need our loss acknowledged.

And so, as part of that acknowledgement, I would like to introduce my son Ben to you. Even though he lived for only ten days, he was my son and will always be a part of who I am.

They say time heals some of the pain; I am sure with the passing of time my pain will become less raw, less unbearable. And hopefully one day I will regain some of who I was before. I will never forget, I will be forever changed, but hopefully I will find some of my old strength.

In the meantime, I appreciate your patience, your kindness and your support.

Tertia

Scary stuff, sending that e-mail! But I feel so much better afterwards, so much lighter. I won't allow everyone to treat me like a leper. And

I want everyone to acknowledge Ben – they can't just pretend he never existed. I won't allow it.

To get better faster, to numb the pain, I up my anti-depressant dose. Big mistake. It makes me extremely anxious. I wake up on a Saturday morning and I feel an anxiety attack coming on. My chest gets tighter; I can't breathe. I feel myself starting to slip again.

Sheila is worried about me. She thinks I may need to be hospitalised. I think she thinks I may do myself some harm. I think she may be right. But I don't want to go to hospital. Hospitals are bad. They bring death, pain, loss.

I compromise by agreeing to an emergency appointment at a psychiatric clinic. Another surreal moment. How did my life ever get so fucked up? What the fucking hell has happened to me? Will I always be so broken – will I always skate so close to the edge?

I ask Marko to wait outside the clinic; I don't want him to see me in a place like this. I need to do this alone. I sit in the waiting room and fight the hysteria. I can do this. I wring my hands together all the time – hard. It is how I keep the madness at bay. Rub, rub, rub. How funny – the people there seem normal, sane. I wonder what has driven them to a place like this?

The psychiatrist on call agrees that upping the medication was a bad idea. He convinces me that I need to allow myself time to grieve. That I can't rush through the process. That I can't force myself better. I persuade the doctor that I really am fine, that staying at the hospital would do more harm than good. I promise that I will come back if I think I'm losing it. I get some sedatives and go home.

I explain this fear of losing the old Tertia – this loss of self – to my friend Sandy. And she says something that makes so much sense, that crystallises things perfectly. So simple, yet so profound.

She says, 'But the new Tertia is everything the old Tertia was, just with so much more. It's the old Tertia – better, wiser, softer, kinder.'

This is a big moment for me. For the first time I realise that all that has happened to me need not make me less – it can make me more – if I choose it to.

And I *do* choose to be more. My son has made me so much more. Even with all the sadness, he has enriched my life enormously. All the fear, the anxiety I have been carrying about losing my self, about never being the same again, starts receding. I feel as if a weight has been lifted. I will be OK. I won't be the same, but I will be better. More – not less.

And slowly I start to move out of the dark, deep, debilitating pain of my grief. I read – a lot. I talk – a lot. I write – it helps. I join grief bulletin boards and support groups. I read a profound book that helps enormously with my healing and at the same time restores my faith and relationship with God. It is that wonderful book by Harold S Kushner, *When bad things happen to good people*. It helps me with the 'why' of it all.

I will always, always miss my son – my first-born. There will forever be a pang in my heart when I speak about him. But slowly, slowly, I start to heal.

CONSIDERING OTHER OPTIONS

As the rawness of my grief lifts towards the end of February, I start reviewing my options. As I have always said, I will do anything to have a child. Having a child is more important to me than anything else. If I could choose, I would obviously like to have a child the old-fashioned way – clearly that is no longer an option for us.

Second prize is to get help to have our own biological child. I'd love to have Marko's and my DNA mixed up to make a child that has our genes. But that is not the most important thing. I just want a child. Whether through my own genes, through donor eggs, or through adoption.

I am seriously wondering whether using donor eggs might not be the answer for us. Although nothing tells us that there is anything wrong with my eggs, I wonder if my eggs aren't just really crap. Dr H doesn't think so; he thinks there is nothing wrong with my eggs, that I have just had really bad luck so far. No shit!

And yet, I can't help but wonder about donor eggs. I have joined several donor egg support groups, and I have thought long and hard about how I would process the mental and emotional side of it all. And make no mistake – there is an enormous amount to process. How many people don't respond to the issue of donor eggs with a comment like, 'But then it won't really be *your* child, will it?' How ridiculous – who else's child will it be?

People rarely stop to think that those donated eggs are just half of the DNA required to make a child – without the sperm, without fertilisation, without being carried in your womb, the child would never exist. Those eggs would just go to waste, as they do every month in almost every woman. When you donate eggs, you don't donate a child.

But it is a big thing to give up your genes. I don't care too much about my own, but I desperately want to carry my parents' genes over to my child. My family, and especially my father and mother, are so important to me – I want to have a piece of them live on in my child. And yes, it would be a little sad to not see something of yourself in your child, but it is not the most important thing. I want a child of my own, a child who will call me mommy.

I would do donor eggs in a heartbeat, if I knew it would work, if there were any guarantees. Even if it gave me a 75 percent success rate, I'd do it. But to spend all that money (a donor egg IVF is much more expensive than a normal IVF), to go through all of that with no extra chance at success ... well, what's the point? And Dr H really doesn't believe it will give me any better chance than my own eggs.

So, for now, donor eggs don't seem like a viable option. But, oh my God, I am getting desperate. I can't do this anymore. I will do anything, anything at all, to have a child. And I need to succeed this year. This year, I'm going to have a child – be it through donor eggs, my own eggs, or adoption. This is the year I'm going to get it right – or die trying.

So, I start furiously researching adoption in South Africa. I phone, I e-mail, I go online, we write up our 'parents-to-be' profiles, full of heartfelt emotion. I tell the potential birthmother about Marko and I, about how much we long for a child, how we have this lovely big home and this wonderful life, completely perfect except for one thing – a child to share it with. I tell the birthmother about my loving family – how much they would love and wel-come a baby into our family. My nephew writes a letter (with a bit of help from his mom) that I include in our profile:

My Aunty Tersh and Uncle Marko
My Mom and I had an interesting chat about adoption and she asked me to write down some stuff I know.

My name is Daniel and my Aunty says I am her favourite nephew. I am seven and going to Grade Two, so my writing is not so good yet. Lucky my mom said she would type this for me.

Adoption is a clever thing. Sometimes moms get babies in their tummies but they are unable to take care of the baby when it comes out. My mom says the babies are perfect but have come at the wrong time in their moms' lives.

Then you get husbands and wives who would love to have a baby and are ready for one but cannot make one. This seems a bit strange but luckily for everyone we have this adoption thing. The mom decides that the other people can give her baby a better fun life and the other people really want the baby, so when it is born the baby gets a new mom and dad.

This is so nifty!

My mom asked me to think of three reasons why Aunty Tersh and Uncle Marko would make good parents.

I can think of lots but my mom is a slow typer and it would take forever.

1. *My biggest one is that they are kind and loving. They always give me cool stuff and even money sometimes. My poor sister Rebeka doesn't get much but she is one-and-a-half, so luckily doesn't know yet. My other brother or sister lives in my mom's tummy, so definitely doesn't get much.*
2. *My second reason is that they have dogs. Dogs are fun to run around with and I wish we also had one. My mom doesn't want one but my dad and I do. My mom is in charge, so no dogs for us.*
3. *My third reason is that we have a very nice family and I would be a fun big cousin. I know lots of stuff and small kids think I'm great!*

My Uncle Marko is cooler than Aunty Tertia because he knows important stuff like how to get Digimon stuff off the computer. He also knows that Pokemon isn't cool anymore. He likes to tease my Pops and play tricks on him.

I think my mom wants a chance to be an aunty so she can spoil my cousin and not have to do the boring mom stuff. She says she won't even make my cousins brush their teeth when they sleep over, but I don't believe her. She likes moaning about teeth brushing.

I have another aunty, so I can't say Aunty Tersh is my favourite in case Aunty Nina gets cross. I do love her second most after my mom and Mimi, though.

From Daniel

PS I will draw a picture of my family later when I feel like it.

I send out my profile to as many adoption agencies as I can, to anyone and everyone I think may be able to help us. I speak to friends of friends who have adopted, I visit their homes, I stare at their beautiful children. I visit gynaes to see whether they don't know of anyone who wants to give up a child for adoption. I spend hours searching and researching. I come away very despondent. The waiting lists are so long, some as long as three years.

I can't wait another three years. It will drive me mad.

Through my research I come across the name of a private social worker who does adoptions. Apparently she is the best in her field and has a fairly good success rate, with a waiting period far shorter than three years. But she's expensive. Adoption is expensive. Everything about infertility is expensive.

Marko and I make an appointment to see her. The two-hour appointment costs us a fortune and we leave feeling very down. Expense aside, very few babies are available, and when one is born many people are waiting. Even then, there are no guarantees. The birthmother can change her mind, even after you've taken the baby home.

Oh, dear God, will we ever have a baby? Why is this so hard?

It takes about two months to complete the paperwork and now it's just a case of waiting to see if and when a baby becomes available. You mean we're just supposed to sit around and wait, doing nothing?

I don't have much faith in the adoption process. I don't know why, but I just don't think it will work out for us. These days, there is much less stigma attached to having a baby out of wedlock, so unmarried mothers either keep their babies or they abort. Babies are in very short supply. The whole process leaves me even more desolate. But I'm glad we've started the process, since it takes so long. For now, it's my back-up plan. Meanwhile, I'm going to do another IVF – one more. I have to. If it fails, at least I will have started the adoption process.

Bun in the oven

HOW TO MAKE A BUN

FROM THE HIP

All you need to make a bun are the right ingredients – ingredients of adequate quality and quantity – and a working oven set at the correct temperature for the desired length of baking time.

However, not all of us are the best bakers in the world. Not all of us are lucky enough to have all the ingredients to hand, and not all of us have ovens that work the way they're supposed to.

Nonetheless, there are many ways to make a bun.

THE QUICK-'N'-EASY VERSION

Some people are very lucky. They decide, 'Let's make a bun.' They look in the cupboard and voila! All the ingredients are right there. They mix the eggs and flour together and pop it into the oven. Set the timer and rinnnggg!!! Out comes a perfectly baked bun.

WHEN A SPECIAL CHEF HELPS

Sometimes the aspirant bun baker has all the ingredients and a perfectly fine oven, but the recipe still doesn't seem to work. This baker needs help from a Special Chef. Special Chefs have really cool gadgets. They will take the ingredients, mix them up in a special way – maybe even add a bit of self-raising flour or some other ingredient – and do the popping-into-the-oven for the baker. Sometimes you just need a little help. And these guys know their stuff!

MISSING SOME INGREDIENTS?

Other bakers really, really want a bun, but the cupboards are bare – no eggs, or they're running low on flour. They then run along to a friendly neighbour or other person and ask if that person might let them have some of their eggs or flour. The kind person says, 'Of course. Here, take some. I have plenty and you guys look like you'd make a beautiful bun.' The grateful baker couple rushes to the Special Chef, who mixes the batter and together they make a beautiful bun.

Then the nay sayers come along and put in their two cents' worth, 'But who does the bun belong to?' Duh! Of course it belongs to the baker couple who really, really wanted the bun in the first place. Without them, there would be no bun. That bun is theirs. The eggs or flour donated by the friendly neighbour are just a teensy part of the whole recipe. I mean, *really*. Everyone knows it takes more than just a few eggs or a cup of flour to make a bun. It takes love and a very willing spirit.

GOT NO OVEN?

Some bakers have no oven, or the oven doesn't work so well. But they also really, really want a bun. So, with ingredients taken either from their own cupboard or donated by a friendly neighbour, they ask another kind person whether they can use that person's oven. Just for a bit, just to pop in the bun until it is nicely cooked. Once the bun is ready, the baker couple thanks the kind person with the working oven and take their bun home to love and enjoy.

Fortunately there are some truly generous people around who can see how much some couples want a bun. Not everyone is lucky enough to have *all* the ingredients *and* ovens in working order *all* the time.

READY-MADE BUNS AS SPECIAL GIFTS

Then there are some bakers who have baked a bun, and although they love their bun (who wouldn't love a bun!), they simply do not have space in the pantry to keep it. They see another baker couple who really, really wants a bun, a special bun (maybe they can't make their own bun, maybe they just want a special bun), and give the bun to the bunless baker. These are very special buns, special gifts. If you had a special bun but couldn't keep it, wouldn't you want it to go to a special couple who really, really wanted a bun?

So, you see, there are many different ways to make a bun. Some buns are big, some are small. Sometimes you even get two buns at once! Imagine that. The important thing is for the bakers who want a bun to get their own special bun, no matter how it is baked.

Recipes may differ, but the bun at the end is just perfect.

BURNING DOWN THE HOUSE

And so, life for the living goes on.

It is now February and our new house is almost ready, two weeks to go. I am slowly starting to heal. The pain is still very much there, but it is not as raw, not as all-consuming.

The pills help. A lot. I manage to go whole minutes without thinking about Ben, without the stabbing pain in my heart. Sometimes it even stretches to an hour. Slowly, I regain a semblance of my old self. But it appears I've lost my mind. Forever.

One hot evening I am cooking. I use the term 'cooking' in the loosest possible sense of the word. In fact, what I'm doing is heating up a pot of oil to make chips. Chips in a bag, mind you, not the actual cutting up of potatoes.

Marko has gone to the new house to meet one of the suppliers. I am to meet him there at five. At five minutes to five, I remember the meeting and race off to the new house, a ten-minute drive away.

As I get there, I realise I've forgotten to switch off the stove. What can I say? My mind is a little fuzzy. I race back with visions of flames bursting from the windows, taking a shortcut through a sandy back road. A very, very bad idea in a low-slung BMW.

I get stuck.

So there I am, house almost surely on fire, my mom's car stuck in the sand – me resplendent in high heels and work frock, running, hobbling, the last kilometre home, crying all the way, desperately trying to get hold of Marko on his cell phone, which he is not answering. So, what's new?

Arriving home, I try to open the garage door with my remote, but because the kitchen is on fire, the electricity has tripped and I have no access to the house. I see flames licking the blackened window.

My screaming brings the neighbours running, who eventually kick down the door and put out the fire.

Why I should not cook

I call my poor parents in a hysterical panic. They complete the 30-minute drive from their home in 15. In a state of complete shock, I collapse in my mother's arms. She takes me home and calls the doctor, who comes around to give me a sedative.

My third brush with emergency medical professionals who have to intervene to save my sanity.

Sigh.

My father and husband are left to deal with the mess. Poor Marko sorts out everything – the insurance, the cleaning people, the removal people. What a mess! I love that man so much. Do you know what he did? He went inside and saved Ben's and Hannah's memory boxes.

It gets better from here, I promise. Not the cooking, though. The cooking never gets better.

FAMILY AFFAIR

Things are really bad between my sister and I. Tense. She is very pregnant, very hormonal. I am very barren, very grieving. It's probably my fault. I just can't be around her. Ben died only a few months ago, and seeing her very pregnant belly is just too much. I decline the invitation to her baby shower and avoid her as much as possible.

I decide the best way to deal with this is to send her a letter:

Dear Melanie
There have been bad vibes for a while now and I know you're upset with me for not being around you more, for not being supportive of your pregnancy. I haven't wanted to say anything, because you're so close to giving birth and I haven't wanted to stress you out more. But I need to clear the air.

I haven't been a great sister or friend to you. I know I've been cold and distant. That every time you try and talk about your pregnancy or the birth, I cut you off or change the topic. I know it must hurt. I am sorry.

However, I ask for a bit of understanding. I simply cannot talk to you about midwives, birthing pools, doulas, water births. About choosing the day you want your child to be born because you don't want birthdays to clash.

I. Just. Can't.

How can I have any type of conversation about such birthing normalities, such pleasures? I would love so very, very much to be able to have a fraction of those things. I can't. And yes, it is not your fault. But please understand. My son died five months ago. Five. It's too soon for me to participate in conversations like these.

I don't think you need me to talk about the birth. You don't need me to be actively involved in your pregnancy. Yes, you'd like me to, you may even expect me to, but I can't. I need to not have those conversations. I need to protect my fragile sanity more than you need me to ooh and ah over your pregnancy and birth.

I didn't go to your baby shower because I simply couldn't – not because I'm sulking. I understand that my problem is not your problem. Just because I'm infertile doesn't mean you have to suffer, too. Just because my child died doesn't mean that you can't be totally overjoyed about yours. But what it does mean is that I need to do whatever it takes to protect myself and my husband against further hurt.

All this has to do with my infertility, and is therefore my problem, my issue, my cause. It's all because of who I am and what I am, not because of who you are or what you are. If we were both fertile, this would not be an issue. But you're normal. I'm not. This is my reality, and I can't change it, pretend it's not there, or wish it away. You either live with it, or you choose not to live with it. I have no choice.

And yes, I am angry. Very, very angry. I feel betrayed by you even though none of this is your fault. You can't help being so fertile – that you've had two kids in the time I've been trying for one. Of course I know that.

I don't want to carry this anger and hurt around. It eats me up like a festering sore. I hate the bad vibes between us. But how do I fix it? Don't think I haven't tried. I've tried to ignore it, hoping it would go away, but that hasn't worked. I haven't wanted to speak to you about it, because I was scared it would hurt you. What use is it telling you I'm angry if it isn't your fault?

Oh, but I'm angry. I'm angry that you got pregnant when I was pregnant with the boys. That was supposed to be my turn. Selfish and irrational? Sure. Call it what you want, but these feelings are real. When you called to tell me you were pregnant, my first thought was, 'I just know I will lose this pregnancy now.' And I was right.

I was angry that you spoke as if we could compare pregnancies. It felt like you were trivialising my past. I wanted to rage against you for even thinking there was anything remotely similar about our experiences.

It is very hard to be around you when you're pregnant. You sub-consciously rub your belly all the time. My eyes keep getting drawn to your belly, like when someone scratches his crotch. You ooze earth-motherness. And it's hard for me to watch. That is why I've stayed away; it's the only way I know how to fix it. I need to protect myself.

I am not jealous of you. I don't want your life. I don't want your children. I want my own.

You've always been my best friend and we've been so close. Now you're the person who innocently causes me the most hurt. There's nothing you could have done differently. I know none of this is your fault, but that doesn't make me hurt less.

I'm sorry I can't be the sister you want me to be, but keeping myself sane requires all my energy. It must be hard for you to have a sister who is infertile. It must make you feel as if you can't enjoy your pregnancies around me. It means your own sister can't come to your baby shower. It means your sister can't get excited and involved with your birth. But as hard as it is for you, it is harder for me. I have to live in this hell every single day. I hope you can understand that.

Above everything, I love you very much. I think we can be best friends again. I'm sorry I can't be there for you. I'm really sorry.

Love
Tertia

It is time for me to leave the pain behind and move forward. My next IVF is just around the corner; Melanie's baby is due in a month.

Fresh start. New hopes. For both of us.

IVF #9

May 2004. Like a dog shaking off the water after being caught in the rain, I give myself a metaphorical shake – trying to rid myself of some of the shit that has stuck to me for the past few months, past few years. It's time to climb back on that horse, or more appropriately, that bloody exam table with the dreaded ultrasound probe. The dildocam, we call it. Time to pull my fat clothes from the closet, prepare for the inevitable weight gain that serious drugs, no smoking and frustration bring about. Time to take out the calculator and figure out what adjustments are needed in order to pay for this IVF. It seems we've just paid for the last one.

Dr H said I had to wait a minimum of four months after Ben's birth to do another IVF. Four months it has been. That means I am physically ready to try again. Mentally and emotionally? Well, that's another story. My family and friends don't seem to think so. But it's not as if I've ever listened to them, is it? I need to do this now. I need to put an end to my journey. I won't rest until I have. So, onwards and upwards we go.

I've lived through all the worst possible scenarios imaginable – even the one I was too scared to verbalise last time – getting closer and closer each time. Surely this time I'll get there? It is this thought that keeps me going, that gives me the strength to do yet another IVF.

Gawd's truth, can you believe I'm doing another bloody IVF? I must be mad.

I've never been pregnant in May. I realised yesterday that I've been pregnant in every other month except for May. Shit – is it a good sign or a bad sign that I am going to be doing a pregnancy test in May?

Things to worry about for the next week or so:

1. Will I get the all-clear to start the IVF this coming Friday when I go for my pre-cycle check? Worried shitless I'll have a cyst or some other alien body that will prevent me from going ahead. Should I even be verbalising this?
2. Will I make six million crappy eggs again? My best cycle was IVF #5 when I made a measly eight eggs, only six of which fertilised. All those other 30-embryo cycles were crap. Quality vs. quantity!!
3. How many do I put back? Most definitely not four again. But three vs. two? Don't want triplets — that would be a disaster. But also want to maximise my chances. Where is that bloody crystal ball when you need it?
4. Will my business trip on CD9, CD10 and CD11 be a problem?
5. Are the meds that have been in my fridge for a year still OK? Every bit helps and I can't bear the thought of throwing them away.
6. Will the transfer be OK? Will my reluctant cervix behave?
7. And my biggest worry — is my uterus ready for a pregnancy? I'm secretly worried that the C-section cut will cause a weak spot that may rupture if I get pregnant. How gross is that?

Blah. So many things to worry about. No wonder I can't sleep.

ALL SYSTEMS GO

I'm in that waiting room (*again*), waiting for the pre-cycle consultation with Dr H. I've sat here so many, many times. Sigh.

Everyone is still avoiding eye contact. I read all the magazines in the waiting room about four years ago. I usually bring my PDA along and play furiously fast games of backgammon against the computer, but this time I've annoyingly left it at the office. So I amuse myself by trying to figure out the life stories of the other people. One couple provides some degree of entertainment. She looks about 42ish and he about 30ish. You *go* girl! The trendy young girl must be a donor (too thin and young to be an infertile). The foreign couple aren't wearing socks and sandals, so I don't think they're German.

Then it's my turn. I pick up my own file from the waiting pile – simple to spot, easily the thickest by far. In fact, it's so thick it's actually two files bound by an elastic band. I stroll into the room.

Dr H and I chat, the usual how-are-you stuff. He tells me I'm looking good. I think he's just happy to see me not crying hysterically. His next question is, 'Are you still on Prozac?'

Yes, I am still on Prozac. There is no way I am going off now. After four months of near insanity, Prozac has been the only thing keeping me sane. I'm staying on it right through the IVF, through any (please, God) pregnancy that may result. I'll go off it when I'm good and ready.

Dr H does the scan, and all my bits are looking good, set to go. I leave a few thousand rands poorer, the drugs for this cycle in my sweaty paws. Ready to shoot up. I've stashed them in the veggie crisper drawer of my fridge.

I feel surprisingly blah about all this. I've never felt less excited about starting a cycle. Usually I am filled with hope and excitement at the beginning of a new cycle. Not this time. This time it really does feel more like a chore than anything else. Maybe I'll get more excited when I actually start with the injections, when things start happening.

Maybe one becomes immune to IVF stress? Probably not. I'll probably be nervous as all hell for my first scan. At the moment, though, it's all just a big pain in the arse.

Only two-and-a-half days left to smoke …

The last cigarette – oh, how I will miss it so

I've had my last cigarette. I'm quite anxious about that. Which makes me feel like having a cigarette, but of course I can't have one, which makes me feel more anxious, which makes me feel like having a cigarette even more. You get the picture. I am consoling myself by eating fudge. Which increases my sugar levels, which makes my heart race, which makes me feel anxious, which makes me feel like a cigarette.

Life is very complicated.

DEAR DIARY

IS IT BETTER TO HAVE LOVED AND LOST
THAN NEVER TO HAVE LOVED AT ALL?

I receive an e-mail from a good friend who has been through about nine IVFs, all negative. She's feeling especially exhausted and sad.

'I know it may sound terrible, especially to say this to you, but I almost wish I at least had one positive result somewhere along the line, even if I miscarried.'

She goes on to say she's really sorry if that statement upset or hurt me. It doesn't upset or hurt me at all. In fact, I agree with her. I have often thought that as bad and heartbreaking as a miscarriage or chemical pregnancy (an early miscarriage) can be, it must be far harder getting negative after negative. In spite of all my losses, I've always felt infertility must be far harder to deal with when you get negative after negative, cycle after cycle. When it seems as if nothing you try works.

How do you keep going, how do you find the strength to try again and again, to put yourself out there when you keep getting negatives – big, fat zeroes? I can't imagine. There is no denying that a miscarriage, or an ectopic or a chemical pregnancy is horrible, dreadful and soul destroying, but at least there's a glimmer of hope. You get to pass begin. With negative after negative you don't get to pass begin, you don't get to collect your 200 bucks, you go straight to jail. You never get a chance, really.

The flipside is that almost-getting-pregnant, or almost-achieving-success makes it very hard to give up, whether that is giving up on your own eggs, or giving up on trying with IVF. Some women say early miscarriages and pregnancy losses keep them in the game far longer than would have been the case if they'd just had negatives. Without almost achieving success, one would move on to adoption, or give up on assisted reproductive cycles like IVF or IUI, or live child-free far sooner. This rings true for me.

My sister says, 'Why don't you just move on to donor eggs?'

I reply, 'Because I damn well keep getting pregnant.'

How do you move on to the next stage when IVF keeps working, working being defined as a positive pregnancy test? Of course you want the baby rather than the positive pregnancy test, but what do you do when you keep getting so close?

Getting pregnant is not the end goal – believe me, I'm under no illusion about this. I'm a childless mother, I've lost many babies and I've been to hell and back. But in my mind, it must be far harder to keep going when you've never been pregnant. How do you face cycle after cycle, never having seen two lines on a home pregnancy test or received the news of a positive blood test? I deeply admire those women, including my friend. I think they're incredibly brave.

In my world, it is better to have loved and lost, than never to have loved at all.

THIS. IS. THE. LAST. TIME.

This is the last time I'm using my own eggs.

The scan showed *no* fucking eggs brewing. None. Zip. Fôkôl.

Apparently this is a fairly common response in polycystic patients – you sometimes get lots of eggs, sometimes none. I am to go for more blood tests to see if my oestrogen levels are rising, and another scan.

Whatever.

If things are not looking good by then, I'm going to cancel this cycle and do a donor egg cycle as soon as I can. I'm so sick and tired of this crap. I'm not going to throw good money after bad anymore. Dr H is not too concerned. Easy for him! He tells me to carry on with the injections. He reckons I could get a whole bunch of eggs growing suddenly.

I just want a baby. Now. Jeez, I am tired of this crap. Up, down; yes, no; pass, fail. Fucking enough, already.

Giving up – When is enough enough?

A question infertiles ask themselves often is, 'How you do know when it is time to give up?' The person asking is nearly always in a really painful and desperate place.

It's such a personal decision. There is no magic number of years of trying, or IVF cycles, or losses. Each person has her own pain threshold – what is bearable for some may be way too much for others.

In a study done in Australia*, a group of infertile women were offered

FROM THE HEART

as many free IVF cycles as they could handle in order to conceive. Do you know what the average number of cycles were before most of them gave up? Three. Can you believe that? Three. After three cycles the average person says, 'Enough. I can't do this anymore.'

I think most people who have done an IVF cycle would say they understand this perfectly. It is very, very hard. It is hell on your relationship, your body, your health, your finances, but mostly it plays havoc with you emotionally and mentally. So, going through all of that three times may seem too much for some. For me, this is just unbelievable. Free cycles and they say enough? I pay for everything out of my own pocket and I am busy with cycle number nine! Am I crazy? Are they crazy?

How many cycles you're prepared to go through is not about how badly you want a child. I think it is about what you're prepared to give up or suffer through in order to have a child. For some people the cost is too high. They are not prepared to risk their mental health, their emotional stability, their marriage and more, in order to have a child.

I deeply envy those people who have come to the point in their lives where they say enough, where they make the decision to live child-free. They get off the roller-coaster and get on with their lives – away from the invasiveness and all-consuming cycles, hormonal drugs, needles, blood tests, hopes and disappointments. They go back to being normal. How wonderfully liberating. It must be like being let out of prison. It is called acceptance.

I envy them. Because I can't give up. Even having been through all the pain, living in this hell every day for the last almost five years, I still can't give up. Why? Because giving up is scarier to me than carrying on – way, way scarier. Giving up terrifies me. A childfree future is just not an option for me. Which means I am never giving up.

I wont. I can't.

Am I brave or stupid? Is it perseverance or obsession? I don't know. All I know is that I am not prepared to live my future childfree. And yes, I will do what it takes to get there. There are many people who think I'm obsessed, that I'm crazy for doing this, putting myself out there time and time again, only to have my soul destroyed and heart broken over and over. They don't understand my need or drive for a child. They say, 'Don't you think you should give up now?' Or, 'Don't you think that god/fate/ nature is sending you a message?'

No, I don't. I am not prepared to buy into the belief that this is my lot in life, that this is my life plan. That I am not meant to have a child. Bullshit. I am not going to accept that. I am not an observer in my life; I am a participant. I have control over my fate, because I have choices. I will have a child one day; maybe not in the way I expected. Hell, what am I saying? I expected to have a shag and end up pregnant – IVF is already an exercise in the absurd. So my child may come to me through donor eggs, adoption, whatever. The how is no longer important. The end result is.

I came close about three years ago, when it consumed my life. Now I am just determined. I will succeed, because the alternative is not an option. Making the decision to eliminate childfree as an option has brought me incredible peace. Because I know, come what may, I will have a child. It makes the daily grind of infertility so much easier, because I know I will have a happy ending, even if I don't know what version that happy ending will take.

So, when is enough enough? I think it is when the pain of trying exceeds the pain of giving up. For me, for now, the pain of stopping is way greater than the pain of trying. And so I can't give up, not now.

* From http://www.psychologytoday.com

Crapcycleupdate

I'm writing this drunk. Thank god for sp0ell check. Oops. Did the blood test today. Cra0p news. Oiops. Oops. Anyhow, bad news. Hormone levels hardly gone up. Dr said he is not worried. Good for him. I'm worried. So took myself off to the bar (on a business trip out of tpown) oops. Had a glass of expensive white wine. Then chap at bar bought me another. Might be infertile but men still want me. Also bought box of smokes. Don't care anymore. Now siting oops in hotel room waiting for room service. Stupid f'ing cycle. Hate ivf. Love wine. Where is my food? F'ing hungry now.

SORRY ABOUT THE BRIEF BREAK IN TRANSMISSION

Oops, sorry about that. So, it looks like this cycle is a bust. All that money spent, down the drain.

And as you've seen, I took myself off to the bar and proceeded to get drunk. Lord alone knows how I managed to inject myself while pissed! I know you aren't supposed to drink wine and smoke cigarettes while you're trying to conceive or doing an IVF. But, you know what? They keep me sane. And right now that is the most important thing.

Dr H says to carry on with the injections. I don't know. I'm feeling very despondent about this cycle. It doesn't look like it is going to work. We can't even get any eggs, for goodness sake.

Blah.

NEW RECIPE FOR SUCCESS IN INFERTILITY – DRINK WINE!

I now know what I've been doing wrong all along – not drinking enough! After a night of moderate wine drinking and two menthol cigarettes, my ovaries were lulled into a drunken stupor and got too tipsy to dodge the medication. The meds sneaked through, gave the ovaries a serious kick up the butt, and I have some (many, small) follies growing. My hormone levels seem to be moving up in the right direction as well.

So, for now I have to carry on with the injections and go back for yet another scan. Marko thinks it is all an elaborate hoax on the part of Dr H to see me again.

I wonder whether the prolonged period on injections could affect egg quality? But Dr H says an emphatic *no*. I'm trying to trust him on this and let him get on with his job, but it's damn hard not to jump in and start giving instructions. Of course, now he's worried about over-stimulation. Nice. First bugger-all eggs, now he's worried about too many.

Dr H *(thick Belgian accent)*: 'I don't vant zhirty eggs.'

Tertia: 'I don't either.'

Dr H: 'You zee, viss zeez type of problem (Polycystic Ovarian Syndrome), you get nussing, zhen all of a sudden, you get zeez explosion of eggs.'

EGGS-PLOSION

We have eggs. Lots of eggs.

The scan shows over 20. My oestrogen level has gone up from 457 to 2 057 in the space of three days. Things are definitely happening, and fast. And boy, can I feel it! Very bloated and sore.

I've had to cut back on the injections, from three amps to two to one. Dr H says we're all set for egg retrieval. Which means The Sperminator (aka Marko) has to do his thing again. He is so looking forward to that. When he complains, I say, 'Tell you what, let's swap. I'll masturbate once a cycle and you have the injections and the bloated feeling.' He says he'd prefer the injections, but he's just saying that. I do feel sorry for him – just not that sorry.

The good news is that if we do end up with 20 plus embryos on cycle day three, we can do PGD, which is actually quite a relief. After three babies with potential congenital defects, I don't want to risk getting pregnant only to have that happen again. The clinic has just started offering PGD as an option to infertile customers. I am going to be their first patient and Dr H has kindly offered to do the PGD testing for free, which is a massive relief because PGD adds about another five grand to the bill. It would have pushed the cost of this cycle up to R25 000. Ouch!

PGD

Pre-implantation genetic diagnosis (known as PGD) is a technique that permits analysis of the genetics of an embryo prior to transferring embryos to a woman undergoing in vitro fertilisation. Its primary use is to permit the selection of normal embryos.

When the embryos are three days old, they have divided into six to eight cells. A single cell is removed from the embryo, leaving five to seven cells behind. This single cell is placed on a slide and treated with chromosome paints. These are compounds that fluoresce in different colours and then are attached to DNA probes seeking each of the chromosomes. Common genetic abnormalities involving three copies, where there should be only two copies of a chromosome, such as Down's Syndrome, Patau's and Edward's Syndromes (Trisomy 13 or 18), and Klinefelters's Syndromes (Y-XY) can be diagnosed. Deletion of a portion of a chromosome can also be detected. By identifying the sex of the embryo, one can eliminate sex-linked recessive disorders such as haemophilia. Polymerase chain reaction techniques can be used to identify single gene defects such as cystic fibrosis. Thus each embryo is biopsied and a report issued.

PGD is very powerful and can be beneficial to any couple expected to generate more than six embryos.

From http://www.drary.com/pgd.htm

HUSBAND BEATER

I feel terrible. My husband is writhing in pain as I write this. See, he's been irritating me. Teasing me. Being a typical, silly, bored male with too much time and nothing to do.

There was nothing worthwhile on TV, so he decided to try to annoy me. You know, trying to pull my shorts down as I walk past, flicking my butt, poking me in the side, laughing – usual teasing stuff. Things are so much better between us; I think he's just relieved to have his wife back.

After a few hours of this, he was getting on my nerves, so when he grabbed my gown as I walked past, I *lightly* backhanded him on the chest and said 'Stop it!' Apparently it was more than a light backhand.

Now he has two cracked ribs. OMG! I didn't even hit him that hard, I really didn't. I swear! I must have connected him in the wrong (right) spot. (That will teach him to mess with me!)

I really do feel bad. Am now officially a husband beater. Feel even worse that my first thought was, 'I hope this doesn't affect his sperm quality.'

He can donate sperm first, *then* take painkillers. Priorities, darling, priorities.

Mother's Day gifts

As you can well imagine, Mother's Day is a particularly difficult day for infertile women. It's a day that focuses on and celebrates motherhood, the very thing you yearn for.

So what can you give a childless, infertile woman on Mother's Day? When I should have been home with my month-old twins, not in the middle of yet another IVF cycle, these were the gifts I received on Mother's Day.

GIFT ONE: THE WONDERFUL GIFT

My mother dropped off the most beautiful bunch of St Joseph's Lilies, with a card that read, 'To my beautiful daughter, a special mother to special babies.' My mother is just awesome. I really do have the best mother in the world. I didn't even cry when I got that. I came close, but I didn't.

GIFT TWO: THE THOUGHTFUL GIFT

A text message from my dear friend Tanya (twin boys through IVF) saying, 'Thinking of you today.'

A text message from Melanie saying, 'Luke, Ben and Hannah are watching over their mother today.'

A really meaningful hug from my husband, which spoke volumes.

GIFT THREE: THE THIS-IS-A-REMINDER-HOW-FUCKED-UP-INFERTILITY-IS GIFT

My good friend Beth's second IVF was a total failure, none of her eggs fertilised. None. My heart goes out to her.

GIFT FOUR: THE COULD-IT-GET-ANY-WORSE GIFT

I get home from lunch with my in-laws to see my neighbour arriving home from hospital with her brand new, naturally conceived boy-and-girl twins. Ouch!

GIFT FIVE: THE GIFT I GAVE TO OTHERS

As a special Mother's Day treat, each dog got a nice, big, juicy bone. What a wonderful mother-to-dogs I am.

GIFT SIX: THE GIFT I GAVE MYSELF

Three fruit dainties, three truffles and a chocolate bar. And a partridge in a pear tree.

PRIMED FOR RETRIEVAL

All looks well in the ovary department, eggs by the dozen and a lovely plump uterine lining. I've done the trigger shot, so hopefully eggs are cooking up as we speak.

Tertia: 'Hi Doc.'

Dr H: 'Hello, Mrs A.'

Tertia: 'Doctor, I think you're seeing other women behind my back. I see there was another woman here before me. What's going on? Are you cheating on me?'

Dr H: 'Sorry I was late. You're looking well.'

Tertia: 'You don't look too bad yourself.'

Tertia hops on exam table. Dr H lays blanket over her knees.

Tertia: 'Why the blanket today? I've never had the blanket before.'

Dr H: 'My patients normally cover *themselves* with the blanket.'

Tertia: 'Oops.'

Dr H gloves up, puts condom on probe, lubes up and inserts probe.

Dr H: 'Tell me what you think of the new machine. Do you like it?'

Panicked moment as Tertia thinks he is asking whether she's enjoying the probe!

Tertia *(laughing sheepishly)*: 'Oh … he-he-he … You mean the clarity of the picture on the new scan machine? About time you got a new machine.'

Dr H: 'So, Mrs A, you're good. I see you keep getting your blood results before I do.'

(Blood test results are only ever given to the doctor directly, never to the patient. The patient is then phoned by the doctor with the results.)

Tertia: 'Well … um … I phone the lab pretending to be your nurse and get the results myself. I hate waiting and you know I know how to interpret the results anyway.'

Dr H *(laughing)*: 'Oh, I don't mind. Hmmmm … eggs, I see. *Baie eiers.*'

Tertia: 'It appears there's no dominant follicle …'

Dr H: 'What do you think of your lining?'

Tertia: 'Looks good to me … triple layer pattern. What is the measurement?'

Dr H: 'Nine-something.'

Tertia: 'Very good. So, it seems you were right.'

Dr H: 'I'm always right.'

Tertia: 'Not bad for a man.'

Dr H laughs. Tertia hops off table, gets dressed and walks back to desk.

Dr H: 'I don't need to explain to you what to expect for retrieval?'

Tertia: 'Nope, see you Friday. Looking forward to those pre-meds and the anaesthetic … hmmm, drugs. I'll pick up my meds on the way out.'

Leaves office.

I really am a low-maintenance patient. I should be getting a discount for knowing all the stuff I do.

SHIT, THIS IS NERVE-WRECKING STUFF

Retrieval is damn painful this time. I must be getting old. But 18 of the 20 eggs fertilised. Nice, sensible number. I'm pleased. The next step is to review what they look like to see how many we have to PGD.

Shitting whole bricks here. OK ... deep breath.

Of the 18, two have developed to only two cells, so they're non-starters. Three are too advanced to biopsy (meaning they've developed to more than eight cells). These are placed in a special medium to grow to five days. Nine are slightly slower, at five to six cells – these will be checked and frozen. The embryologist has managed to biopsy four excellent embryos. She says they only biopsy excellent eight cells with no fragmentation.

I'm not sure what to make of this. I'm a little disappointed that only four embryos have been biopsied. Lord knows what we will transfer now. I hope I haven't made a mistake by telling them to freeze the nine. I don't care about the FETs. I want fresh embryos. Lots of them.

So I have seven embryos to work with, to try to take to day five. We also have the three advanced embryos that look good and the four biopsied ones. Shit, I hope that's enough. The biopsy process is all new to me.

I ask the embryologist, 'Will we have at least two good embryos to work with?'

'Definitely,' she says.

Shit, I hope so. Aargh!! Nervous now.

And I'm having a real dilemma about how many embryos to transfer back into my womb. I want to maximise my chances, but I obviously do *not* want to make the same mistake again and end up with quads or triplets. It's just too dangerous. Even I know that. Dr H doesn't even want me to have a twin pregnancy. I think if he could, he'd transfer only one embryo, but I'm having none of that. What if there is something wrong with that one? No, I want to transfer either two or three. But I don't think Dr H will let me transfer three. OK, two it will be, then. That is if we have two decent ones to transfer!

Bugger! This is enough to drive anyone to drink, except *I can't smoke or drink now*! If ever I've needed a cigarette, it is now.

CAN YOU BELIEVE THIS SHIT?!

Just got a call from the lab. The PGD process was a bit of a fuck up. As I mentioned, I'm their first patient and there are obviously some issues that still need to be sorted out. Long story short: they biopsied four of my embryos. One embryo died after the biopsy, two results came back as invalid and the only result they got is that the fourth embryo has a chromosomal abnormality, not viable. The invalid results were probably because of some kind of delay in getting the cell slides to the lab on time. Great.

So now what? The embryologist says the two we didn't get results for are the strongest-looking embryos. If we hadn't done the PGD, she would have picked those two to transfer. But of course I am paranoid now. What if there is something wrong with both or either of them? I can't believe that we risked losing the embryos by doing the biopsy and still have no idea whether the two embryos are chromosomally normal or not. Fuck. I'm just going to have to trust Dr H, the embryologist and God/nature/fate that those two are OK.

Can you believe this? It never bloody ends. Can I not get some good luck, ever? Just once?

EMBRYOS BACK TO THE MOTHER SHIP

Embryo transfer is a breeze. I swear my cervix and the catheter are so well acquainted that the former starts opening at the merest whiff of the latter. In and out, like a bad lover.

We decided to transfer the two embryos that were biopsied, even though we didn't get results for them. The embryologist felt that they were definitely the strongest looking embryos and she felt that if they could survive the biopsy process and still thrive, then they'd be strong, hardy babies. I hope she's right. So, in official terms, Dr H transferred two 'excellent', expanded, hatching five-day-old embryos back into my womb.

It's actually quite an anti-climax after all the drama. What now? How am I going to pass the time for the next ten days? Have no money, so can't shop. Can't drink, can't smoke, can't have sex. Bored already. Tap, tap, tap.

FROM THE HIP

Let's talk about sex, baby!

I need to discus this whole sex thing. Or lack thereof.

One would assume that when a couple is trying for a baby they're having a lot of sex. Afternoon sex, morning sex, sex in the lounge, sex in the bedroom – a regular shagfest. The reality couldn't be further from the truth. I've never had less sex in my life.

When you first set out trying for a baby, you do it the old-fashioned way, by having sex with your significant other. And, yes, for the first few months you probably do have sex quite often.

But after a few months of nothing happening in the baby depart-ment, things become a little tense. You stop associating sex with fun and start associating it with trying for a baby. Sex becomes about timing, cycles and ovulation. It becomes a chore, an obligation. For both part-ners. And then, if you're not careful, sex becomes associated with failure, with duty, with angst. Hardly romantic stuff. As hard as you try *not* to make sex all about trying for a baby, it is impossible to just forget about that part. It's hard to stop yourself from saying to your partner, 'Just skip the foreplay, darling. Let's get it over with.' I swear I've never said that. Well, not a *lot*.

Then, once you realise you can shag till you're blue in the face and it is not going to result in a baby, it's tempting to shelve the whole sex thing all together. Of course, once you move on to assisted reproductive tech-nologies like artificial insemination and IVF, you start having sex even less, if that is at all possible. Not only because you really don't feel like it and what's the point, really? But because you're not supposed to have sex during that time.

Although some clinics no longer insist on it, there are many clinics that tell their patients to avoid sexual intercourse from the time of embryo transfer until the first pregnancy test. So for half the month, you're not allowed to have sex. Of course, before then you're very hormonal (read witch-like) and your ovaries are so swollen and bloated, the last thing you feel like is something poking around down below.

Then, if by some miracle, you do get pregnant, you're so bloody para-noid about losing the baby that there is absolutely no way you're allowing anyone's penis anywhere near it. Once you're past the scary first trimester, things get a little easier and you can have sex if you want.

Unless, of course, you're me, in which case sex is banned throughout the entire pregnancy. My pregnancies are deemed high risk and on doc-tors orders we're on a shag-free diet.

So, for half the month while we were doing the IVFs, there was no sex. While we were pregnant, no sex. After the ectopics, miscarriages, D&Cs, births, no sex for at least eight weeks while I recover. Add to this the Bartholin's Gland removal, the two laparoscopies and assorted other fanny operations and you can begin to see why we probably had sex about four-and-a-half times in five years.

Poor Marko. Poor, poor Marko. No wonder he has a permanently pinched expression on his face. The man deserves a medal.

THE UTERUS, SHE'S AFRAID

Warning: Esoteric touchy-feely, incense-burning, deeper-meaning, tree-hugging, tie-dyed stuff.

As I lie on the acupuncturist's table with the plinky-plonky, water-falling, bird-singing music playing in the background, I wonder how I can pass the time. I know I'm supposed to be relaxing, but I get so bored just lying there.

Maybe I should practise a bit of visualisation. Visualise my embryos nestling into the plush lining of the womb and all that touchy-feely shit. Send energy to my nether regions. But alas, I have never been able to do that stuff properly. I keep forgetting to visualise and start thinking of things I need to do, compiling To Do lists in my head.

As I'm trying to visualise my embryos cosying up to my receptive womb, I suddenly think, 'What if my uterus senses my fear and rejects the poor wanting-to-nestle embryos?'

You see, here's the thing … I am petrified to get pregnant again. There, I've said it. I'm scared shitless about it. Getting pregnant after what I've been through is the scariest goddamned thing ever. Nothing is guaranteed; every second of every day will be fraught with worry and fear. There will be no safe point where I can relax and say, 'Well, things should be fine from here.' Not at the end of the first trimester, not at the second. Not even in the third trimester. I've lost too many babies at too many stages to ever feel safe, at any stage.

While I'm going through the motions of doing the IVF, I can steel myself against most of the pain. But once pregnant, matters are out of my control. No matter what I do, there is no guarantee the baby will be OK. If staying on bed rest for the full eight months would help, I'd do it in a heartbeat. But how on earth do you prevent things like placenta failure, or premature rupture of the membranes? You can't.

What terrifies me most of all is the fear that I may end up back in that dark, scary place where I was after losing Ben. I came so close to insanity, the thought of going back there terrifies me. Because I don't know if I will be able to stop myself from falling into that dark pit.

Now, I'm not one who normally believes in touchy-feely shit, but I have to say I'm a little worried that my fear of pregnancy may prevent these embryos from implanting. That my uterus will sense my fear and shrivel up like a dried prune. So I try to visualise the embryos settling in and all I experience is a slightly gassy feeling. And, clearly, farting in the acupuncture room is a no-no. God, I hope I am wrong.

What a crap time to decide I'm a tree-hugger. Where's the hedonistic, pragmatic capitalist pig when you need her?

I DON'T THINK IT'S WORKED

Well, it seems this IVF hasn't worked. I've had a feeling that it hasn't worked since the weekend and Vicky basically confirmed it during my acupuncture appointment. She reckons my pulses have dipped – they're very weak. She knows my body very well, having correctly predicted my pregnancies as well as my negative cycles. So, I'm about 99 percent sure the IVF is a bust. Obviously, I'll carry on with the hormone injections and do the pregnancy test, but Vicky has not been wrong before.

So where to from here? As I lay crying on the acupuncture bed, a million emotions and thoughts run through my mind. I'm so tired, my soul so fatigued. I am bone weary of putting myself out there time and time again and just hitting heartache over and over and over. I don't even know whether I should carry on trying. Me – who vowed never to give up. But how much money can one pour down the drain? If this was all free, I'd carry on until I got it right, but it's not. It's fucking expensive.

And what about more IVFs? What do I do now? Do I do another cycle with my own eggs or do I move on to donor eggs? I honestly do not give a shit about genetics anymore. I. Just. Want. A. Baby. Now.

If this cycle is negative, it will be the first negative since we sorted out the fertilisation issues. So, is there life in my old eggs? Or will donor eggs give me the edge? The reason I hesitate to move on to donor is the cost. And, given the very small increase in potential success rate, do I want to risk spending even more money?

Can I do another cycle? Do I have it left in me? I'm starting to get embarrassed at how many cycles I've done. Do people look at me and think I'm pathetic and should have moved on long ago? I wish I had the courage to give it all up, to accept a childfree future. I just can't. I won't be stupid enough to stop the medication and injections, but I know in my heart it hasn't worked. Sometimes you just know.

All the grief of the previous hurts and losses floods back. I'm overwhelmed by it. I feel as if my heart will tear in two. I'm just so tired. So very, very tired of it all. This hurts. A lot.

The chosen few

FROM THE HEART

I need to talk about the whole faith/religion thing. It's been bugging me. People love to throw the God thing around. Glibly. It's easy to be glib when you're OK. When you are not the one whose life is being shattered.

I have a big issue with people who say, on having their wishes granted, like getting a positive pregnancy result, or their premature baby surviving, 'See, God *does* answer prayers.' It really gets up my nose because, well, what exactly do they mean?

That God has somehow *chosen* not to answer my prayers? It's not as if I haven't been praying – believe me, I pray. I pray and pray and pray. I've said so many prayers over the years – for positive pregnancy results, for not miscarrying, for having 'two healthy babies at term'. I've said that one many, many times! And recently, my most desperate prayer of all: 'Oh God, please, please, please don't let my boy die. Please let him be OK.'

Would those glib folks like to comment on me and my prayers?

God did not answer my prayers. Am I therefore to assume that God answers *their* prayers only? Or *some* prayers only? That I'm not praying hard enough? Impossible, by the way. I beg, I plead, with my whole heart.

But I know what they'd say. They'd toss me the slippery faith ball. I don't have enough faith. *They* do. All I can say to that is it's easy to have retrospective faith, faith after the fact. Don't tell me you've never had any fears, any doubts. Bullshit.

The thing that gets up my nose most is the underlying insinuation that somehow they are more deserving, because *their* prayers are answered – their baby lives, their result is positive. Somehow, if I tried harder, prayed harder, became more deserving, then my prayers would be answered, too. This is the part of Christianity that irritates me. That sense of moral superiority, that culture of deservedness, the 'look at me, I'm so good/pious/worthy' stuff.

God doesn't work that way – not a loving, caring God. It can't be about deservedness; if you deserve the good stuff, then surely you deserve the bad stuff that happens in life as well?

Not true. Ben did *not* deserve to die. Cancer patients do *not* deserve to get cancer. The granting of prayers has nothing to do with deservedness.* It is not 'God's will' to grant some people babies and others not. It is not God's will to let some babies die. The God I know would never have it as his will to let innocent babies die, or to let children suffer. You can't have the good without the bad. You can't say all the good that happens is because you deserve it, but the bad is because ... well, just because.

I honestly don't believe God answers prayers with a 'No'. I don't think he sits up there and says, 'Tertia ... umm ... well, I think this time I will say no. But come back again next time. I may just say yes. OK, Sally, you can have a yes today. Why? Oh, just because I feel like it. Let me rephrase that: it is Part of My Plan. The plan that is bigger than you – one day you'll understand.'

I believe God created us with free will, and having free will implies choice, and a certain amount of randomness in the world we live in. And free will does not come with conditions attached. As in, 'You can have free will, but only until I decide to intervene.' You can't have it both ways. You either have free will, or you don't. And you can't have free will without the consequences that go with it.

I have to believe in the randomness of the world; otherwise abused children, genocide victims and women who are raped are part of a Plan. And I can't believe in a God who has a plan that says, 'Let this little nine-month-old baby be raped. It's OK – it's part of my plan.' These things happen, every day, all over the world, to good people, to innocent children. You can't ascribe everything to that nebulous 'God's Plan'.

So why do things happen? Because they just do.

Why is it so difficult for people to accept the answer – just because? Maybe it's because throughout our lives we are programmed to believe input = output. Cause = effect. Being good = reward. Hard work = good payment. Being godly = being blessed. The harder I push this pedal, the faster it will go. We need to make sense of our lives. We need to believe in fairness, justice and logic.

Then, when tragedy strikes, we are lost. We have an effect here, so surely there must be a cause somewhere? There can be nothing without reason. And because we don't like to say (out loud) that 'well, maybe you deserved it' (input = output), we scramble around looking for a reason – any reason that will restore order and logic to our lives. So we use the esoteric part-of-a-bigger-plan reasoning. Because admitting that there is no cause and there is no reason turns most people's belief system on its head. And that is almost impossible for some people to bear. If they have a reason, an answer, even a blame to apportion, then they can go back to thinking the world is in balance, that things happen for a reason, that good is rewarded and bad is punished.

It is difficult to live in a random world, one where there is no discernable pattern. It is frightening, to say the least. If there is no logic or fairness, why should anyone strive to be good? If being good is not rewarded, and being bad is not punished, then surely being bad is a whole lot more fun? It is also difficult to prepare and protect yourself in a random world. Because nothing you do can prevent the bad things from happening, no matter how good you are. So all you can do is live your life as best you can, doing things that feel right and make you feel good. And pray to God for strength to deal with the shit that happens in everyday life – to pray to be gracious and humble in times of prosperity and good fortune, and strong in times of challenge and hardship.

Because, no matter how hard you try, no matter how good you are, Shit. Just. Happens.

Ask me, I know.

* See *When bad things happen to good people*. Harold S. Kushner. Avon

I'M OK

I'm OK because I have to be. Don't have a choice, really.

Either I am amazingly resilient, or amazingly stupid, but I'm not giving up trying for a baby yet. I'm just annoyed about the R15 000 I've just pissed against the wall on this IVF. And this was a cheaper cycle thanks to medication donated by a good friend. A normal IVF cycle costs around R20 000. God, all that money we've burnt!

I send Dr H an e-mail asking him what I should do. Once again he says donor eggs will improve my chances only slightly. Here is his e-mail so you can see what a divine man he is:

Hello T
My crystal ball is still glowing nicely, so I am still hopeful. Donor eggs will give you a better chance, but not by much. We will see, and keep hoping.
Dr H

Time is marching on – rapidly. I take a month's break and do my next cycle. I don't normally take only a month's break, but I feel it will be OK. My fertility is already blown to shit according to the stats that say your fertility declines after 35. Mine must be plunging like a rocket in reverse. The only question that remains is, donor eggs or not ...

Shit, I wish I knew what to do. The not knowing, the uncertainty of it all, is sometimes the hardest part of infertility.

THE GOOD EGG

I have a long chat with the embryologist. I tell her I don't think it's worked. This genuinely upsets her. She says she's been thinking of me and my pregnancy test all week. This sweet woman has hundreds of patients and she cares about me as an individual. She says she's been working on my embryos for so long, she feels personally involved in my cycles. What a kind woman.

I say, 'If you were me, would you do donor?'

She replies, 'Mrs A, you always produce beautiful embryos, excellent ones. I've been working with your embryos for four years now; I know what excellent quality you produce. In fact, some of our donors don't produce such good quality embryos.' She thinks it is just a matter of time until I get pregnant with my own eggs.

This gave me so much hope. There is so much damn uncertainty and so many unknowns in this game, it is just bloody nice to get some good news for once. Even though this cycle is a bust, I now have hope again that we will succeed – one day. I'm still concerned that my embryos may have a high number of chromosomal abnormalities. That's why I want to do the biopsy testing again. I want to remove as much of the unknown as possible.

I will go to Dr H to plan my next IVF. Then I will take one month's break and do my next (oh God, it will be IVF #10!).

At least I can drink and smoke to my heart's content for a while. Small confession: Since Vicky told me the cycle hasn't worked, I've been drinking and smoking anyway.

Might as well enjoy myself. Can't be barren *and* miserable.

HE WAS RIGHT, SHE WAS WRONG

Scene: Tertia at restaurant with work friends, enjoying a glass of crisp Chardonnay and a lovely menthol cigarette – those indispensable I-am-barren accessories. Phone rings. It's my darling Dr H. Pleasantries are exchanged.

Dr H: 'Vicky was wrong.'

Tertia *(struggling to hear over din in restaurant and slight buzz produced by Chardonnay)*: 'Pardon?'

Dr H: 'She was wrong. It's positive.'

Tertia *(convinced that either wine is causing auditory hallucinations, or she's experiencing acid flashbacks)*: 'Pardon?'

Dr H *(now laughing)*: 'She was wrong. It's positive. The pregnancy test is positive. Your count is 164.'

Tertia *(in complete disbelief)*: 'Are you sure?'

Dr H: 'Yes.'

Tertia: '*Absolutely* sure?'

Dr H: 'Yes.'

Tertia: 'But I've been drinking and smoking!'

Dr H *(more laughter)*: 'Well, stop immediately. Go for a repeat blood test and call me for the results. Good luck.'

Tertia starts bawling her eyes out. Total and utter disbelief. Then abject terror.

I was so totally and utterly convinced it hadn't worked. Not only because Vicky had said so and I trust her implicitly, but because I felt nothing. Nada. Not an iota of a symptom. In fact, I was so certain that I wept my tears, got over it and made a follow-up appointment with Dr H to discuss my next IVF. I'd worked out my finances for my next cycle. I was absolutely convinced it hadn't worked.

So convinced that I smoked almost a pack of menthol cigarettes and drank almost an entire bottle of wine. I took my two big, rambunctious dogs for a walk, got home, cleaned out the cat litter box, stopped all the medication and even had sex! I didn't even bother to do a home pregnancy test, because I didn't want to waste 20 bucks. That's how sure I was.

What's more, I almost didn't go for the blood test. It was raining and I thought, bugger that! But I knew Marko would be pissed off if I didn't go. Usually I phone the lab pretending to be the nurse in order to get my results. I didn't even bother doing that, because I knew it was negative.

Imagine my surprise. I've already mourned the negative result, the failed cycle. I've been through the whole process, and here I am – pregnant and in shock. The emotion is just too much. The elation, the fear, the terror. All the memories come flooding back – of the past, the losses, and especially of Ben and his death. Now I am petrified. I can't go through that again. I won't make it out the other side again.

I phone Marko, crying so much he doesn't recognise my voice. He manages to calm me down, sadly enough by reminding me that it all could *still* go wrong so easily. In a strange way, that makes me feel better. OK, don't be too happy, it could still all go wrong. Loss is what we know, what we're used to. We have a positive pregnancy result. So what? We've been here before. We have about another 999 steps to go. I can go back to my state of disbelief.

I can't sleep. I keep thinking the lab must have made a mistake. At five I get up and fish out an old home pregnancy test left over from an earlier cycle. I want to make sure that the lab hasn't made a mistake, or the implanted embryos haven't suddenly died. The test is positive.

Good Lord, I'm pregnant. The cycle worked! What the fuck?

Of course, this is only the first pass/fail point of many more to come. The count has to double within 48 hours. Do you have any idea how long 48 hours is? It is very, very long.

I arrive at the laboratory before it even opens. I wait the painstaking five hours until Dr H phones me with the results. The waiting is killing me, so Marko and I go for breakfast at the mall. I get more and more agitated and anxious as the morning progresses. Why is he not phoning?

I can't stand it anymore. I call the laboratory. *What the hell is going on?* The lab people say they've been trying to get hold of the doctor, but he isn't answering his phone. He. Is. Not. Answering. His. Phone. Do I have to kill the man with my bare hands?

I phone Dr H on his cell. No answer. I phone him at home. (Yes, I have my doctor's home number – that's how far we've come.) He is in the shower. *In the fucking shower?* I'm dying here and he has time to shower?

He calls me back within five minutes – 305. It's gone up. I'm still pregnant – though it hasn't exactly doubled. That feeds my paranoia nicely. Even if it's as close as dammit. But, of course, once bitten (or a million times fucked over), twice shy. Did one implant and not the other? Is one of them dying? Is this a weak pregnancy? Is there something wrong with the embryos? Did the sex hurt the embryo? Did the smoking and drinking put the pregnancy at risk? On and on the thoughts churn in my mind.

For now, for this moment, I seem to be pregnant. But it's my fourth pregnancy out of the last four IVFs and still no baby. So forgive me if I'm a little paranoid. This is just the first step in a long and scary process. I'm still in a state of disbelief, waiting for the cards to come crashing down.

Oh and so much for those who love to tell us infertiles to 'just think positively' or 'just have faith'. I've never before been so positive it was negative.

A randomised study into alternative infertility solutions

In an attempt to finally prove or disprove the validity of several popular alternate infertility solutions espoused by assorted fertility experts (cleverly disguised as perfect strangers or well-meaning friends and family), we enlisted the help of volunteers Jack and Jill.

Although the sample size was small *(n=1)*, we believe it was sufficiently representative of the general infertile population, and that based on the findings of this controlled double-blind research, we could extrapolate the findings to the general populace *(p=01)*.

The sample

Jack (age 38), diagnosis: slight morphology issues, slightly lower sperm count, otherwise healthy.

Jill (age 35), diagnosis: Polycystic Ovarian Syndrome (a fairly common medical condition), Stage Two Endometriosis and some adhesions, otherwise healthy.

Jack and Jill have been trying to conceive for four years. They have no living children.

Hypotheses

HYPOTHESIS ONE: JUST RELAX

This hypothesis suggests that if Jack and Jill *just relaxed,* they would get pregnant. The inference is that by not consciously relaxing, they are permanently stressed and tense, and the tension is somehow preventing the sperm meeting the egg, fertilising the egg and the embryo implanting in the womb.

The couple was rather surprised and said they did not feel particularly stressed or tense at all, but were willing to go along with the experiment.

We asked Jill, in particular, to just relax. The reason we focused on Jill is because it is common knowledge that it's the woman who causes the stress in the bedroom when trying to conceive.

Initially, Jill was puzzled as to how she should just relax, but after a few glasses of wine and some pot, she seemed to get the hang of it.

The findings: Jill reported back that despite being so relaxed, she fell asleep twice during sex and once during foreplay, and still did not manage to conceive.

Unfortunately, it seems that just relaxing will not clear up endometriosis or assist with fertilisation.

Jill was advised to continue with the wine and pot by all means, if that helps.

HYPOTHESIS TWO: JUST DON'T THINK ABOUT IT AND IT WILL HAPPEN

Similar to the first, this hypothesis suggests that by the subject not thinking about the fact that she is trying to conceive, she will automatically get pregnant. The inference is that constant thinking (read obsessing) about efforts to conceive actually prevent it being accomplished.

Much anecdotal evidence has been supplied by local fertility experts, each of whom apparently knows someone who just stopped thinking about it and, voila! They got pregnant.

The researchers were somewhat at a loss as to how to suggest to Jill she just not think about it. Clearly, the well-meaning fertility experts have on-off switches in their brains that can be flicked at whim to terminate certain trains of thought. There is no truth to the rumour that most of our experts have their switches permanently switched off.

Our intrepid volunteers soldiered on regardless and tried their best. Jill said she totally ignored ovulation by taking several happy pills, thereby numbing herself to its signs. She also ignored her period and pretended she did not take any notice of the stages of her cycle. That led to matters becoming messy and embarrassing at times. When asked at a social function whether she planned to have children, she became vague and said, 'Children? What do you mean? What is this 'children' you speak about?'

The findings: Unfortunately, this did not seem to work either. The researchers requested the fertility-experts-cleverly-disguised-as-well-meaning-friends to put forward practical suggestions on how just not to think about something. Short of having a lobotomy, this proved nearly impossible.

HYPOTHESIS THREE: WHY DON'T YOU JUST ADOPT?

At this stage of the study, the researchers noted the steady use of the word *just*. Which seems to imply that, really, the solution is painfully obvious and simple and the subjects are a bit thick not to get it.

The hypothesis is that the subjects can just adopt and then stop moping around, hankering for a child.

The findings: Jack and Jill discovered that there is nothing *just* about adopting. Not only is this an enormous decision that affects their and the child's future, but also there is nothing *just* about the adopted child, since it is not a commodity or Band-aid to be pasted on a stubbed toe.

Moreover, adopting is extremely difficult and rather costly. Babies cannot be ordered off a catalogue, COD.

HYPOTHESIS FOUR: JUST ADOPT AND YOU WILL GET PREGNANT

Ah! The inference here is that the adoption and, by implication, the adopted child are expendable tools used merely to get pregnant with the subjects' *own, real* child. The adopted child in this hypothesis is reduced to little more than a voodoo doll or fertility statue. The subjects may consider rubbing the head of their adopted child three times and placing him facing the front door. The experts, well-meaning to the last, also seem to be suggesting that the adopted child is somehow second best, not quite good enough, the runner up. The researchers are baffled as to what the fertility experts want the subjects to do with their adopted child once they are pregnant.

The findings: Despite seemingly endless anecdotal evidence by our experts, in the manner of 'Susie, Mary and Thelma adopted and boom, they conceived', statistics show absolutely no difference in pregnancy rates between those who have adopted and those who haven't. Really. Promise.

HYPOTHESIS FIVE: WHY DON'T YOU SLEEP WITH ME/MY HUSBAND? I/HE WILL GET YOU PREGNANT

This hypothesis was difficult to prove or disprove, as our intrepid volunteers were reluctant to test its validity.

However, after much persuasion (read more wine and pot), we managed to convince Jill to sleep with Bob, her fertile friend's husband. Oddly enough, her endometriosis did not clear up, her Polycystic Ovarian Syndrome did not disappear and she did not conceive. Jill was overheard saying she would rather have no children than have to shag Bob ever again. Fertile or not, he was a crap shag.

The findings: Contrary to popular belief, it appears that fertility has nothing to do with sexuality, virility or even getting an erection and sticking it in an orifice somewhere.

HYPOTHESIS SIX: ARE YOU SURE YOU'RE DOING IT RIGHT?

By *right* the researchers assumed that the expert meant shagging in the correct manner, as well as taking care to shag without contraception. After discreet questioning, we found that, in fact, Jack and Jill did not use condoms or birth control pills. They seemed to be aware that such behaviours could interfere with conception. Surprisingly astute, our volunteers.

The methodology was empirical. The sexual act was examined according to a complicated checklist to ensure that Jack and Jill were, in fact, doing it right:

- ☑ Penis – check
- ☑ Vagina – check
- ☑ Penetration – check
- ☑ Ejaculation – check

All the bits seemed to be there. Jack and Jill were doing it right. For good measure, we added the legs-in-the-air-afterwards trick.

The findings: Nope, did not work.

HYPOTHESIS SEVEN: ARE YOU SURE YOUR DOCTOR KNOWS WHAT HE IS DOING?

The researchers are not sure whether the expert is implying that they would do a better job, or that the credentials of the (well-known, respected and accomplished) doctor are invalid.

It was established that Jack and Jill's doctor *was* qualified to practise.

The findings: You guessed it.

Conclusion: After rigorous testing and many hours of exacting research, the researchers are forced to conclude that, in fact, fertility-experts-cunningly-disguised-as-well-meaning-friends, while meaning well, did more harm than good with throwaway advice and hypotheses. We strongly suspect that they, in fact, are the ones who don't know what they're talking about.

Moral of the story? Don't ever, *ever*, tell an infertile couple to *just* relax, or *just* be positive, or *just* have faith. In fact, don't ever tell an infertile couple to *just* do anything. There is nothing *just* about infertility.

HOPE ADDICT ON SPEED

Hope Addict is a term coined by my friend in the computer, Julia. It's the part of the infertile's persona that is addicted to hope, the part that keeps you going on this terrible journey way longer than you ever thought possible.

Well, my Hope Addict has gone absolutely crazy. She's on speed, coke and Ephedrine. She's bouncing off the walls. And she won't shut up. She keeps skipping around, hair in pigtails, holding her dress by the hem and chanting, 'We're pregnant! We. Are. Pregnant!' I can't hear anything else above the din.

Today's count is 732. A beautiful, more-than-doubled number. A perfect number. A desirable number. A number that, if you were a number, you'd aspire to be.

What happened to taking it one day at a time? What happened to being cautious? What happened to the disbelief, the dread that it can all go wrong? Oh dear, things are totally out of control here in Hope Land. I've just ripped open my chest and exposed my heart to the elements. Oh God, not Hope. It's too scary. Where is Ms Fearful, Ms Terrifiedoutofmymind? Fearful I know and understand. Hope scares me.

But no worries – I'm sure Ms Terrified will be back. By tomorrow I'll be paranoid again, convinced it will all go wrong. Today's result was just too delicious, too wonderful, too full of hope.

I am pregnant!

MY CHAKRAS ARE SPARKLING CLEAN AND ALIGNED

You won't believe this. Me, of all people, the quintessential anti-tree hugger! Five weeks pregnant and I go to see a healer. Vicky recommended this healer woman to help with my anxiety about the pregnancy. Being a sucker for anything, absolutely anything at all, that will help with the baby-making business, I decide to give it a go.

I'm such a cynic when it comes to touchy-feely, tree-hugging, moon-worshipping shit. I'm an I'll-believe-it-when-I-see-it kind of a gal. I don't even do poetry, let alone esoteric, somewhere-out-there stuff. I run a mile at the sight of a sliver of crystal or a dream catcher. Then there's the hangover Catholic thing – about it being a sin. So I'm more than a little sceptical. But what the hell! What's another 150 bucks when you've spent thousands? And to be honest, I do think I'm carrying around an unhealthy amount of fear and anxiety. Perhaps the healer can unblock whatever is preventing me from losing the anxiety.

It's not too bad. The healer is what you'd expect. Softly-spoken, tie-dyed purple leggings, big turquoise shirt (natural fibres), long crystal-chandelier-type earrings, beads, spiky hair, the works. Luckily no pointed hat and wart on her nose.

We speak a bit, I lie down on her bed and she spring-cleans my Chakras. Or my aura. Something. Something gets cleaned. Or aligned. Or just generally tidied up. Anyway, I'm aligned and spruced up. Apparently I have lots of stress (no shit, Sherlock!) and blockages. Speaking of blockages, she never mentions my constipation, a major blockage in my life at the moment.

Apparently I am way too stressed and should try to relax more. I know this. I can't sit still, not even for a moment. Must do things, all the time. Busy, busy, busy. I can't even sit still in a waiting room for five minutes. She says I should try to meditate for 20 minutes every day. I can't do that. I can't clear my mind. My mind is the most stubborn, obnoxious thing around. How on earth do you clear your mind anyway? As soon as one thought leaves, another pops in.

It goes something like this: Are my boobs sore? Maybe not, could be nothing. I wonder how long this will take, hope the pillow-slip is clean, wonder how much money she makes? What's that smell? Is it incense or a candle? Wonder if she shaves her armpits? What are we going to eat for supper? Will I miscarry? Oh shit! Clear mind! Think of nothing! What's nothing? Is nothing something? Can there ever be nothing? Shut up! Think of nothing. Am I thinking of nothing yet? No, I'm not, because I'm still thinking. Stop it. Stop thinking. Have I stopped thinking? *No,* if I'm asking that question it means I'm still thinking. *Stop fucking thinking!*

I can't do it. Apparently you can buy a book to help you. I don't feel like buying the book, because I think meditation is silly. Why meditate when you can pack and unpack your dishwasher, fold your laundry, read a book, moan at your husband, make fudge, tidy up, reload the dishwasher, write up shit for your journal?

I'm not going to meditate, but I think the Chakra healing thing did kind of help. Could be totally psychosomatic, of course, but I feel much happier and calmer. At worst I'm R150 poorer, but at least I have tidy Chakras.

HAPPINESS ON HOLD

I feel so flat. I hate that I feel this way – that I'm not all happy and excited. It is just that I've been here so many times before.

The scan shows one heartbeat, two sacs. I'm disappointed that we don't see the second heartbeat. I thought it could be twins – the count was high enough to make that a possibility. I want it to be twins. The Dr H is happy; he thinks it's twins, but he can't be sure until the next scan.

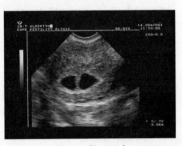

Six weeks pregnant

This is so bittersweet. I miss my boys. I want those babies. OK, deep breath. It's good. There is one heartbeat. Hopefully the other one will catch up. I just wish I could be more excited and less scared. When do I get to be happy and excited?

CAN'T TALK

Can't talk. I'm seven weeks and three days pregnant and very nauseous (which is good). When I open my mouth I feel sick. Of course
I'm glad to be feeling sick; if I wasn't feeling sick, I'd be crying
about not feeling sick and see it as a bad sign. So I'm happily sick.
If that is possible.

Pregnancy: normal vs infertile

WHAT HAPPENS WHEN A FERTILE PERSON DECIDES TO HAVE A CHILD

1. Have sex.
2. Get pregnant (immediately).
3. Do a home pregnancy test when she finally notices her periods
   are late.
4. See two lines to indicate a positive result (immediately).
5. Tell everyone the good news, buy pram, paint nursery, have baby
   shower, be happy.
6. Have trouble-free pregnancy, go to gym, eat what she wants,
   carry on life as normal.
7. Have healthy baby, no mess, no fuss.
8. Live happily ever after.

WHAT HAPPENS WHEN AN INFERTILE DECIDES TO HAVE A CHILD

1. Have sex.
2. Don't get pregnant.
3. Have more sex.
4. Still don't get pregnant.

5. Repeat points one to four for a year or so (in the meantime all her friends and family will have babies).
6. Stop having sex. What's the point?
7. See a doctor, have all sorts of tests.
8. Do all sorts of invasive procedures.
9. Don't get pregnant.
10. Spend more money, do more procedures.
11. Don't get pregnant.
12. Get fat.
13. Cry, scream, hate the world.
14. Still don't get pregnant.
15. After repeating points seven to 13, sometimes over a few years, if she's lucky, get a positive pregnancy result.
16. Immediately think lab has made a mistake or she heard doctor incorrectly.
17. Start squashing boobs hard against chest to see whether they're sensitive or painful. Do this until they become sensitive or painful.
18. Over-analyse every twinge, thinking it is her period coming.
19. Run to the toilet every five minutes to check for blood in underwear.
20. Spend the two days between first and second blood tests, convinced the embryo has detached itself and is now dying.
21. Even after the second blood test result, still don't believe it could be true.
22. Do anything and everything not to jinx the pregnancy.
23. Stress out about whether the embryo is normal.
24. Worry about miscarrying.
25. Be unable to think of anything else but the pregnancy and whether it will last.
26. Worry about whether the first scan will reveal a heartbeat, or an empty sac.
27. Worry that hormone levels are strong enough.
28. Worry that all that worrying is bad for the pregnancy, leading to more stress, which causes worry.
29. Try not to kill people who say, 'just relax and have faith'.

Shit, being infertile is exhausting!

HOPE ADDICT BACK IN ACTION

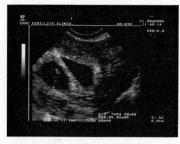

Seven weeks pregnant

Right. I'm hopeful again. It is twins. Two heartbeats, both babies measuring OK.

Now begins two weeks of waiting hell until my next scan. *Two* whole weeks. What's Dr H thinking? Sadist! What will I do for *two* whole weeks? Besides drive myself crazy with the 'what ifs'.

Luckily I'm still feeling as sick as a dog, so that is reassuring. Only 32 weeks to go. A walk in the park, really. Can do it with my eyes shut, one hand tied behind my back.

Not.

NO-MAN'S LAND

It amazes me how people think that because I'm pregnant now, I must blithely forget about the past and be deliriously happy. I can't. It still hurts like hell when I hear about people getting pregnant at the drop of their underpants. I still don't do baby showers. In the four years of trying to have a baby, my sister has had two baby showers. She is due again in a few weeks and has her third baby shower. And even though I'm pregnant, I still don't go. I can't. You can't undo years and years of pain in an instant. Or even a lifetime.

Being infertile and being surrounded by infertile people – even if only in the cyberworld – is all I've known for so long. I'm part of the club, the sisterhood. It is comfortable and comforting. It's the lot of us against the world, sisters in arms. My infertility world is my home, my safe haven.

Moving on to the normal pregnant world is impossible. They speak another language there. It's all hope and confidence that all will be OK. Their pregnancies are planned. Unlike me, they haven't gone through blood, sweat and tears as their foreplay. It is an alien world, this normal, happily pregnant place of baby showers and moms-to-be. You don't suddenly forget all you've been through once you get pregnant – you don't suddenly become 'normal'. Once an Infertile, always an Infertile. The scars run deep.

I know I will pass a point where hope starts at least to equal fear, but I'm nowhere near there yet. Maybe after 12 weeks, maybe 16 – maybe much later. Then I will find a new home. For now, I guess I'll live in No-man's Land for a while longer.

DEAR DIARY

Scan update: Slow, but good

Looks like my kids are destined for the special class. Two heartbeats, two good-looking (bit like their mother) sacs, two normal-looking babies. But, just to keep me on the edge of my seat, they're measuring a day or two behind where I think they should be. Dr H is not worried at all. I'm going to try not worrying about it. Ha-ha-ha-ha! Sure I won't worry. Right. And what's with the slacking off of the nausea? Mind fuck! The nausea is what keeps me sane – have morning sickness, will be pregnant.

FROM THE HEART

Differing styles of grief

I receive an e-mail from a friend – one of those friends whom you know for years, but speak to only once in a blue moon. It sends a chill down my spine.

'Our son, Ben, was born three months early, and after fighting bravely for ten days in NICU, the fight became too much for him and he died …'

When I read the words, I go cold. I can't process what I'm reading. For a minute I think it's the e-mail I sent to her earlier and that she somehow sent back to me by mistake. Very bad déjà vu.

Then I read it again, carefully. I realise that this poor woman has gone through exactly the same thing as I did, just four months later. Our stories are eerily alike – both our sons were named Ben, both lived for ten days. Both died in our arms.

We go for coffee. We just speak. And speak. I can't tell you how good it feels to speak to someone who's been through what I've been through – not that I'd wish it on anyone. Her grief is a lot fresher than mine, but I can relate to every single thing she says.

Once I leave her, so many of the memories come flooding back, memories that I've been suppressing. The day I heard the news that Ben was dying. The incredible highs and lows of the NICU stay. The birth. It's hard to believe I went through all of that and came out the other side (semi-) sane. I haven't stopped thinking about Ben for the last 24 hours. That's OK, because I don't ever want to forget him. Even if the memories are painful.

But what was interesting about the discussion was the stark difference in how we grieved. Grieving is a process and pretty well most of us will go through the various grieving phases. But her approach to it may be better than mine. She surrounded herself with family and friends. She had them stay over, she got together with her friends, she had people around her all the time. Her friends and family supported her, and she grieved with them and in front of them.

I was totally different. I retreated so far into my cave that no one could find me. I couldn't be around anyone, and besides my mother, I grieved alone. I was too scared to let people see how raw I was. It felt as if I had no skin. I grieved out of sight even of Marko. It's not my family or friends' fault; it is just how I am – a cave dweller through and through. And that is how I get stronger, by being by myself until I feel stronger.

I'm not sure whether her way really is better – perhaps there is no better way. She did what worked for her. I did what worked for me. It's just that, well, maybe her way is an easier way to heal. It must surely have made it easier for her family and friends, because she invited them into her world.

ACT 4, SCENE 3

In which Hope makes her reappearance after a long absence.

Setting: Waiting room. Dr H is 30 minutes late. An anxious Tertia is writing up bad-news journal entries in her head. 'Dear Friends and Family, I am sad to tell you both babies have died.' 'Dear Friends and Family, I am sad to tell you one baby has died.' 'Dear Friends and Family, I am so sad ...'
    Receptionist: 'Mrs Albertyn, you can go in now.'
    Tertia enters consulting room.
    Dr H: 'How are you doing?'
    Tertia: 'Ask me after the scan.'
    Dr H: 'You really are cautious, aren't you?'
    Tertia lies down on the bed. Dr H scans her belly.
    Tertia: 'Just tell me already. Can you see the heartbeats?'
    Dr H looks for heartbeat in first baby. Well-behaved child immediately jumps (acrobat!).
    Tertia (*with huge relief*): 'OK, that one's alive. The other one?'
    Dr H looks for heartbeat in second baby – equally well-behaved child jumps and waves his arms. Phew!
    Door opens with a loud crash and in skips Hope, singing at the top of her voice:
    Hope: 'La-la-laaaaaaaaaaaaaaaaa!!!'
    Tertia: 'Where the hell have you been, you fickle bitch?'
    Hope (*with puzzled look on her face*): 'But you told me to go away and leave you alone?'

Tertia *(grudgingly)*: 'Well, you can hang around for the next day or so. Can't promise anything longer than that. Now stop singing so loudly. We're only ten weeks and three days. We have a very, very long way to go.'

HOPE, SHE IS BACK

It's the day of the big scan. Marko is with me. We arrive at the foetal assessment centre both nervous as hell. We both keep sighing – deep, heavy sighs. So many horrible memories. I'm reminded what a horrible place Tygerberg Hospital is. It's gross, yucky, dirty and depressing. But I'm looking forward to going back to Dr G and her excellent staff. She is, very possibly, the best in her field.

As I lie on the table I mentally square myself for what is to come. I can't even look at Marko, because I can't bear to see his fear. It's hard enough for me to deal with my own. We see both babies bouncing around. So they're both still alive. Phew.

Dr G then does a thorough analysis of each baby, spending 30 minutes on each. All I want is for her to get to the nuchal measurement, that all-important neck measurement. She eventually measures the first baby's neck – it is 1.6! I'm stunned. That's a brilliant measurement – perfect! We have one normal baby, at least. Everything else measures fine. Nasal bone, skull, brain, spine, abdominal wall, bladder, hands, feet, placenta – all 'appear normal'.

The second baby's nuchal measurement is even better – 1.5. Everything else also fine. Heartbeats at 167 and 161 beats per minute – beautiful.

The news is far, far better than I could ever have hoped. The boys' nuchal measurements were 2.7 and 2.9 respectively!

Based on these measurements and various other factors (including the fact that I've had a previous Down's baby), Dr G places my odds at having another Down's baby at one in 275. But if we take the previous Down's baby out of the equation, the odds are something like one in 600. Music to the ears of a woman whose previous odds were one in 15.

Had the neck measurements come back iffy, we would probably have had to do an early amnio, a procedure known as CVS. This carries a one to two percent risk of losing the babies, so we were planning to do it only if there was concern. Based on the brilliant results, we don't have to do the CVS. But we'll do another extensive scan at 16 weeks to double check everything. If any abnormalities are picked up at that stage, we'll do an amnio.

I am so unbelievably grateful. Unbelievably relieved.

So, Hope is back.

DEAD BABY THOUGHTS

I have terrible Dead Baby Thoughts. It all started when Vicky told me that my body was incredibly exhausted and that I needed to rest more. Of course, she wasn't trying to freak me out or anything, but it doesn't take much to set me off.

Then, to complete the happy picture, a colleague at work says, 'God, what's wrong with you? You look terrible.' Sensitive bunch I work with. I tell her I'm just really tired.

'You'd better be careful,' says this thoughtful co-worker. 'My friend's friend got toxaemia from being tired and her baby died.'

Thanks a fucking lot. Now I can't even sleep. I lie awake for hours, panicking about not sleeping, which makes me even less able to sleep. Then I doze off only to wake up thinking, 'Oh well, the lack of sleep has now surely killed my babies.'

But it's true – I am tired. I'm 35, feel 85 and look 95. I am pregnant with twins, gave birth just six months ago and had a child die straight after. I am stressed as hell at work, I burnt down the kitchen five months ago, moved house four months ago and in general am slightly fucking insane. It's tiring being me.

I wake up at five in the morning to puke, feel much better, thinking, 'Yay! I'm still pregnant!' Then I think, 'But what if the babies are actually dead and it's just the left-over pregnancy hormones making me puke.' So, the puking euphoria lasts about two minutes.

I do my wifely duty and have sex. So, if my earlier lack of sleep hasn't killed the babies, this will surely do for them. Later I don't feel nearly sick enough, and then I feel far too normal again.

So, now I'm paranoid my babies are dead. I wish I'd ordered that damn home Doppler thingy, the thing that allows you to hear the babies' heartbeat. And my next Live Baby Check is days away. Can I wait until then? Maybe I can go to the local clinic and ask for a heartbeat check. But what if it's too early to hear the heartbeat with the Doppler thingy? Then I'll be even more stressed. Arrgghhh!

Of course, we all know Dead Baby Thoughts add to your stress, which causes Cortisol to rush through your body, which stresses out your foetus. So, if the lack of sleep, toxaemia and bonking haven't killed the babies, the stress of worrying about all of the above surely has.

Reasons for not having an emergency Live Baby Check

1. I feel sufficiently pukey to assume at least one baby is alive. Hopefully.
2. If both babies are dead, having a scan won't change the fact that they're dead.
3. Most importantly, I've already had so many scans that I'm convinced these babies are going to come out with satellite dishes as heads and ears like Dr Spock. They will pick up radio waves through their dish-like heads. I will be able to have conversations with aliens by positioning them carefully.
4. If I go for an early scan, it means a longer period until the next one. The maximum time I can stay (semi-) sane between scans is 14 days.
5. I'm trying to be sensible. This is a big thing for me. Being sensible does not come naturally.

DEAR DIARY

BREAKING UP IS HARD TO DO

Wow. Breaking up sucks. Especially when you have to a dump a really nice guy. I broke up with Dr H today. I felt like crying. We've been together for so long. Through thick and thin (literally). He's seen my fanny more times than my husband, knows me inside out, so to speak. How can you not get close to someone who knows your organs intimately?

Dr H is an amazing doctor, an amazing person. He's sweet and caring. I am distraught. He is a funny guy with a great sense of humour. The other day he looks at my cervix, (the one with the kink in it) and says, 'Wow, I'm good to get the embryos through there.' He's good, all right. Very good. My cervix knows him and likes him.

I would love to have stayed with Dr H, but his rooms are just too far away from where I live. I've moved and I can't do bed rest for two months so far away from home. It will be a nightmare for Marko and my mother to travel the distance every day.

But the deciding factor, the big, *big* reason, is that I want to be at a hospital with the best NICU possible. Chances are pretty strong that these babies are going to come early, and I will do everything in my power to make sure they get the best care available. The new hospital has the best NICU in the Western Cape.

Dr H was really cool about the break-up. I warned him by sending him a 'Dear John' e-mail a week ago. He was so understanding. He agrees that being near a top-class NICU is vital. He even offered to phone my new guy and give me a glowing reference and background history.

I can't believe it's over. I feel so sad. He kissed me on the cheek and said in his soft voice, 'Good luck, Mrs A.' I nearly wept. How am I going to survive without him? He's been my rock, always there for me. And I was his special patient. I know I was.

Sob

LOSING THE PLOT

I am 14 weeks pregnant and I've lost the plot. You will not believe what I've done. I've bought baby stuff. Me. Have I totally lost the plot? Have I developed sudden amnesia and forgotten that this is my fourth pregnancy and look ... no baby!

Of course, I won't be taking the labels off anything. In fact, everything will go straight into the cupboard and I won't take it out to look at and dream. Or maybe I will. Just a little. Perhaps I will hold it a little, press the soft cloth against my cheek and dream about my some-day babies. I can always give it away as gifts if – heaven forbid – something happens.

Why buy now, after four-and-a-half years of not buying a single baby-related thing?

Well, I have a perfectly good reason – Woollies is having a big sale and everyone knows when Woollies has a sale you must be there at sparrow fart to wait outside the doors with your fellow Woollies fans. I was there, waiting with my shopping sistas.

Woollies' baby stuff is gorgeous! I love it. And it was *on sale*. I can't resist a sale. I'm addicted to sales. And once I'd picked the first thing (a pair of hooded towels), all resistance crumbled. I bought stuff. Cute stuff. Lots of stuff. *Baby stuff.*

So now I have bags full of baby stuff in my car. All gender-neutral pale greens, yellows and whites. My neck has developed a nervous rash and my palms are sweaty. What if I've jinxed things?

To be honest, whether I buy baby stuff or not is not going to make losing the babies any easier or harder. I always thought that if I didn't buy any baby stuff, then the miscarriage or neonatal death would be easier to deal with. I wouldn't have to pack away baby clothes. It makes no difference. My heart will be just as broken.

So, for now, it feels good to think things may just work out OK. I'm not brave enough to cut off the price tags. But maybe I won't take it back yet.

And speaking about losing the plot – a woman at the sale was buying similar stuff. Being completely flat-bellied, I thought she was buying for a friend. We started chatting and she asked me how far along I was. I told her and then asked tentatively, 'Are you pregnant?'

Her answer? 'I think so. I only test in five days' time, but I think I could be pregnant.'

Oh. My. Word. She has not yet tested and she's buying baby clothes! What it must be like to be fertile and so supremely confident. Not sure who's lost the plot more, her or me.

Isn't it amazing? I'm pregnant, yet I'm still insanely envious of people who get pregnant so easily.

NIGHTMARE

In the two hours I manage to sleep, somewhere after my midnight feed and third pee, I dream that I go for a scan. I'm told it seems that the babies are dying. The ultrasound technician tells me this news casually, as if it didn't matter. I'm hysterical, running around, begging someone to give me a definite answer, to do another scan, but all they do is say, 'We'll have to wait until the morning to see whether they're dead or not.' This is all my miscarriages and losses rolled into one.

I remember from my previous scans – when you hear those dreaded words, 'I'm sorry, Mrs A, there is no heartbeat. Your baby has died.' The sense of disbelief – that feeling that the world around you has been muted out. Time slows down and it feels as if you're drowning. Drowning in the most unbelievable pain, where a voice inside your head is screaming, '*No, no, nooooo!*' Your heart feels like it is being ripped in two, so very slowly, painfully. You can't breathe. And that silent scream that deafens.

All those horrible memories and feelings come back to me. I wake up drenched in sweat. The most overwhelming feeling is one of abject terror. I'm scared a new loss will break my heart forever. My fragile heart and soul are pieced together with scraps of tape and old glue. One more blow and it will shatter forever. I'd never mend. In the dream, the wave of terror, pain and anguish come rushing towards me so fast, so furiously, I don't have time to steel my heart, to gather resolve and find strength. It's too enormous. Insanity looms. I fear I will drown. Last time I skated so close to the edge of insanity, I nearly lost it, but I managed to claw myself back. Next time, I fear I will slip, slide, rush straight into the dark abyss and there will be nothing to grab onto to stop myself.

It's taken everything I have to get to this point. I've borrowed up to my limit on my strength and resolve. I don't think there is anything left.

I *HEART* MY BOOBS

I love my boobs. One of the good things about pregnancy, besides the bit about getting a baby at the end of it all, is that your boobs get bigger and fuller. My boobs feel fantastic. I feel them all the time. I can't believe they belong to me. I feel positively Baywatch-ish. I feel like running on the beach in slow motion in a red swim-suit, clutching that plastic lifesaver thingy.

I have boobs. Yay!

I KNEW IT. IT'S BEEN TOO EASY

I knew it's been too uneventful up until now. Too easy. Things are never easy with me. I should have known. I have my big 16-week scan with Dr G to check all is well with the babies. Everything is fine with Baby A – head, heart, kidneys, fingers, toes, jawbone.

But Baby B has what appears to be a small hole in the heart. Dr G isn't entirely sure, because their hearts are so tiny at this stage – the size of your fingernail. By itself, the hole is not of great concern. It's a fairly common condition and many of these defects repair themselves in utero or once the baby is born. If not, then an operation is possible to repair it. The rest of the baby is perfect. But! A heart defect, even one as small as this, is an indicator for Down's. Down's babies often have heart defects. And that is worrying.

We decide to do the amnio there and then. It's horrible and scary. And sore. Dr G, competent as ever, does a single-entry, double amnio. This basically means the probe enters each baby's sac through my belly once. Now I have to wait to find out whether the baby is chromosomally normal or not.

If the baby is chromosomally normal, they'll watch the heart with regular scans. If the baby is not chromosomally normal …Well, I don't even want to think of that.

Please, please, please, let both babies be fine.

NORMAL!!!!!!!!!!!

Normalnormalnormal. Both babies are normal. I'm overwhelmed and elated at the same time. And so very, very grateful.

Still a long way to go. As Marko so succinctly puts it, 'Now we just have to keep them in there.'

Oh God, thank you, thank you, thank you!

Oh, and it's a boy and a girl. How absolutely amazing is that? I am pregnant with a boy and a girl.

I am a lucky, lucky woman.

The never-ending Two Week Wait

Any infertile person will tell you that one of the most difficult times in a trying-to-get-knocked-up cycle is the 14 days (give or take a day or two) between ovulation, or IUI, or IVF and the dreaded pregnancy test. This period is (un-)affectionately known as the Two Week Wait, or 2WW. The fact that the acronym is just slightly different from that of World War II (WW2), a time of immense suffering, is not lost on me.

Never does time go as slowly as during 2WW. Days seem like weeks, minutes like hours. And while time slows down to a crawl, your mind accelerates to warp speed. Am I? Aren't I? What does that twinge mean? Does it mean my periods are coming, or does it mean I'm pregnant? On and on and on it goes – you drive yourself crazy. You scour the Internet for early signs of pregnancy (a fruitless exercise, as you will either make up the signs, or you will have your own signs or lack of signs).

Then some lucky souls get a positive pregnancy test and that's it. End of horrible, worrying period; beginning of blissful happiness and decorating the nursery.

Then there are the others, usually people who have been around the infertility block one time too many. They worry endlessly about that first count. What does the number mean? Is it a good number? Is it too low? Could it mean ectopic? Could it mean twins? The waiting, the worrying and the schizophrenic mood swings don't stop there for these people. Because the next big wait is the wait between your first pregnancy test and your second count, to determine whether the pregnancy is moving in the right direction. The number must double. Time slows down proportionately.

Depending on the level of your paranoia, you will have another test a few days later. Repeat previous cycle of hysteria while waiting for the results.

And then.

You wait for the first scan, usually another two weeks later. You spend those two weeks furiously squashing your breasts against your chest to check whether they're sensitive (a known pregnancy symptom, yet not everyone experiences it; this statistic does not stop you from believing that painless breasts means bad things). You do this so often your breasts become sore from all the squashing. You also pull down your panties at every available opportunity to check whether you've started bleeding. If you're like one of my friends, you wouldn't even bother to pull down your knickers. Don't ask.

If this is your first pregnancy, you will be scared but excited about the scan. If you've had previous losses, you will be scared shitless. Then, hopefully, you get to see something that looks like a cross between a bean and a blob. With a blinking bit in the middle that is the heartbeat. That's a euphoric moment. For some, the euphoria lasts for the duration of their pregnancy. For others, only a day or two.

For the lucky ones who haven't lost a pregnancy before, this is mostly where they get off the 2WW train. They start relaxing and believing.

For the rest of us nut cases, it becomes a never-ending 2WW between scans. Lord alone knows how some women manage to wait *four* weeks

between live LBCs (Live Baby Checks). And heaven forbid you need invasive genetic testing like CVS or amnio. The time between test and results
is a particular kind of hell. I don't wish it on anybody.

People ask when I will start relaxing and believing. I think that will
happen only when I hold my babies in my arms. In the meantime, I'm
living in a continual 2WW punctuated by scans and brief moments of
euphoria, but characterised mostly by fear and a deep longing to find
that damn fast-forward button.

SELF-CONTROL = ZERO

Have I mentioned that I'm an instant gratification kind of girl?
I've never ever been able to save half my chocolate bar for later.
Unlike Sis Melanie, who would save hers, then eat her other half
in front of me later. This did not endear her to me. Of course,
infertility is the biggest cosmic joke ever to someone like me. You
say you want kids now? Ha-ha-haa-haa-haa-haa! Wait, sucker!

I think about waiting for my next scan, about being strong and
staying positive. But I cave. I have to have a Live Baby Check (LBC).
Now. *This minute.* I can't wait another week. I send an e-mail to
my ex – Dr H, my most favourite doctor in the whole world:

Hi Doc

I'm seeing Dr New next Thursday, but not sure I can wait that
long. I need a sanity-saving scan just to check both babies still alive.

Please can I come see you one more time? I'll be very quick,
just hop on table, check heartbeats and hop off.

Txx

I know, I know. I am a pain in the arse. A paranoid pain in the
arse. Luckily he says yes and fits me in between two laparoscopies
and a twin C-section. I'm pathetic. I can't even wait two weeks.

But both babies are still alive. *Yay*! Dr H also says I'm most
likely out of the danger period for any potential loss caused by
the amnio, which has been worrying me. It was just a quickie, but
very satisfying.

Seven more sleeps till my next LBC. Then I will really try to wait
for two weeks between scans. Promise. I will be calm and Zen-like.

NAMING THE OFFSPRING

It's time to start thinking of names. What a bittersweet exercise – I've gone through this before.

I'm a firm believer in each to their own, do what makes you happy, but I can't do the whole cutesy, rhyming, same-letter names for twins. Bobbi and Boston. Allan and Alanna. Kyle and Kail. It just doesn't do it for me. Plus I don't go for spelling seemingly ordinary names in unusual ways by adding lots of Ys, like Brytannyy. Ditto fashionable names like Madison or Sky or Cloud or Cumulonimbus. Marko and I are simple, plain people.

As for naming your child after the place he or she was conceived? Well, Newlands Surgical Clinic doesn't quite have the same ring as Brooklyn, does it? And what will I call the other one? Newlands Surgical Clinic II?

Some people do that naff thing, combining the parents' names in some convoluted way to make up a new name. Somehow I don't think a combination of Tertia and Marko is going to work. Terko? Markia? Termarko? Sounds like Tomato. Nope. None of the above.

I think we've chosen names we like. I say think, because I told Marko the two I liked, and that he could now suggest a few he liked. So he came up with a few, to which I responded, 'Too naff, too common, revolting, stupid, no way, you must be joking, no, we're not calling our son after your first dog, sorry.'

He says, 'Why are you asking for my input when you've made up your mind already?' A bit rude, if you ask me. Am I not allowing him to participate? If he hates the names I pick, would I not pick others?

I'm not going to say them out loud yet. You know ... that jinx thing. If my next appointment goes well, I might just say them out loud. Maybe.

DR NEW

Seventeen weeks pregnant and I have my first appointment with Dr New. It feels so strange to see someone other than Dr H. I've been so nervous. These constant visions of one or both babies dead.

I warn Dr New that I'm a pain-in-the-arse, high-maintenance patient. He doesn't seem fazed. But he's been warned. I take no further responsibility for any pain or suffering he may go through in his dealings with me and my paranoia.

We speak about lots of things – my fears, bed rest (up to me when), putting a stitch in my cervix to try to prevent my cervix opening and going into early labour (not a good idea), how to stop pre-term labour (they have some wonderful new drugs apparently). He wants to know what really worries me. I say dead babies and early labour.

I'm sitting there thinking, *'Just scan me already! If both babies are dead, this conversation is pointless.'* But I can't carry on too much, because Marko is with me and, as you know, he doesn't quite realise the extent of my paranoia. He thinks I'm only mildly insane. So, chat, chat, chat – blah, blah, blah. Then urine check, pap smear, internal cervix check (yuck!). *Eventually* the scan.

Dr New says, 'I can see why you're so uncomfortable – you're quite big already.' That's me, baby. Big. As my mother would say, a strapping lass.

Jelly on belly, paddle on skin and there I see them again: two beautiful heartbeats, two gorgeous, adorable *live* babies. They're lying butt to butt. You can see their profiles so clearly, she (Baby

B) on top, he (Baby A) at the bottom. They measure perfectly – he is a day or two bigger than his sister.

I'm a very, very happy camper. Maybe, just maybe, things will turn out OK. Maybe we'll end up with live babies. So very, very close now.

So my dears, I would like to officially introduce you to my beautiful babies, my twins – Adam and Kate. Those are the names we've chosen for them. We wanted strong, simple names, and we think Adam and Kate are exactly that.

It's too late to protect my heart. I'm afraid I'm in love already.

CONFESSIONS OF A CHEATER WITH NO SELF-CONTROL

OK, I confess, I've cheated on Dr New again. It was just a quickie, I promise. Really! It means nothing. In and out (of the office!) and it's over with. I can't help going back to Dr H. He's my first love, after all.

I know, I know, I'm pathetic. No self-control. But Marko said it was OK. In his quiet, patient, my-wife-is-completely-fucking-unhinged way, he said, 'Sweetheart, if it will make you feel better, go.' I went.

And the babies are fine.

My sister says, 'Maybe there's a most-scanned baby competition. You could enter and win a gazillion dollars. You could retire.'

Marko says, 'So, dear wife of mine, how long will the good feeling last this time?'

'Oh, I think it should last about five days, probably till Tuesday,' I say.

Me? Paranoid? No way.

I'M SCARED. AND MORE THAN A LITTLE IRRITATED

I'm scared. As if my Dead Baby Thoughts aren't enough, I'm now petrified of pre-term labour (PTL). I'm 18 weeks pregnant and it is way too early for the babies to come.

I suck at being pregnant. I'm crap at it. I suffer all sorts of maladies – if there's a shit pregnancy side-effect, I suffer from it. Perhaps it's because I'm older, perhaps it's the twin thing. Who knows? None of that rosy, glowing shit for me. I get the bleeding gums, pregnancy tumours in my mouth, nose-bleeds, backache, rib ache, irritable uterus. But of all the symptoms, what is of most concern is the severely traumatised bladder. Not only is it damn painful, but if it gets even slightly full (like as in two sips of water) and I don't pee immediately, my uterus starts to complain. Add an irritable uterus to a traumatised bladder and what do you get? *Contractions.*

A contracting uterus is *not* what you want when you're already at risk for pre-term labour.

Risk factors for PTL include one or more of the following:

1. Multiple pregnancy ☑
2. Older than 35 ☑
3. Previous PTL ☑
4. Previous surgery ☑

One puts you at risk, all of them = shit. A contracting uterus could lead to PTL, which could lead to cervix opening, which could lead to babies falling out and babies dying. In other words, contracting uterus = v. v. bad.

For some reason my bladder is now particularly irritable. So instead of waking every two hours to pee, I wake every hour with a highly irritable and ratty uterus, a crampy, tight, feels-like-I'm-going-into-labour uterus. Horrible. Scary.

Then, I wake up to find some fluid in my panties. And we know fluid is v. v. bad. Fluid = potential rupture of membranes = potential dead baby = PTL = all babies dead.

It's hard to distinguish a normal pregnancy discharge from the potentially Very Bad Stuff. The very last thing I want to see is fluid in my broeks. Lots of awful memories. My heart sinks when I see the wetness in my knickers. I am scared. Very scared.

BAND-AIDS AND GRIEF

I fret and worry, building up to near hysteria, as I try to convince myself that the fluid is nothing – normal stuff. It's not working. My anxiety just increases. I go backward and forward with myself.

'Just phone him, you idiot! You know you'll feel better once you've done it.'

'But I hate bothering him for nothing.'

'Don't be an arsehole, just phone.'

For the sake of what's left of my sanity, I eventually phone. Dr New has an efficient but very protective receptionist who acts as his gatekeeper. Getting through to speak to Dr New personally is rare, but she must have heard the urgency in my voice. I tell him about the fluid, how scared I am. He says, 'It doesn't sound like cause for concern, but come in and we can check.'

That's when I lose it. I start crying and shaking. I'm shaking so much, I can hardly pack up my stuff at work. A colleague offers help, but I can't even reply, I am crying so much. I haven't sobbed like that since, well, since the horrible times at the beginning of the year. You see, this is exactly what happened that day, the day before I found out Luke had died. Déjà vu. The fluid, the call to the doctor, the exact same reply, 'Doesn't sound like cause for concern, but come in and we can check.' I went in for the quick visit and came home five weeks later with two dead babies. All of that comes back to me.

I know I shouldn't be driving, but I need to get to the doctor *now*. Work colleagues offer to drive me, but I need to do this alone. If

I'm going to face dead babies again, I need to do it alone. I call my mother and tell her what is going on. She says she'd meet me at the doctor's rooms immediately. I can hear the concern in her voice. The fear. My poor mother. I SMS Marko, telling him I'm going for a quick consultation. I don't want to speak to him – I don't want him to hear me crying like this. I don't want to make him scared. But Marko has a sixth sense when it comes to me.

It's a 20-minute drive to Dr New. I cry all the way. Marko calls me. I can hardly speak. I keep saying, 'I'm scared. I am so scared.' He tries to calm me down, tells me to drive carefully. To phone him as soon as I know something.

My mother is waiting for me at the doctor's rooms. She must have flown there. I love my mother. She hugs me. We hold each other tightly. Masses of emotion pass between the two of us. Terror, memories, fear, love, strength.

Dr New is wonderfully calm. He knows I don't want to talk. That I want to be scanned right away.

And the babies are OK. Both of them. Oh, thank you, God!

Dr New checks my cervix – closed. He tests for infection – none. Tests for amniotic fluid – none. Cervix closed. Babies fine. Perfect. Beautiful. He doesn't know what the fluid is, but it's nothing terrible.

They're so gloriously alive. Alive. They're kicking each other. Kate kicks Adam on the head and he punches her. My mother says Adam looks like Marko.

We are so relieved. And I am absolutely exhausted.

I realise now I've stuck a Band-aid over my grief and hurt. When Luke died I had to try to stay sane for Ben's sake. I told myself that when Ben was born, I'd lock myself in a room and cry and scream for the loss of my little Luke. I couldn't do it then – I had to try to stay strong and calm for Ben.

Then Ben died. I immediately put myself on anti-depressants. I stuck on a Band-aid so fast, the wound never had a chance to air. Then I dived into this IVF and got pregnant. This all on top of four years of infertility – four years of continuous heartache and grief. That grief hasn't gone anywhere. It's all still there. So much of it, there is no space for any more. The whole process has rubbed me so raw, stretched me so thin, that all that stands between me and insanity are my gritted teeth and white-knuckled fists.

I am worn out from the long journey, from being brave, from swallowing the hurt. Wearied from fighting and jumping into the lion's den over and over. Most of all, I'm tired of being scared. Now, instead of relief at the reassurance the doctor's visit gave me, I am just tired.

Dr New wants to book me off work from the end of September. I'll be 22 weeks then. The plan is to do home bed rest for October and then perhaps hospital bed rest from the beginning of November, when I'm 26 weeks. If I manage to keep the babies inside until January, I will have done really well. That's my goal, babies in January. My official due date (not that *that* means anything in my life) is 4 February 2005. So, babies in January would be a real blessing.

Thank God everything is OK. For now. I hope with all my heart it stays that way.

MAGIC MARKER

For people who have experienced prior losses, there seems to be a point, a magic marker in the pregnancy, that they just want to get past before they start relaxing about their pregnancy. The magic marker is normally the stage at which they lost their last or longest pregnancy.

For some people it is eight weeks, for others 12 weeks (I think even people who haven't had prior losses regard 12 weeks, or the end of the first trimester, as their magic marker). Several of my now pregnant, infertile friends have their own magic markers. For one friend it's 14 weeks – she's nearly there. Another lost twins at 18 weeks and four days. She has just passed that point and is now a little more confident.

A big marker for me is 21 weeks. That's when I found out Luke had died. As I head closer to that time (I am 19 weeks now), I get increasingly nervous. I'm filled with dread, a sense of impending disaster. Of course, once I'm past that point, the next biggie will be 26 weeks, when Ben was born. These are fraught times.

I'm going for a big anatomy scan at 21 weeks. I am fairly anxious about it, firstly because of the timing, with all the associated bad memories and, secondly, because we will get the next diagnosis on Kate's heart.

Roll on 32 weeks. That's my new magic marker. Babies born at 32 weeks have an excellent chance of a healthy outcome.

Where is that fast-forward button?

Is this your first?

I hate this question, even though it's a perfectly legitimate one to ask. I hate it because I'm so conflicted about what answer to give.

After I lost Ben I went looking for support on Loss Boards on the Internet. I didn't stay there too long, because the length and depth of the grief on these boards were overwhelming. I didn't want to be a sad person forever. Those people were very sad and very angry for a very long time afterwards.

However, one of things they discuss there is what to answer to the question, 'Do you have any children?' Or, 'Is this your first?' They are, on the whole, quite aggressive in their approach. A lot of them are still very angry, very raw – even two or three years later. They insist on mentioning their dead babies, to make sure they are acknowledged and remembered.

It's a hard one to answer. Because it isn't my first child or first pregnancy. I had a son, I gave birth to him. He is and always will be my first-born. So, if I answered yes, am I doing him and his memory an injustice? Am I saying he is not worth acknowledging? Yet, do I really want to get into all of that with strangers? I honestly don't want or need their pity or sympathy. Even worse are people who brush it off as if he didn't exist. 'Oh, you had a son who died? How awful. Well, let's not discuss tragic things like that. Let's just move right along, shall we?'

I'm sure it's not easy to hear, 'I had a son, but he died,' but there is such a simple response. All you need to say is, 'Oh, I'm so sorry, what a terrible loss.' There. Simple. Acknowledge my child, acknowledge my pain and let's move on.

Usually, I judge the situation. If it's a stranger, I answer, 'Yes, this is my first.' If it is someone I may see often, or someone whom I can tell will take it the right way, then I say, 'No, I had a son but he died a few days after birth.' I try to say this in a way that will not make the person feel uncomfortable. I try to indicate that I'm not about to burst into tears – that it's OK to talk about it.

Marko always says yes. He's not prepared to get into discussions with other people about our lives. But then, discussion/talking/chatting and Marko don't go together.

I don't want anyone who knows us ever to forget about Ben. He had such a short time on earth, he deserves to live on in our memories. On the other hand, I don't want to be aggressive and in-your-face about it either.

In my head, in my heart, the answer is perfectly clear – this is not my first. My firstborn is Ben.

LIVE BABIES AND HOLE-LESS HEARTS!

Well, it all makes sense now. I've been having terrible Dead Baby Thoughts for the last few days, because I've been feeling kicks on one side only, almost all in one spot. I was convinced I had one dead baby in there. The other was definitely fine, because I've been kicked plenty – lots of kicks, really hard ones. But only in one spot.

The Live Baby Check showed them lying like two Cs, forming a circle, with their heads facing each other, low down to my right, resting on my bladder – thanks babies! Their bums are positioned in the opposite direction, with their feet coming together in the same spot to the right of my belly button. No wonder they're kicking in one spot. Naughty babies for stressing your mother out!

This Live Baby Check is, in fact, the big 20-week growth scan. And I couldn't have asked for a better result. Both babies are growing beautifully, slightly ahead of their dates, Kate seeming a wee bit bigger than Adam. They weigh 450 and 415g respectively – almost as much as a tub of margarine each.

The best news of all (well, besides having two live babies) is that the hole in Kate's heart has either repaired itself or is too small to cause a problem. I am not out of the woods yet but, for now, I'm damn happy. My heart wants to explode with love and happiness.

Back to the mantra – healthy-babies-in-January, healthy-babies-in-January, healthy-babies-in-January.

BREEEAAATTTTHHHHHHHE IN,
BREEEAAAAAATTHHHHHHE OUT

Well, I've done it! I've booked us into an antenatal class. You know, those childbirth classes where they teach you more than just about pushing. Well, I hope so because I ain't pushing anything out of anywhere. Give me science and drugs, baby. They teach you stuff about pregnancy, birth and babies. Clearly the pushing and heavy-breathing bit is going to be a waste of time, but maybe I will learn some other stuff. If this isn't going to jinx things, then nothing will.

Last time, I was too scared to do anything of the sort. This time I think, bugger this – I'm pregnant and I'm doing as many normal things as I possibly can. I hope the classes aren't too naff. I haven't told Marko yet. He's going to freak *out*. Marko absolutely hates any touchy-feely shit, and apparently there are visualisation and relaxation classes on the agenda – ha-ha-ha-haaa (nervous laughter). Bloody hell, is he ever going to freak out! The man hardly bonds and shares with me – can you imagine him being forced to share and bond with a room full of potbellied chicks and their nervous husbands, talking about vaginas and blood and stuff. Shitting myself to tell him!

PTLTS > DBTS

My worry quota is full, and when your worry quota is full, you just have to let go of some things. They don't go away completely, but they can't hog the top of the list anymore. Somehow, in the last week or two, worries about dead babies have given way to fears about things like pre-term labour (PTL), closed cervixes and the like. Obviously, movement does help to reassure one somewhat. It seems to be a progression of some weird kind. You go from worrying about whether your baby is still alive to whether you can keep him/her in there long enough to be fully baked.

PTL, and worries about it, is a particularly familiar friend. We spent a lot of time together in my last pregnancy. I am paranoid about PTL and therefore hyper-vigilant about any signs that may indicate its presence. Especially since I missed the signs so badly last time. (Oh, so *that* is what a contraction is supposed to feel like?)

Today is one of those days. My irritable uterus and surly bladder are in particularly bad moods. My uterus keeps tightening all the time. This freaks me out. And an irritable uterus can degenerate into PTL in no time at all, if things get out of hand. Add to this the fact that I'm now 21 weeks and four days. I lost Luke and my cervix started opening last time at 21 weeks and three days. This time last time, I was in hospital already.

I fret and I worry. Should I call Dr New or not? In the end, I cave in and call him. Thank God, he says I can come for a check-up.

All is fine. Cervix is long and closed. My dear son has his head resting very comfortably on my bladder, lying on his back, legs crossed, feet in the air. I am just going to have to live with the irritable uterus and crotchety bladder. It's all part of the twin pregnancy thing and it's just the way I do pregnancy.

Dr New is fantastic. I am slowly falling in love with him as well. Of course, it's not the same as with my first love, Dr H, but Dr New is great. He doesn't make me feel stupid. He says I'm special (I *love* hearing that) and that we need to monitor me closely. Very reassuring. I tell him that I can't wait two weeks in between visits, I won't last, I'll drive myself crazy. I need to see him once a week, a week is as long as I can last between scans.

He says, 'But you'll get sick of me.'

'Oh no, I won't,' I say. 'Give me half a chance, and I'll move my bed into your office. In fact, that exam table looks very comfy.' Dr New laughs.

Marko says, 'The bizarre thing is the doctor doesn't realise you're actually being dead serious!'

Now I'll see Dr New once a week for a cervix check, and depending on how my cervix is behaving, we'll decide when to hospitalise me for bed rest. As long as my cervix stays closed, I can stay home.

I feel better. I think I can manage once a week. It is also a huge comfort to know that my cervix is being so closely monitored. I can monitor contractions, but I have no idea about what is going on inside.

It doesn't get any easier, the worries just change.

LEAVING WORK

It's my last day at work until May next year, hopefully. If all goes well. If we have babies in January. What a brave, bold, jinxy step to pack up my desk! I'm terrified that I will go on maternity leave and things will go wrong again. That I'll be back, babyless, in a few weeks' time. Babyless and broken. Last time I was back before I was even due to go on maternity leave.

My bosses have been amazing. I'm going to be off work for seven months and I am grateful for their support and understanding. Seven months is a long time. It's a massive relief to know that my job is safe. My company has really been there for me through all the ups and downs, time off, operations, tests. I am lucky to be working for such a decent, caring organisation.

Work is where I'm safe. Stupidly, I keep thinking that if I don't change too much in my life (like go on leave, buy baby furniture), it won't hurt as much if I lose the babies. How stupid is that? No matter where I am or what I've bought, it will always hurt like hell. By going on maternity leave you kind of announce to the world that you're pregnant – that you may even have a baby. Or two.

I'd love to be wealthy enough not to *have* to work, but I love what I do and I love the people I work with. I'm very fond of my bunch of techie geeks. We have lots of fun, always laughing and joking around. And I work for a really great company. I love them; they love me. What if they forget about me when I am gone? I'm scared that if I'm not there to remind them daily how witty and divine I am, they'll forget and replace me with a younger, better, funnier model.

But this is the right thing to do. I have to do whatever it takes to make sure I get healthy babies at the end. Right now that means stopping work and doing some time flat on my back.

I'm going to miss my co-workers. Lots. John, Frans, Dave, Kevin, Jamiella, I adore you guys. You make me *want* to come to work every day. Don't forget me! Promise!

LADY OF LUXURY

I could get used to this. Being on modified bed rest means that I don't have to lie down *all* the time. There are a few things I can do. And believe me, I am being careful. I would never take a chance. I'd rather err on the side of caution.

For the first week, I allow myself one outing every day. What fun! I get to sleep in, rest during the morning, shower at 11am, go for lunch with a friend or my mom, come home, rest a little more, make supper (i.e. heat up a meal in microwave), clean up (i.e. throw away boxes, stack dishwasher) and chill in front of the TV.

The only crappy thing about modified bed rest is trying to type lying down. It's hard. The first step to success in finding the correct typing-while-lying-down position is to ensure my snacks and ever-present water bottle are within reach. Water is very important, as it helps keep the uterus hydrated, which in turn can help prevent pre-term labour. Next, my cell phone and mobile landline handset need to be in close proximity, because, without fail, just as I'm getting into typing-while-lying-down position, the phone will ring. The final step is to pile pillows in a two-across (lower back support), one upright (preventing head smashing against headboard) fashion.

Once all this has been arranged, I sit down and put another pillow on my lap for my laptop. Trying to position the laptop at a comfortable distance is tricky. It's all about positioning it in a way that my arms can stretch past my enormous belly to reach the keyboard. My arms can't go over my belly – they simply won't reach.

I also can't pull the laptop closer because of aforementioned obstacle. So my arms have to go around the obstacle, on the sides, which shortens their reach.

So, in order to reach the laptop and get more comfy, I slide down a little. This in turn causes my panties to slide up my bum. Which is highly uncomfortable and will drive me crazy unless I do something about it. So I sit up again, causing my carefully arranged setup to fall apart, pull my panties out of my bum and start over again.

Then, just as I get comfy, this time having slid down slowly enough to prevent my knickers from creeping up my arse again, I realise I need to pee. Ignoring it won't work, as my full bladder just triggers those scary contractions. I eventually give up, get up and go to pee. And start all over again.

Funnily enough, sitting at a desk is hardest and the thing that causes the most contractions. Standing is fine (although I can't do that for too long because of pressure on my cervix). Lying down is optimal and half lying, half sitting is not too bad. But if I sit at my desk for longer than an hour, I suffer badly. I don't think my uterus, cervix and bladder like being squashed. If I squash my insides, they bite back with a contraction. So, just as well I am off work.

Right. In the time it's taken me to type this and get comfy, I need to pee again.

Here we go, from the top again …

CLASS ONE

'If they come with that crap of having to stand up and say your name and do all the bonding, touchy-feely shit, I'm outta there.'

Oops. Marko is not amused. I've been waiting for the right moment to tell him about the antenatal classes. Of course, I've been so nervous to tell him about it that I left it to the last minute.

'Of course,' I say, always the submissive wife. I've neglected to mention the breathing and visualisation class scheduled at the end. Tee-hee – should be fun.

Marko grumbles all the way there. He keeps asking why we're going.

'To make friends and learn things,' I explain. Which is mostly true, but there is another reason I want to go. For so long, all I've wanted was to have a normal pregnancy, just like everyone else. I want to do normal things – go to antenatal classes, read baby books, buy stuff.

Ten couples are already waiting when we arrive, all sitting on plastic chairs. We're a bit late and the eager beavers have taken all the front seats, leaving a spot for us at the back. Just perfect. Marko's body language is screaming discomfort. I try to ignore it – I'm determined to do this. For once he can just socialise and let go a little.

We do the admin, filling in forms and stuff, then it's time to start.

'Let's all introduce ourselves to each other,' the midwife says. Marko's nightmare begins. He shoots me a filthy look. By now, I'm nervous about what's coming. Personally, I couldn't give a shit what people think, but I know how much he *hates* this sharing shit, so I start laughing. I can't help it.

Luckily for Marko, the moms do the talking. We introduce ourselves and our partners and tell the group about our due dates. I'm tempted to tell them our history, how special this pregnancy is, how hard we fought for it. But I don't. I tell them that I am pregnant with twins. They ooh and ah, and that makes me feel special anyway. I tell them that I have no idea when the babies will come, but that we're going to try to keep them in for as long as possible.

So far, so good. Marko is slouching in his chair, trying to be as inconspicuous as possible. Then the dreaded moment – a sharing exercise.

We're divided into groups of three, husbands separated from their wives. We have to *share* the things that make us smile. By now I'm wetting myself with laughter, and Marko is shooting daggers at me, swearing under his breath. Ha-ha-ha-ha-ha! The poor bugger is placed in a naff group that takes the exercise very seriously. They're all dead keen on sharing.

My group asks what makes me smile and I answer, 'Seeing my husband in a group exercise at an antenatal class makes me smile.' I can't stop giggling.

'I don't care what you say, I am *not* coming again,' Marko says through gritted teeth when the exercise is over. I stop laughing. I can see I'm pissing him off, but it is just so *funny*!

I embarrass him further by asking whether they accept credit cards as a method of payment (who on earth still carries cash?). That's after I made the whole class wait while I have a pee and after I start yelling and screaming halfway through the class because an enormous moth flies towards my head.

It gets better after a while. He gets over the trauma of all that sharing and once we start going through baby and pregnancy stuff, he relaxes. By the end of the class, he says he will come back to one more class. Here and there, he manages to see the funny side. When they start talking about what is considered normal weight gain in a pregnancy, he pokes me hard and raises his eyebrows at my massive girth.

So, we'll go back. I tell Marko we can skip the breathing and visualisation exercises, and he is somewhat mollified by that.

Can you believe it? We – Marko and I – went to an antenatal class. Us. We. The infertile couple. For all its naffness, it was just divine.

FROM THE HIP

IVF Currency

Not only is infertility such an insidious disease that it affects your whole life, your looks, your health, wealth, happiness, relationships and career, but it also has its own currency. You know how economists use the Big Mac index to indicate currency parity and the relative cost of living in various countries? Well, forget about that, we have IVF currency – the universal currency of the globalised infertility world.

After a while, your local currency, the dollar, pound or rand, becomes secondary and IVF currency takes over. This is especially pertinent while you're still trying, but as I've subsequently discovered, it is hard to give up calculating things in terms of IVF currency.

I remember calculating the amount in my savings/investment account in terms of IVF. For example, I would say, 'I have an IVF-and-a-half in my savings account, and my bonus this year should be about three-quarters of an IVF.' Or, 'We can't go on that holiday, are you crazy? That's at least an IVF.' I always tried to have an IVF-and-a-half in my savings account for back-up if the current cycle failed.

Of course, the value of a unit differs depending on your individual situation. A normal infertile person (is there such a thing?) will probably do an IVF that costs half of my cycle. That is because I need stronger, more expensive drugs and special treatment. My IVFs normally cost nearly double that of a starter pack, a normal IVF.

We buy a stunning new lounge suite, very expensive, good quality – about an IVF-and-a-bit's worth. Suddenly our other furniture looks, well, out of place. So we buy a new coffee table (four days of drugs) and some side tables (six days of drugs). Then our dining room doesn't match at all, so we buy a new dining room suite (half an IVF), a server (one artificial insemination), new mats (two days of drugs), pictures and so on.

It freaks me out to spend so much money on non-IVF things. I worry as my back-up IVF fund dwindles. I still have one. You know, what if ... This is what our life has been like for so long and it's hard to break the habit.

But the shopping was fun.

CLASS TWO

This time we deliberately arrive early to make sure we get seats at the back of the class. We also bring pillows, because the plastic chairs are hard on Marko's skinny butt and I need about 75 pillows to get comfortable at any given time.

Class two is better. Not too much sharing. We have one group exercise, each of us having to write on a piece of paper what we hope our babies will inherit from our spouses. I think about the things I love about Marko. I write down, 'his strength, his drive and ambition, his brains.' We swap our pieces of paper. Marko has written, 'brains, kindness and eyes.'

What? He can't think of a third characteristic and the best he comes up with is eyes? Bastard. I notice something small written at the bottom of the paper and squint to read it. '*Not* her nose.' Very funny. Double bastard.

Tough shit, Marko. I think our babies are going to have big noses. At least they will look like their parents, then!

Twenty-five weeks and three days

This is a big week for me. It's the week I went into labour with Ben. I was 25 weeks and six days then.

Both babies are growing well, with Kate still lying on top of Adam. Boy, I hope having a million scans is OK, or else I'm totally fucked and these babies will really be born with big satellite dishes for heads.

I'm not totally skippy happy – still too scared. I'm going to be even better about lying down.

But I've made it.

DEAR DIARY

This is the longest I've ever been pregnant!

Twenty-six weeks and three days! What an achievement! I don't want to fry the babies' brains more than I already have, so I settled for a quick LBC. Both hearts beating, still plenty of fluid. Dr New says to continue doing whatever it is I'm doing. Which means lying down and eating fudge and chocolate.

DEAR DIARY

NO MORE CLASSES FOR US

We're not going back to antenatal classes. Such a pity. Not only because I paid for the full course and I *hate* wasting money, but because I so badly wanted to be *normal* and do *normal* things. The harsh reality is that sitting for two hours is just too much for me now. It's getting harder and harder to do anything but lie flat on my back. On my side, actually.

I was very crampy after our third class and woke up with a contraction – probably just a Braxton Hicks (practise contraction) – but still, it was enough to terrify me into lying awake for hours, worrying about going into labour. I guess I just have to accept that *normal* and *Tertia* don't go together.

Marko is naturally very upset at the thought of no more classes – *not*! I suggested he go without me, but strangely he didn't think it was a good idea. Probably didn't want to have fun without me. That must be it.

Ah well, more and stricter bed rest it is.

I will miss seeing Marko's reactions to the group tasks. Last night as we got there we had to split up in groups of men and women and write down the five best and five worst things about being pregnant. I cringed when she said we had to do a group exercise, waiting for Marko's stormy looks, but he dived in with gusto.

When it was time to share what each group had written, I immediately recognised his contributions. The good bit was, 'They (the wives) sleep more often and bother you less,' the bad bit, 'You have to do more chores.' The other men said naff things like, 'Wife looks

so beautiful,' and, 'The prize at the end.' Not Marko. Funny guy.
I *do* like him.

The other men complain about being kept awake by their wives
constantly getting up to pee and the snoring or insomnia. Marko
leans back, folds his arms and says, 'I don't have that problem.' The
other men are all amazed.

'How come?' They ask.

'Simple, I just kick her out of bed.' Now they all think he's a hero,
sniggering among themselves and slapping one another on the back.
Bloody hell – I'm the one who chooses to sleep in the other bed –
to get some, not because he kicks me out.

They think Marko and I are very odd. Which we are. Match
made in Oddball Heaven.

TERTIA HAS A BABY SHOWER.
WHO WOULD EVER HAVE GUESSED?

My mother walks into the room ahead of me. I have to duck off to the loo first (obviously). What she sees is too much and she bursts into tears. The room is filled with people – my work colleagues. Gifts are stacked all around. This is the first time Mom is meeting my work friends.

'I'm so sorry,' she sobs. 'It's just that Tertia has come such a long way.'

The moment is overwhelming for her. Special. For both of us. Poor mother, I love her like mad. She really has been my rock through all of this. She has grieved with me and on her own. She's had to carry her own pain as well as mine.

She sits to my side, so that I can't see her face. She hides her tears from me throughout the shower so that I don't get upset.

This is my first baby shower. I've been very anxious in the days leading up to it.

Why, you ask? Well, because:

1. I've avoided baby showers like the plague for so long that it feels plain weird going to one, let alone my own. All that baby talk, all that fertile, normal stuff. I'm just not used to it.
2. I *hate* being the centre of attention (believe it or not). I love social occasions, but not when everyone is focusing on *me*.
3. I am scared to jinx my pregnancy.
4. I've become extremely leaving-bedphobic, which is the fear of

leaving one's bed when on bed rest. I get scared if I travel too far from my bed. My bed is safe. When I'm near my bed I will be OK.

I'm so anxious, I even consider not going. I wake up in the morning feeling crampy – a bad sign. I'm not sure whether the cramps are causing the anxiety or the anxiety the cramps. All I know is it's freaking me out. The whole morning I vacillate – should I go, shouldn't I go? Eventually I decide I have to go – my work friends are so wonderful. How can I let them down?

My darling mother has appointed herself my chauffeur and picks me up for the baby shower. She won't let me drive myself. Not that I can at this stage, anyway. On the way, I have a huge contraction. *Shit!* It freaks me out even more. Maybe it's just a Braxton Hicks, but my face goes bright red and I get all hot. I tell my mother one more and we are turning around and going home, back to bed to lie down. Thank goodness things calm down.

I'm pleased I came. The shower is lovely. Helen, my best friend at work, organised it. Helen, who is super-fertile, has three kids and has never had to deal with any infertility issues. *She gets it.* She totally gets it. See, there are people out there who just get it, fertile or not. I love Helen to bits.

I get lots of cute gifts – clothes, products, bottles, baths, you name it. Lots of stuff. I am really spoiled. That's the cool thing about being out of the closet about my infertility – everyone at work knows my situation and they are all rooting for me. And they care. Such cool people I work with.

But it's an emotional day and when I get home I'm still very crampy and my uterus is extremely irritable. I nearly, nearly go to hospital. I have the phone in my hand, finger poised over the fast dial button, ready to call Dr New to tell him I'm giving in, I'm off to official hospital bed rest.

But then my uterus calms down. Things go quiet down below.

It makes me realise I can't go out any more. Unfortunately I am resigned to staying at home, in my bed. And that's OK. I'll do whatever it takes.

I wish I could have relaxed more and enjoyed the baby shower more, but I was just so overwhelmed. I am glad my mother was there with me – she's been with me through so much of the bad shit, I'm glad she's had a chance to see the good stuff as well.

Together, Marko and I ooh and ah over every little gift. Marko unpacks, while I lie on the bed. We look at and hold each little outfit. This is wonderful. I feel almost guilty at how much I'm revelling in the moment. It's all so surreal. I can't believe this is actually happening to me, to us.

I had a baby shower! For me! How fucking unbelievable is that? After nearly five years, I had a baby shower. A baby shower. *My* baby shower.

A letter to my mother

MY DARLING MOTHER

Having a mother like you while growing up was the greatest gift and biggest advantage I could ever have had. It is because of the confidence and values that you instilled in me that I am who I am today. Thank you for shaping me into a person who I like and am proud to be. Thank you for letting us believe that we could be whoever we wanted to be, do whatever we wanted to do, that there were no limitations except our drive, ambition and creativity.

Having had you in my life throughout my infertility was a life and sanity saver. If there were a textbook on how to be the perfect mother to an infertile daughter, it would have you as the role model.

Thank you for your unwavering support throughout my long, hellish journey.

Thank you for reading all those infertility, grief, pregnancy and baby books and thank you for learning about a world that must be so foreign to you.

Thank you for taking me to hospital and sitting with me through all those retrievals and transfers. Remember how excited we were at first? You were such a calming influence.

Thank you for always having hope for me when I didn't have for myself.

Thank you for telling me not to give up when I said I couldn't do it anymore.

Thank you for never giving up on me when I went through the dark time. When loving me must have been like trying to hug a cactus. Thank you for loving me through all of my rejections of help and love.

Thank you for always thinking about how Marko must be feeling – so many people forget about him because he doesn't talk much.

Thank you for mediating between Melanie and me. It must have been very hard for you to be stuck in the middle of the tension. Thank you for never taking sides, for being there for both of us, equally. I can't wait for my kids to love you as much as my nieces and nephew do. They love their Mimi very much.

Thank you for saying to me, wholeheartedly and with absolute conviction, that you would love my future child 100 percent, even more, no matter where that child came from.

Thank you for coming to visit me when I was in hospital after having lost Luke. Thank you for sitting in the chair, entertaining me with stories from home or just sitting quietly. Thank you for washing my underwear, for bringing me books, special treats. You gave me some dignity. Thank you for bringing the nurses vegetables from your garden – I was their favourite patient.

Thank you for rushing to me when I went into labour, I needed you there. All I wanted was my husband and my mother there.

Thank you for having Ben's picture in your bedroom, pride of place among the rest of your grandchildren. For always talking about him, for crying with me and on your own about him. And, oh God, Mother, you never got to hold him, never got to touch him – our special boy. That's not right Mother, you never got to hold him. Remember how proud we were of him when he used to roll around and kick on the scans? Remember how we laughed when we saw his dangly bits? How you told Dad and Paul that our boy had big balls?

Thank you for being there for me, when other people didn't know what to do with me or for me when I was so raw with grief. You just sat and held me and let me cry and wail. You let me be raw.

Thank you for the flowers and beautiful card on Mother's Day. Thank you for doing this when other people couldn't even look me in the eye. When people told you not to because I wasn't a mother. Thank you for standing up for me, for telling them that I was a mother, that I had a son. Thank you for thinking of me on a day when I should have been celebrating you.

Thank you for loving Kate and Adam as much as I do.

Thank you, for everything you have done for me, for everything you have said, and for all the times when you said nothing and just listened.

Thank you for being my good luck charm, my muse, my hero, my saviour, my therapist, my chauffeur, my cook, my personal shopper and my bed-rest nurse.

Thank you, thank you, thank you. For a million things, for everything. I don't know what I would do without you. There are so many more things, small things, big things.

I love you very, very much. If I could be half as good a mother to my children as you are to your children, I will have done exceptionally well.

Thank you, Mother. I love you, more than words can ever express.

THE WOUND STILL ACHES, SO VERY MUCH

I love little Ben so much. I always will. He will forever be my first-born, my special, brave boy. My heart breaks that his time was so short. He never even came home. I can't stop crying. I just miss him so much.

Where are you now, my boy? Are you happy? Mommy misses you, brave boy. I will love you forever. Forever. Don't you ever forget that.

Will this wound ever heal? Each time I lift the Band-aid to take a peek, it's as raw as ever. I don't know, maybe it's better to rip it off completely, to let it all out so that it can get better. But not now, not while I'm pregnant and on bed rest. When, then? If I don't touch the Band-aid, I'm OK. Is it OK to live with a patch over your pain forever, do you think? I know taking it off and letting everything out is best, but if I can't, might it slowly heal on its own?

As I write the letter to my mom, I remember again. I sob my eyes out. And while I'm weeping, Kate and Adam start to kick, as if to say, 'Hey Mom, we're here. We love you, too. Don't cry.'

And I do love them, with all my heart. But there is no limit to love, and I will always love and miss my firstborn. Children aren't replaceable or interchangeable. Having more children never makes up for the ones you've lost.

MY UTERUS AND THE TERRIBLE TWOS

Poor Marko. If you see a chap walking around with a severely pinched expression on his face due to extremely high levels of sexual frustration, that would be my husband. Dr New says there is to be no uterine activity – no orgasms for me, no sex.

'Oh no!' she cried.

Marko comes up with several suggestions on how we can work around the no-sex rule. I tell a small white lie and say the doctor specifically said no blow jobs as well. He doesn't look convinced.

A lot of time and energy have been focused on my cervix. And rightly so – it's been our main cause for concern. However, the real pain-in-the-arse, sulky brat in the family is actually my uterus. The cervix is the quiet one, gamely struggling along, trying its utmost to do its bit for the greater good.

But my uterus … What a sulky bitch she is! As mentioned earlier, I suffer from an irritable uterus (it's a real thing, a medical thing – really). But my uterus takes this medical diagnosis a step further – it's just plain bratty. My ute is like your typical toddler going through the terrible twos.

My gorgeous niece, who is two, and my uterus are at roughly the same stage of development. Little Rebecca's entire vocabulary seems to be made up of the phrase, 'I don't like it' – spoken in an extremely whiney tone. If you offer her orange juice, she doesn't like it and wants berry juice. Yesterday's favourite dish? She doesn't like it today. Cheese? I don't like it. This dress? I don't like it. Ah-doan–laaaaak-ittt! That's my uterus. But worse. Everything irritates her – full bladders, lying on one side for too long, clothes that hug my belly, the list is endless and, sadly, it is growing.

The equivalent of the throw-yourself-on-the-floor-in-a-tantrum behaviour exhibited by my uterus is for it to tighten up and get hard in the manner of a Braxton Hicks contraction, frighteningly similar to the real thing. In other words, behaviour requiring my most immediate and urgent attention. Behaviour that, if not placated, will start off labour. My uterus has got me by the balls, so to speak.

As the list of I-don't-like-its gets longer, my world gets smaller. My uterus has now decided that it absolutely cannot stand for me to sit for longer than about 45 minutes. At a certain point, it will make its displeasure clearly known and force me to lie down. So even my favourite weekend pastime of going out for breakfast with my husband is no longer a possibility.

Apparently, sitting in the passenger seat of a car is also no longer acceptable. 'Ah-doan-laaaaak-ittt!!!' Anything longer than a ten-minute drive and I get a big Braxton Hicks. Which means I can't attend the family gathering on Sunday for my brother-in-law's birthday, or drive to the baby shop to get more stuff. Funnily enough, my uterus doesn't mind me standing or walking around. I just may *not* sit, as this squashes it and it doesn't 'laaaaak-ittt'. And of course I can't do lots of standing or walking because of my long-suffering cervix.

So lying down it is. Which is a pity, because I would love to use this time to write, but even half lying, half sitting is a no-no. Now even my last little luxury – a facial – is also no longer acceptable. After the last facial, my uterus performed the whole day. I have never met a sulkier brat in my life. Apparently, lying on my back forces my uterus to squash and press down on my bladder. My uterus hates my bladder about as much as it hates being squashed – Lord knows why – so now it hates facials as well. If my poor bladder gets even slightly full and should *dare* to encroach on the uterus' territory, the uterus will respond with a vicious tightening, even though it is actually taking up space previously reserved for the bladder. The bladder is petrified. As am I, to be honest.

And don't think this sulky-brat behaviour ends at night. Oh no. We will go to bed with everyone on apparently good terms – my cervix, bladder, uterus and I – when sometime during the night, my uterus will decide my bladder has upset it somehow. Cries of 'you're in my space' and other whinging follows. And beware the consequences if I dare suggest that I may be a bit fatigued, and could I possibly just get some sleep. Oh no. A mother of all tantrums will follow with a tightening that basically forces me to get up, have a quiet word with my bladder, empty it to make space, make sure everyone is happy again, rearrange the pillows and hope we can all go back to sleep. This happens repeatedly at night – 11p.m., 12a.m., 12:20a.m., 2am, 4a.m. and 5a.m. And I can't just put any old pillow under my belly. 'Ah-doan-laaaaak-ittt!!!' The uterus is very fussy about pillows – only certain pillows will do. I just love night-time.

Sometimes it gets so sulky I'm not even allowed to rest my hands on my belly to feel the babies' kicks and movements. Oh no. It just wants to be left alone. 'I vant to be alone.'

I can fairly easily recognise the signs of a tantrum coming on and attempt to distract my uterus immediately. The only time I can't is when I'm sitting, because then there's no stopping the irritable cow. Sigh.

So, while my cervix is the one forcing me to take it easy, it is my uterus that is completely ruling my life and defining my world. I am a slave to the whims of my uterus. Fickle bitch that she is.

PREPARING FOR HOSPITAL BED REST

Boo hoo! I don't want to go to hospital for bed rest. It's horrible there and I will have to share a bathroom. I hate sharing bathrooms. I suffer terribly from performance anxiety. I may never do a number two again and die from constipation. What a cruel and torturous death. Death by poo. Or no poo, to be precise.

But I think I may just have to give in and go to hospital this week. I'm getting plenty of Braxton Hicks contractions every day. So many, I'm almost getting used to them. This is normal (almost all women get them in late pregnancy), but I think I may as well be as close to help as I can be. And yet, being home is so much more relaxing, for me and my uterus, I honestly don't know what to do.

I will see what my next check-up brings. If my cervix is still intact, I will stay home for another week. If it's started to funnel or shorten, I'll go to hospital. Meanwhile I'll prepare myself, just in case. I'll get things in order, so that I'll feel better about being away from home.

So far, I've cleaned out the nursery, packed away all the clothes and blankets into appropriate piles, marked clearly what must be washed. Kind mother will do this for me. I've drawn up a list of what I still need and kind sister will do my last shopping. It makes me a little sad that I don't get to enjoy the shopping-for-baby-things thing, which is such a divine part of the whole preparing-for-baby-thing. C'est la vie.

The nursery furniture is due to arrive in a few days and I've shown Marko where I want what, given him instructions on what must be cleaned, paid all outstanding accounts, sorted out queries. I think I'm good to go. The only thing I need is something to wear. At home I wear old T-shirts or just underpants to bed, but I guess I can't walk around there with my underpants showing, can I?

The thing that keeps niggling at the back of my mind is that hospital bed rest didn't stop me from going into pre-term labour last time. Although I now know more and will insist on drugs the minute I suspect anything amiss. Last time they dismissed my fears as just an irritable uterus. Next thing I was five centimetres dilated and contracting. In hindsight I am completely pissed off at the nurses, because I now know I passed my mucous plug as well, which I showed them and still they said it was nothing.

Ah well, no point in looking back.

My dad is pretty damn wonderful too

It seems grossly unfair to write that long letter to my mother without at least a little adoration thrown my father's way.

I've always been Daddy's girl. We are four kids. I'm the eldest and my siblings always tease me that I'm Dad's favourite, which is not true. He doesn't have favourites. Although if he did, I'm quite sure it would be me, being so divine and all. What is true is that we have a very special relationship.

Because I got married fairly late, at the age of 31, for a long time the only steady man in my life was my father. He was (and sometimes still is) the first person I call when I have a problem, or I have to make a decision. There isn't a decision I make without speaking to my father first. Not because I can't make a decision on my own, but because I respect his experience in life so highly.

He is the guy I called when my car broke down in the middle of the highway, probably because of something I'd done wrong. He is the guy I called from a nightclub in the early morning hours the first time I got very, very drunk. He got out of bed to come and fetch me without saying a word. He is the guy my sister and I called, crying, from our first camping trip because we'd forgotten to pack the tent poles. He calmed us down, told us what to do and arranged that a driver deliver them to us the next day – a five-hour drive away. My father has come to our rescue more times than I can even remember.

I grew up in a pretty traditional household – my mother never worked, my father was the breadwinner. When he got home, we were always bathed. Mom wore lipstick and we were well-behaved at the dinner table. My father was kind of old-fashioned in the way that he believed girls should act like young ladies. Burping and farting was frowned upon, unless it came from Paul. Then it was very funny. He wasn't restrictive – we had lots of fun – just traditional in some respects.

I never discussed girl stuff with Dad. None of us girls did. Tampons and sanitary pads were kept out of sight. I also didn't go into much of the detail around the infertility things with him. We would speak in more general terms. My dad has never been good with girly stuff. And yet, now, when my father calls to see how I'm doing, as he does every day, and I reply, 'OK, just feeling a little anxious,' he says without blinking an eyelid, 'You aren't spotting, are you?'

Oh. My. God. My father – Dad – asking whether I'm spotting. He who can't even look at a closed box of tampons without feeling extremely uncomfortable. I feel touched and guilty that my poor father has to endure this, has to worry about his daughter spotting.

My father is also the one who pushed me, gentle as ever, into therapy when I was at my lowest. He said, 'Do it for me.' I can never refuse my father – he asks for so little. I went and am glad I did.

A while ago, Dad went to get some things from the supermarket. There he bumped into a woman pushing twins in a pram. He stopped to talk to her about her twins and told her about his daughter who had been pregnant with twins, but lost them and went through such a hard time.

The woman said, 'You're Tertia's father aren't you?' It so happened that this was an infertile friend of mine who did IVF for her twins. She told me afterwards how lucky I was to have a father like mine who so obviously cares about me and what is happening in my life. And I am. I'm very, very lucky.

I love my daddy, very much. I am truly blessed to have such wonderful parents.

STOCKHOLM SYNDROME, OF ANOTHER KIND

I've been getting increasingly anxious about the babies arriving and being able to cope with them and doing the right thing. But there is something else clogging up my worry quota. This is something that is really hard to articulate. And I don't want to sound ungrateful. I'm not.

The truth is, in a strange and warped way I am scared to leave Infertile Tertia and the world of infertility behind. Infertility is all I've known for the last five years. I've lived, breathed and eaten it. It has defined who I am, it's become an integral part of my personality. Infertility is what I know. I'm really good at it – I know stuff, I know lots of infertile people. I have a master's degree in infertility. Infertility has given me my friends; it's defined my social space. I've become damn good at living in this world. As shit as it's been, it's what I know. This is where I feel safe and connected.

Oh, I will always be infertile, but because I will not be trying for any more children (God forbid!), I won't be living in that world anymore. For all this time I've wanted nothing more than to leave that hell behind me. And yet, as I'm about to leave, I feel naked, vulnerable. Incomplete. Suddenly I'm no longer special, no longer different. No longer part of the club. Weird and twisted, I know, but the world of infertility has become me. Taking it all away will leave a gaping hole. Who will I be, now? I know nothing about this new world, this world of normal and motherhood.

I most certainly don't want to be battling with infertility anymore, but I also don't want to ever forget and move on without a backward glance. These past years have left such indelible marks on my soul that I can't ever be the same person again. To forget the past would be to pretend the last five years have never happened – that Ben, Luke, Hannah and the other little ones never happened.

Yet, I am no longer welcome in that world.

What will I do? What will normal life be like? Will I ever find a closer, more caring group of people than my infertile community? Those people to whom I am so strongly bound? I've been so proud to be a part of such an amazing group of women. The future seems so unknown, feels so scary. If I am not infertile Tertia, who am I?

Every right-thinking infertile woman will say to herself, 'Just shut the fuck up and be grateful you're no longer living in this hell.'

Oh, but I am. Grateful, that is. However, it's like languishing in jail for a long time. When you're a prisoner, all you dream about is being free. Then, on the day of your release, suddenly the big, wide, open world seems so scary – the cold, hard routine of prison life strangely comforting. You'll never willingly go back, but it is with huge trepidation that you take your first steps to freedom.

Another – awful – thought lingers. What if reality is nowhere near as wonderful as the fantasy? What if the prize is not what I expected? After putting happiness on hold for so long, what if the hole isn't filled?

It's terrible thinking these thoughts. I hate myself for it.

Mixed emotions

When I talk about Ben, or am sad about him, some people tell me to 'focus on the good things – think of Adam and Kate.' I know their intentions are good in that they don't want to see me sad. But I want to say to them and to anyone else who is tempted to temper my emotions, my feelings for Kate and Adam have nothing to do with my feelings for Ben. They're totally separate children, totally separate emotions.

When I lost Ben, I in fact mourned two losses, both intensely. The first was the loss of the opportunity to have a child. And this is the loss that almost all infertiles mourn each month when they start to menstruate, or each time a cycle fails, or each time they miscarry. Those who are not infertile should understand that this is what infertile people experience over and over again in their quest to have a child. It is very real. It is just all the more tragic when the loss occurs later in the pregnancy.

The infertile is grieving over yet another stillborn opportunity – a chance to end this hellish journey, to fill the hole, to stop the pain. This is the loss that the fact of being pregnant with Kate and Adam does help. Because, thank God, it spells the end of your grief about not having a child. Today, a year later – thank God – I don't have to mourn the loss of any hope at all to have a child.

But then there's the grief about losing Ben. This has nothing to do with Kate, Adam or anything else. This is about that special little boy. Ben. This is not even about me, or what I went through. This is about the fact that this baby boy, whom I loved intensely even before he was born, never got to experience the things all parents want for their children. He never got to run outside in the warm sunshine, feeling grass beneath his feet. He never got to laugh from his belly, he never got to run to his mom or dad and jump into their arms to give and receive tight bear hugs. He never even received one. This is what makes me most sad. It is about Ben and what he never had. As a mother, this breaks my heart.

Neither Kate, nor Adam, nor a million other children can ever replace Ben or make me feel better about what he never experienced. Some people, even people close to me, just don't understand this. Ben is Ben. It is Ben I mourn. Ben I miss. He is my firstborn son. Kate and Adam cannot and will not ever make up for losing Ben. Ever. What they do make up for is being childless. That is different.

At the same time I feel such joy, happiness and excitement about Kate and Adam. Thankfully, love is not finite. I can love Ben and miss him completely, and love Kate and Adam and enjoy them completely at the same time. I am sure I'm not unique in this. It's part of being human. We are able to experience complexities of emotion. We can have two conflicting emotions simultaneously. Joy and sorrow can exist side by side. Both are equally important.

Happy Tertia and sad Tertia co-exist in the same body. That's life. There can be no healing in suppressing sorrow. And there can be no fulfilment in denying joy.

A DATE WITH DR NEW

I booked my C-section date. Me! I booked a delivery date. Booked. After 13 weeks of bed rest and living with my own and both my doctors' fears of pre-term delivery, *I booked my delivery date*. Surreal. Our date is 17 January. In two weeks' time. *Min dae!*

Of course I may deliver before then. But I got to book a delivery date. And who knows, I may just end up with big, healthy, term babies on the scheduled date.

Surreal, absolutely surreal.

I am over the moon, beside myself with joy. I am jumping out of my skin here. I have to lie down and take it easy, but I want to run, shout, scream from the rooftops!

THE LITTLE GIRL WHO WAS NEARLY MY DAUGHTER

You will never believe what happened a minute ago. I just got a call from the adoption social worker. Remember? The one I saw almost exactly a year ago.

'Hi Tertia,' she says. 'This is Ms Adopt. I have a little girl for you. She's due next week.' My legs go weak. I have to sit down. This was the call I'd been waiting for, longing for. It's the call I'd dreamt about for so many years. It was the call that came eight months late.

I start to weep. I just know how absolutely, totally, wonderfully happy some other couple is going to be tonight. The next-on-the-list couple. Tonight, another infertile woman's dreams are going to come true.

I rub my belly and thank God that tonight, there would be two couples fewer in the infertile world to cry, to feel empty, to despair. Marko and I, of course, and the couple who will become the parents of that very special little girl who is about to be born.

Go well, little girl. May life bring you every wonderful blessing you deserve.

Life is beautiful.

MARKO AND TERTIA ARE PROUD TO ANNOUNCE …

They are here. Our babies are here.

It all started on a warm summer's morning. When the scorching heat of the day had not yet begun it's stranglehold on the air outside, the last remnants of the cool night air still lingering.

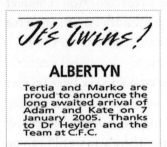

It's Twins!

ALBERTYN

Tertia and Marko are proud to announce the long awaited arrival of Adam and Kate on 7 January 2005. Thanks to Dr Heylen and the Team at C.F.C.

It is Friday, 7 January. I get up to the sounds of sparrows farting gently in the breeze and my normal morning routine. Pee, pour glass of milk, have some cereal, dial up to the Internet, browse around, download my mail. The usual.

After about an hour, my back gets really sore. I go to lie down. Fifteen minutes later I feel a gush of fluid and jump up.

'Fuck!' I think. 'I hope I haven't wet the bed – I've just washed the sheets!'

Then I think, 'Yay! I know what this is.' It's my water breaking, of course, which means, according to the books, my babies should be arriving in about eight to ten hours or so. I am only 36 weeks, but that's fine – they're more or less fully baked.

Even though it is not yet seven o'clock, Marko is at work already. I call him.

'I think the babies are coming today.'

'You think so? Why?' I explain what's happened and say he needn't rush, but perhaps he should start making his way home.

'Fine,' he says. 'I'll come as soon as I've been through my e-mails.'

I can't believe my babies are coming today! I can't wait to meet them. I'm excited about the whole water-breaking thing. Almost like a real labour. How cool! I'm a little nervous, but mostly I'm just damn excited. I can't believe it is finally happening. Feels like I've been pregnant for years.

I call Melanie, who has had three babies and knows about babies and birth stuff.

'My water has just broken,' I giggle over the phone. 'I've told Marko to come home once he's finished with his e-mails.' At that, I get a strong contraction. (Oh, so *that's* what a contraction feels like. Flashback to the one I had with Ben. Wish I'd known then that I was having contractions and not just a crampy bladder!).

'Are you crazy?' My sister shouts. 'Get to the hospital! Now! Have you forgotten that you had a C-section a year ago? You shouldn't be going into labour at all. Not unless you want your entire uterus to rupture and bleed to death.'

Fuck!

I call Marko. 'Get home straightaway! Mel says I need to get to hospital *now*!'

Shit. OK. Maybe I should stop walking around with this cheesy grin on my face and start doing something. There's no way I'm going to the hospital all stinky and with dirty hair, so I have a quick shower. Washing my hair, I have another contraction. Damn, they're getting worse. As I get out of the shower, the rest of my water breaks. Getting a little nervous now.

I phone the hospital and explain that I'm on my way, and that I'm 36 weeks pregnant with twins. They had bloody better make sure Dr New is there when I arrive.

Great excitement as Marko drives in the emergency lane all the way to the hospital, hazard lights flashing. Just like in a movie. Meanwhile I'm becoming less and less enthralled with the whole contraction business. They're getting fucking sore. I white-knuckle clutch the dashboard as they come. I can't believe people actually do this for hours. It *hurts*.

Everyone, including Dr New, is waiting for me at the hospital. I am completely effaced, four centimetres dilated, with fluid coming out. Babies are on their way.

I will be the first one to admit that I have a very low pain threshold and am a big poop when it comes to pain, but oh, my fucking fuck, the contractions are fucking terrible. So damn painful and so damn frequent – every two minutes, now. But all I can think about is my previous C-section wound rupturing. I start to feel nauseous.

'Have you eaten anything this morning?' Dr New wants to know. Of course I've eaten! I'm pregnant with twins, it is eight in the morning, I've been awake for hours. He tells me this is a problem, because if the epidural doesn't work, they will have to administer a general anaesthetic. And if they do a general and I've eaten, I'm in danger of puking the food into my lungs and dying. Great.

He asks me to try to hold on, to see how long I can hold out, the longer the better, so that my food can settle, to prevent this whole lung-puking, dying thing. By quarter to ten, the contractions are so strong I'm prepared to take any chance. *Give me that effing epidural, already!*

As I'm wheeled into surgery, I become extremely anxious. I'm scared the epidural won't work and I will feel everything. Which is silly, because I had an excellent epidural last time. I'm also scared about the babies being OK. Oh God, please let them be OK. Please let nothing be wrong with them.

Then it stops being fun and exciting. It becomes scary. There's a lot of action around me – doctors, anaesthetists, paediatricians. I start shaking really badly and am very nauseous. I am worried the shaking will cause the epidural needle to puncture my spine and I will be left paralysed and won't be able to look after my babies. You, know, all the normal thoughts one has.

The epidural isn't pleasant. I can feel the touch sensation, which completely freaks me out. The anaesthetist tries to reassure me that this is normal and although I can feel touch, I won't feel any pain. I don't believe him. How can I feel touch and not pain? Last time I felt nothing.

Marko and I are incredibly tense as Dr New starts cutting. Terrified. I lie there, unable to see what the doctors are doing, but I can feel tugging.

Then the miracle ... I hear a baby scream – a lusty, healthy yelp. Oh God, thank you!

A minute later, I hear another.

JUST LIKE BEN

It was that lusty yell of his that did it. Even though Adam was a big boy at birth, his lungs were immature and one lung tore. The paediatrician noticed that he was losing colour and becoming increasingly weak in the incubator. He was X-rayed and immediately rushed off to the theatre for a drain to be placed in his lung. Now he's on a ventilator to help him breathe.

Just like Ben.

After the birth, Marko goes to the nursery to take some really cute video footage of them together in the incubator. Then he runs to tell my family the good news and returns to the nursery to look at the babies.

There is only one. Kate is alone. Adam is missing. He asks the nurses where Adam is. They tell him to ask the paediatrician. Marko starts to panic. No one is able to help him. Where the fuck is his son? As I've said before, he is not at his best at hospitals and airports and the combination of the morning's events have left him frazzled.

He establishes that there is something wrong with Adam and that he is in the neonatal intensive care unit. He tries to go in, but they won't let him in because they're working on Adam. When they work on a baby, no one is allowed in.

Eventually he is told to wash his hands with the sterile solution and to put on a gown. Adam's bed is at the far end of the nursery and Marko has to walk past all the tiny babies on their warming beds. All he sees are pipes and machines and monitors and alarms. Adam looks just like Ben and all those terrible memories come

rushing back. Marko is finished, broken – a wreck. He
fears the worst.

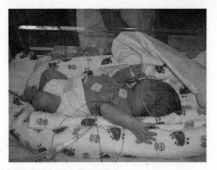

Adam – a few hours old

He rushes around looking
for someone who can tell him
what is going on. He rushes
around looking for me. No
one knows where I am. I am
languishing in the recovery
room. I've been left behind and
forgotten about. I have plenty of time to think about what Dr New
told me while he was stitching me up. He said it was just as well
he did the C-section when he did it – my uterus had started to
rupture at the site of the old scar. He said it had started tearing
and that he could actually see the babies through the wall of my
uterus. Scary shit.

By now Marko is almost hysterical. Eventually he finds me.
He's a wreck. I try to calm him down. There is just no way I will
believe that anything can go wrong now. Yes, our boy is sick, but
everything has been too good to be true up to now anyway. It's
been too easy.

The paediatrician tells us we will have to wait to see how Adam
does. For now, he's in a serious condition, but he's being monitored.
He wont be coming home with his sister, not now. That is all he
can tell us.

Adam is a sick boy. He needs help to breathe. He is on monitors
and has to be fed by a tube through his nose into his tummy. He
has pipes everywhere.

Just like Ben.

But unlike Ben, I won't let him die. Not this time. Not ever again.

MY DAUGHTER IN MY ARMS

I feel the weight of her tiny body in my arms. It feels wonderful. I hold her close and drink in her smell. I brush my lips against her head. Her soft, downy hair tickles my face. My daughter is gorgeous, tiny, minute.

It is ten o'clock at night and the frenetic activity of the maternity section is winding down. Marko has gone home, the poor guy. He's finished. The whole experience with Adam has exhausted him. I am still on a drug-and-birth high. And bed-bound. I haven't seen Adam yet. As soon as I can, I will get up to go and see him. He will stay in hospital for a while longer, but he will get better. Every day, he will get a little bit better. And then he will come home to us.

I know that. Adam is the biggest baby in the NICU. God, how wonderful is that? Ben was the smallest, weakest baby. This time we have the strongest, biggest baby.

I hold Kate against my chest and slowly lower myself onto the bed. I lie back and close my eyes, my mouth still pressed against her head. We spend our first night like this – bodies pressed together, my arms around her.

THERE!

Adam came home today, two weeks after his birth. I finally see my babies together. At home. My *babies*. *My* babies. Our family is complete. I can't imagine it any other way.

In a perfect circle of completion, we were discharged today by kind, gentle Samantha. Samantha, the NICU nurse who prepared Ben for his goodbye. Samantha who placed him in my arms. Who took him from my arms again after he had passed on and who then prayed over his little body.

'I'm so glad you get to take your baby home with you today,' she said as we left.

The last baby she handed me was so heartbreakingly still. She handed me a baby so that he could die peacefully in my arms. Today she handed me a wriggling, moaning, healthy baby boy so that he could go home to join his sister and father and mother. Our family is complete.

What a day. What a journey. What a ride. After being so close for so long, I have finally arrived.

Surviving infertility: An infertile's guide

When you're infertile the last thing you want is advice from everyone and anyone – especially fertile people, or even infertiles who are now pregnant. So, what follows is not intended as advice, but rather strategies that kept me relatively sane and functioning during my years of infertility treatment. Use what you can, discard the rest.

YOUR LOYALTY LIES WITH YOURSELF

Life is too short, and sometimes too damn hard, to do things because of social niceties or out of obligation. When you feel you can deal with the situation or the company, by all means go to baby showers and other social occasions. But if you're feeling fragile, *don't go*. Of course your friends would *like* you to be there, but they don't *need* you there.

Besides, who has the greater need? If your pregnant sister or friend is in a bad way and *needs* you, you can and should make an effort to be there for her. But if your pregnant sister or friend simply *wants* you to listen to her talk about pregnancy stuff, your need *not* to listen might be greater.

Sometimes you need to protect your own heart more than you need to do the 'right' thing. The right thing for you right now is to look after yourself.

DECIDE WHETHER YOU'RE IN OR OUT OF THE CLOSET

Do you reveal your infertility to the people around you or not? The advantage of being out of the closet is that your friends and family know why you don't attend baby showers and other events. What may be perceived as anti-social behaviour becomes a little more understandable. My friends and family gave me a lot of leeway because they knew my situation. If there was going to be lots of kids and babies at lunches or other social events, they would warn me. That way I could decide whether I was up to it or not, and they understood.

The disadvantage of being out of the closet is that it feels as if you're letting down a million people each time you have a failed cycle. Instead of one phone call, the one to your husband, you have to make eighty. Perhaps compromise and limit the amount of detail you share.

EDUCATE THOSE AROUND YOU

The more your family and friends understand about your situation, the easier it will be for you and for them. Just sending them a link to an informative website will help them become a bit more sensitive. Getting just one person to understand how hurtful the words 'just relax' are to someone who is infertile will be a step in the right direction.

EDUCATE YOURSELF

I swear I could practically do my own cycles if it wasn't for retrieval and transfer. I found that educating myself made me feel more in control. And control is so hard to come by on this ride. But remember – a little knowledge is a dangerous thing. Don't Google yourself into a frenzy. No, you do not have all of those scary problems you've just discovered on the Net. Discuss your theories with your online friends, or, better yet, your doctor.

GET SUPPORT FROM LIKE-MINDED PEOPLE ...

There's no shortage of online support. I made some life-saving friendships on bulletin boards and in chat rooms. It is such a relief to be with people who *get it* and to be able to bare your soul to kindred spirits. Try it: there are groups of many different flavours to suit your personality. Some are upbeat and positive, others are filled with cynical humour and the occasional swear word. Find one where you feel at home. If you can attend a local support group, even better.

... BUT LEAVE WHEN THE GOING GETS TOUGH

Hopefully you will be among the first to get pregnant, but if not, and it hurts to stick around, leave. Find another support group, maybe for people who have been around a little longer. Remember, your loyalty lies with *yourself* first. I left a few support groups as the last woman standing, and still managed to keep a few of the friendships. Don't hang around pregnant people, even former infertiles, unless you *want* to.

GET HELP IF YOU NEED IT

About two years into the process when things got really bleak for me, I finally bowed to gentle pressure from my family to get help from a therapist. I didn't want to go. I didn't see how it would help. But, while it certainly didn't change my reality, it did help me deal with it. The treatment proved to be a lifesaver. The anti-depressants didn't obliterate the sadness, nor did they make me blissfully happy. But the pain, sadness and anger no longer threatened to overwhelm me and were much more manageable. I actually managed to laugh again. Be warned, though, you may have to kiss a few frogs (disguised as therapists) before you find your prince.

TAKE BREAKS BETWEEN CYCLES

This is important, mentally and physically. I firmly believe the body needs a break from the stress of an assisted reproductive cycle. The worst treatment cycles for me were those done back to back. The breaks between the cycles are an opportunity to live like a normal person and not think about trying to conceive. Don't let your loudly ticking biological clock rush you into doing repeated treatments without taking breaks.

DON'T COMPARE YOURSELF WITH OTHERS

Yes, apparently there are some people who conceive on their first or second IVF. Unfortunately not all of us do. Don't compare yourself with other infertiles or, even worse, fertiles! It will get you nowhere.

NEVER CONSIDER YOURSELF LESS WORTHY

Pregnancy is not confined to people who are 'worthy' of it. Being infertile is not your fault, nor is it because of something you did in the past – even if the diagnosis is blocked tubes caused by a wanton lifestyle. If everyone who shagged around or had an abortion in their youth was punished by becoming infertile, there would be a whole lot more of us around. So stop blaming yourself. It gets you nowhere.

Never allow yourself to question your femininity based on your reproductive ability. The last time I checked, the requirement for being categorised as female was having XX chromosomes, not a sparkling uterus and nice, shiny eggs.

DOING IVF IS NOTHING TO BE EMBARRASSED ABOUT

Don't be embarrassed about how many IVFs you've done. Who cares? I mean, really – having sex to get pregnant? How last season! Some people may think you're obsessive (so what?), or that you don't know when to stop. Wrong. Do as many cycles as you want or can afford. I applaud you for your determination and strength. If it's only one, that's your choice. I honestly don't give a flying fuck what other people think of my efforts. Let them walk in my shoes and then we can talk.

DECIDE ON HOW MANY DIFFERENT VERSIONS
YOUR 'HAPPILY EVER AFTER' COULD TAKE

For some people anything beyond sex is too much. For others, IVF is a bridge too far. We're all different, but the most liberating thing for me was the decision that I would do whatever it took to have a child, whether that meant donor eggs or adoption. Not everyone will make that decision, but never having to face the end of the road helped me stay on the road.

ALWAYS HAVE A PLAN B

Having a back-up plan kept me sane. I was so anal about my Plan B that at the beginning of each cycle I had the money saved up and time allocated for the next one. Having something to look forward to made the setbacks just a bit easier to deal with. It was my way of trying to wrest some semblance of control from this crazy, chaotic situation.

DON'T LIVE LIKE A NUN

Drug-addicted teenagers get pregnant while jumping on trampolines. I'm not the best example to follow (that overwhelming fondness for wine and cigarettes), but make use of the breaks between cycles to eat sushi, drink wine, bonk for fun and just be normal for a while. Going through this shit is hard enough without having to live like a nun.

HUSBAND STUFF

I was very fortunate that our infertility brought us closer together. Of course, it doesn't always work that way. Make sure you and your partner are on the same page. This infertility shit can wreck a marriage quicker than an affair.

BE KIND TO YOURSELF

Infertility is fucking hard. It sucks. It is fucking unfair. I wouldn't wish this on my worst enemy. So you're allowed to be sad, to cry, to shout, to feel sorry for yourself. You don't have to be brave and strong all the time. Get help, go online and chat to your online buddies. It's hard, but you don't have to be alone.

DON'T DEVELOP AMNESIA

When you eventually succeed, or decide to get off the roller coaster, don't forget what it was like to still be struggling. Be kind to other infertiles. Remember how hard it is for an infertile to be around pregnant people, even if the pregnant person has struggled for ages and did six million IVFs. You are pregnant – she is not. Sometimes this means telling your friend you'll wait for *her* to contact *you* when she feels strong enough.

Good luck, sisters! May all your dreams come true, one way or another. I wish I had that elusive magic wand to grant all of your wishes. I'd do it in a heartbeat.

Want to know what Tertia, Marko, Kate and Adam are up to today?

www.tertia.org